CHALLENGES ARE OUR BUSINESS

Planeta

GUSTAVO CISNEROS

CHALLENGES
ARE OUR BUSINESS

Adapting, reinventing and thriving
across a century of change

 Planeta

© 2024, Editorial Planeta Mexicana, S.A. de C.V.
Bajo el sello editorial PLANETA M.R.
Avenida Presidente Masarik núm. 111,
Piso 2, Polanco V Sección, Miguel Hidalgo
C.P. 11560, Ciudad de México
www.planetadelibros.com.mx

First edition printed: june 2024
ISBN: 978-607-39-1051-4

Printed in Impregráfica Digital, S.A. de C.V.
Av. Coyoacán 100-D, Valle Norte, Benito Juárez
Mexico City, P.C. 03103
Printed and made in Mexico - *Impreso y hecho en México*

INDEX

On December 29, 2023, my father, Gustavo Cisneros, died quite unexpectedly. He was 78.

Many people called my father a visionary. It's true that he had an uncanny knack for seeing around corners and into the future. He spotted opportunities that were invisible to others. An idea might seem impractical or impossible — or, such as when he broke our decades-long partnership with Pepsi-Cola to switch to Coca-Cola, unthinkable. But he would grab onto that elusive thought and, as he often enjoined, "double-check and triple-check" until what initially looked like a crazy risk began to seem not just achievable but, in fact, the smart course of action. And often, it was. As my mother said, "The most remarkable thing about this man is that he's almost always right."

Where did that extraordinary ability come from? If I had to name the character trait that best defined my father, it would be his insatiable curiosity. It was something he inherited from *his* father and tried to pass on to his children and grandchildren: to keep your mind open to everything and everyone.

My father was fascinated by people who excelled at their work. It didn't matter whether you were a business magnate, an orchestra conductor, an art historian, a writer, a gardener, a yoga instructor, or a doorman; if you were good at what you did, he would always find common ground for conversation. He engaged with everyone because he wanted to understand the world through their eyes, whether they were a small farmer in the Dominican Republic or the head of one of the world's largest beauty companies. He would treat them both the same: with respect, kindness and genuine interest. That's the kind of man he was.

Of course, being the kind of man he was, he often found a way to turn those conversations into business opportunities. He never knew what or where an idea might come from, which was one of the reasons he was open to everyone and everything.

He fueled his curiosity through books. The term "voracious reader" was no cliché for him. Some people buy books by the yard; my father *read* books by the yard. His offices were lined with bookshelves crammed with books in both English and Spanish, with more stacked chest-high on his desk. You could be certain that he had read every one of them. As a young girl, I remember watching him pack for business trips: There would be a suitcase or two for clothes — he was always a snappy dresser — and a suitcase just for books.

He always read two or three books simultaneously. He had taken a speed-reading course in college and would divide titles into two categories: books to be read fast and those to be savored slowly. He knew there were some books that he just wanted to extract the main points from and others he wanted to delve into.

One of the latter was my last Christmas gift to him: *The World: A Family History of Humanity*, by Simon Sebag Montefiore. It's literally a chronicle of humanity through the stories of influential families, from ancient dynasties to modern fortune-makers like our family. When we returned home from the hospital after he died, there it was on his desk — on top of some 30 other books he had planned to start the new year with.

Another way my father honed his curiosity was by taking walks. My father was like a tourist in life. Just going for a walk with him was an education. We were in Sao Paulo for an art show when he invited me to visit a local shopping mall. He was definitely not intending to buy anything — he never carried a wallet. Instead, he was shopping for ideas: What were people buying? What were the popular Brazilian brands? Which American brands were most prominent? We'd go on these walks and he would ask questions that would make me observe and learn. And then he'd always stop for an ice cream.

Although my father was a proponent of seizing a teaching opportunity, he could be a father as well as a teacher. Of course, as someone in charge of a global business, he was a very busy man. We all understood that he and my mother couldn't always be with their kids on a day-to-day basis. They made up for it by ensuring there were plenty of opportunities for them to be fully engaged with us in other ways. Some of these experiences were extraordinary, like our annual trips to the Amazonas region, where we lived with indigenous people for weeks on end. Many were low-key but special nonetheless. Our beach house in Los Roques deliberately had no telephone, no television, not even a radio for distraction. (Of course, there were books!) It was just us, going spear-fishing or swimming or sailing together — undiluted bliss.

He especially enjoyed having one of us kids join him on his business trips. In this book, he describes how he took me on a tour of South America when he launched DirecTV. Twelve countries in twelve days. I was 14 and he thought the trip would be a cool way for me to expand my geographical perspective. I learned so much more than geography. That was when the seeds were planted that led to my becoming the third generation to lead Cisneros.

My dad often talked about the importance of having a sense of purpose. Planning for me to succeed him — and for me to succeed at doing so — became his favorite project. Unlike so many patriarchs, he didn't wait until time forced him to start making tough decisions; instead, he used the time to his advantage by starting the process when he was young and capable and full of energy, then letting things develop naturally. Our relationship, too, evolved, and we were both so happy with it.

Even though he stepped back from operations when I became CEO, his interest in my success only grew. He began each day excited to see what I'd do and was thrilled to help me do my best.

At the last conversation I had with my dad, he said with a little smile, "I feel so lucky to have in you a daughter who is also my boss and my best friend and my *compinche*." I replied, "I'm so lucky to have a father who is my best friend and my boss and my *compinche*."

My father signed off on the final version of this book just a few weeks before he died. This was a man who never left for tomorrow what could be done today, especially when it involved a project that he knew would be so important to us. My family and I feel so fortunate that his wisdom and his zest for new challenges — both in business and in life — live on in this valuable gift to guide us into the future.

As he embarks on his next great adventure, I wish him "Godspeed, *compinche mío*."

ADRIANA CISNEROS
January 11, 2024

"Gustavo, I'm going to teach you to be an entrepreneur"

In 1959, when I was 14, I accompanied my father to a business dinner at the Hotel Delmonico in New York City, where he said to me, "Gustavo, I'm going to teach you to be an entrepreneur."

Thirty years earlier, in 1929, my father, Diego Cisneros, had taken his entire savings of 1,000 *bolívares* (about $250)— painstakingly accumulated on a monthly salary of 250 *bolívares* — and made a down payment on a dump truck in the Venezuelan capital of Caracas. He was only 18, so his mother had to sign the documents to guarantee the loan.

It was an exciting time in Venezuela for a young man with ideas, ambition and determination. Oil was discovered in 1914, and by the late 1920s, the country was the world's leading exporter of petroleum.[1] Caracas was expanding; roads were being built and highways paved. Opportunities abounded, if you could just grab onto them.

Diego's mother knew the man who had the contract to pave the road from Caracas to Antímano, a nascent industrial zone eight miles from the city center. She knew that he needed trucks to carry the materials. They had a conversation. The result: He hired Diego at a fee of 20 *bolívares* per run. After expenses, there was just enough money to make the loan payments.

Whenever my father reached this point in the story, he would always pause, then say, "That little truck was the gateway to the world of business."[2]

Over the following years, as the world's demand for oil boosted Venezuela's economy, Diego expanded his business: refitting the dump truck as a bus, then developing a regional bus network; selling spare parts for the cars and other vehicles that his countrymen could increasingly afford to buy; setting up dealerships for top consumer products such as Norge refrigerators and Hamilton appliances to stock their homes; then, in 1940, in partnership with his brother Antonio, obtaining the exclusive right to market and sell Pepsi-Cola in Venezuela, only the second Pepsi franchise outside of the United States (Cuba was the first.)[3]

Powered by Pepsi's profits, by the evening of our dinner at the Hotel Delmonico, Cisneros & Cia. had become an economic dynamo in Venezuela. My father leveraged the expertise developed in bottling, marketing and selling Pepsi into a variety of related businesses: building carbonation plants, manufacturing bottle caps, designing and producing plastic shipping crates, creating other soft drinks using local flavors, and more. Knowing the importance of cold refreshments in a hot country — "A cold drink is a sold drink," he liked to say — he established an ice cream company, later known as Helados Tío Rico, and became the country's largest ice cream maker.

The 1959 edition of *Economic Geography of Venezuela* listed Cisneros & Cia. as one of the principal businesses in the country.[4] (The company has been known by various names over the years. To avoid confusion, from now on we'll call it by its present name: Cisneros.)

In short, my father had a lot to teach me about being a successful entrepreneur. And I was eager to learn. That evening at the Delmonico was the first time my father said to me, "I'm going to take you seriously. I'll give you the tools, the recommendations, the connections and my advice."

At the time, we weren't talking about my succeeding him. I had two older brothers, so I always assumed I would go my own way. But he was basically promising to help me forge my path.

I don't think he cared *what* I did as much as *how* I did it. My father firmly believed that a business existed within the context of the country in which it operated and that a business leader had a responsibility to improve not just the bottom line but also the lives of the people touched by the company — our employees, our customers and our partners. He taught me to broaden my focus and always consider the greater good, no matter what I was doing.

To everyone's surprise, including my own, I followed in his footsteps — and much sooner than anyone expected. I became Chairman and CEO in 1970, at the age of 25. My father's precepts helped guide me as Cisneros grew into a global enterprise and one of the largest privately held businesses in the world.

Just as my father trained me to succeed him, I was delighted some 35 years later to train my daughter Adriana Cisneros to take my place. She became the CEO of Cisneros in 2013 at age 33. I continue as Chairman.

Together, we look forward to celebrating some 100 years of a family business that started with one small dump truck in Caracas and today owns or holds interests in more than 30 companies, serving millions of English-, Spanish- and Portuguese-speaking consumers in over 100 countries on five continents, with operations ranging from media and entertainment, telecommunications and digital advertising to travel resorts and real estate development.

This book describes our journey through a century of change. It is not a comprehensive record of every deal and negotiation; rather, it is both a memoir and an illustration of the precepts that have guided and shaped us, and can guide and shape *you*, whether you head up a multinational corporation or are in charge of a company of one.

In addition to those leadership lessons, four fundamental values first embodied by my father became the wellspring we draw on to nourish and refresh us in good times and bad, in calm seas and in what can seem like endless whitewater. Those values are: reinvention; resilience; responsibility — to our family, our employees, our partners and, most of all, our customers; and, ultimately, a sense of adventure that enables us to constantly seek out new opportunities.

These values have become embedded in our DNA. I hope they will serve us long into the future. And I hope they will inspire you on your own leadership and life journey.

Notes

1. Tinker Salas, Miguel, *The Enduring Legacy: Oil, Culture, and Society in Venezuela*, Duke University Press, 2009, p. 6.

2. Bermúdez, Alfredo, *Diego Cisneros: A Life for Venezuela*, Fundación Diego Cisneros, 1992, p. 54.

3. Bachelet, Pablo, *Gustavo Cisneros: Pioneer*, Planeta, 2004, p. 22.

4. *Ibid.*

Part I

LESSONS I LEARNED FROM MY FATHER

Why me? Why did my father select me to share his thoughts and wisdom with? My father invited all of us kids to be part of his life and business, but I was the one who best understood him and knew what he wanted. I'm not being conceited. We just had extremely good chemistry. As a result, we spent a lot of time together and consequently, our partnership developed naturally.

My father was a big fan of the "teaching moment." He never missed an opportunity to give us kids "one-on-one seminars," especially when we accompanied him on his business trips around Venezuela and to the United States. Some of my siblings made it clear that they'd rather go to the movies than listen to a lecture.

I understood that if I wanted to learn from him, my first task was to get along with him. My second task was to get along with him. And my third task: to get along with him. As long as that worked, I would have the finest professor in the world. I chose him and, in return, he chose me. It wasn't easy.

When he and his brother Antonio first came to Caracas, the society girls nicknamed them "*los manguitos*" — a word that translates as "muff," but implies something soft and cuddly. In fact, he was anything but. He had a booming voice and commanding presence that took over any room he entered. He had a magnetic personality — and he used it. When he concentrated on you, you knew you had been charmed but you couldn't resist.

He could also be very demanding and didn't suffer fools gladly. If he saw you were interested in what he did, he would spend hours with you. But if you weren't paying attention, he quickly got bored with you. There were always two versions of my dad: My sister thought he was remote and my brother Diego didn't always see eye to eye with him, but I genuinely enjoyed being around him.

He was a one-man tornado. When he visited the plants — he was constantly on the road — he had a team of both male and female secretaries trailing him and writing down his observations and orders. He always had an agenda and by the time he finished a visit, he had generated so much work for everyone that they were ready to collapse. He only seemed more energized.

He was obsessed with finding the brightest people to hire and searching for the best ideas. No matter where they came from — Germany, France, the United States, wherever — he would copy whatever behavior or custom could give him an edge. He particularly liked the European habit of regularly visiting a spa for a week of relaxation and rejuvenation, so once or twice a year he would go to Rancho La Puerta in California, where he practiced yoga and tried marijuana. No one else I knew in Venezuela did anything like that.

His doctor had warned him that he might have a stroke, but he continued to burn the candle at both ends. Consequently, as he began to age, he dressed even more elegantly than he had when he was younger. He'd say, "My body is much older than my physical age, so I have to appear younger. I have to look vital." Then, because there was always a lesson to be learned, he'd add, "I don't know how long I'm going to live, so pay attention." I did.

He liked to sit up late and talk with me while slowly sipping a glass of his favorite Glendenning single-malt scotch. Then he'd wake up very early — at 5 a.m. or 6 at the latest — and he'd want to take a walk or have a coffee and talk some more. I was an early bird, too, but I was also young and enjoying the nightlife in Caracas and New York. The hours could be grueling — at least, for me. Part of our unspoken deal was to organize myself physically and mentally to keep up with him. I learned to take cat-naps and, even now, I take one or two short naps every day.

There was always a lesson with him: "Look at this, Gustavo. How would you make it better?" When we went to the theater or a movie, he would review the performance with me and we'd discuss whether it was good or bad. If I admired someone, like Aristotle Onassis or Stavros Niarchos, say, he'd say, "Let's examine that. Are they really successful? Look at their personal lives. One is killing his wives, the other is screwing around. Is that the model for you?" I learned to look for the good in someone without feeling I had to emulate them in every way.

He always surrounded himself with interesting people with incredible expertise. He provided the key to a world that I could join because I was his son. In return, I learned to keep my mouth shut and my ears open.

Sometimes, my father would tell me, "Take this guy out to a restaurant and ask him about such-and-such." Meanwhile, he'd tell the person I was having dinner with, "Teach Gustavo how to deal with this." It was a fantastic education — and all for free.

My father liked to be thought of as a person who was transferring knowledge to the next generation. I would follow his lead with my daughter Adriana.

Here are the most important lessons he taught me.

Foundations

My father was probably the most positive person I've ever known: always open to people and possibilities, always eager to learn something new, always ready to adapt to changing circumstances.

Much of his fundamental philosophy — about business, lead-ership, social responsibility, government and his approach to life — was rooted in the experiences of his early years. Necessity honed his determination to work hard and do well. Growing up in Cuba, Trinidad and Venezuela — three countries with three very differ-ent cultures — gave him a cosmopolitan perspective early on: Rather than inhibiting him, the idea of expanding beyond borders intrigued and excited him. His initial entrepreneurial successes, however small, gave him the confidence and courage to try for something bigger. He refused to be intimidated by the uncertainty of venturing into the unknown.

These experiences shaped him profoundly and, consequently, shaped me.

* * *

"Be a cultural chameleon"

My father was a cultural chameleon both by circumstance and inheritance. Born in 1911 in Havana, Cuba, his early life was characterized by upheaval. His father died of tuberculosis when he was just three; his mother, born María Luisa Bermúdez Martínez, was left on her own to support him and his older brother, Antonio José, then only seven. (I should mention that although Diego was born in Cuba, his mother's family had been in Venezuela since the 18th century and she always considered herself — and, consequently, her sons — to be Venezuelan.)

María Luisa had few marketable skills: Like most girls from "good" families, she had learned just enough cooking, sewing, writing and arithmetic to keep house when she married. Now, she resolutely put those meager skills to work by painting fans, knitting, doing embroidery and selling homemade cakes and confectionaries. When that didn't bring in enough money, she took a job selling household goods at a department store, directly contravening the convention at the time that "nice" women didn't work outside the home. Even so, her earnings still weren't enough to keep her small sons fed. My father remembered that his aunt Caridad, one of his father's sisters, regularly sent over food for midday and evening meals.[1]

In 1918, María Luisa and her sons, now seven and eleven, relocated to Port of Spain, the capital city of the British colony of Trinidad. It was a homecoming of sorts. María Luisa had family among the large community of Venezuelans who had fled political upheaval at the end of the 19th century. She had friends, from when she and her husband had lived there during the first seven years of their marriage. Most importantly, she had connections through her former church, the chapel of the College of the Immaculate Conception, to one of the finest schools in the British Caribbean. Though money was tight, María Luisa was fiercely determined — my father would say "obsessed" — to give her sons a top-notch education. Through her connections, she convinced the principal of the College of the Immaculate Conception, commonly known as St. Mary's College, to provide both her boys with a scholarship.

Thrown in the deep end, my father quickly became fluent in English and thrived, attending St. Mary's between 1921 and 1927. The school was run according to the British education system and inculcated British values in its students. It was there that my father learned to admire a system of government marked by political stability, freedom of speech and respect for human rights. These elements would become defining beliefs, both for my father and for me.

When my father was 17, the family moved back to Caracas, where he and his brother Antonio quickly found that a first-class education and mastery of English opened opportunities for jobs with top multinational companies. Antonio worked for Shell, one of the largest oil concessionaires, and Diego initially was employed by the Royal Bank of Canada, then by the Chrysler car and International truck dealership. An important part of his job was to send accurate requests for machinery and parts to the United States in accordance with the catalogues which, in those days, were written entirely in English.

Even then, my father was comfortable socializing with the representatives from the many international companies establishing themselves in Venezuela. He understood the importance of seamlessly shifting languages and mindsets: He could be Cuban in Havana, English in Trinidad, American in New York, and Venezuelan in Caracas.

He became a cultural chameleon. This would prove an invaluable asset in winning the Pepsi-Cola concession and building his business empire. It was a lesson he passed on to me early on, although I wasn't altogether thrilled at the time. I was an honors student at San Ignacio, a traditional and demanding Jesuit school in Caracas when, at the end of sixth grade, I was called into the office of Father Fernando María Moreta, S.J., my spiritual adviser.[2]

"Gustavo, you're doing well at school," he said, "and I want to congratulate you." "Thank you, Father," I replied. "You have special qualities, my son," he went on. Again, I thanked him. Then he pounced. "The house of God could derive much benefit from your special qualities. Would you consider studying at a seminary?"

I felt flattered and eagerly related his comments to my parents. My father's reaction was definitely not what I expected. Most Catholic families would have been delighted to have a son take holy orders. But while my father was unabashedly Catholic and married to a deeply Catholic woman, he was skeptical of Catholic doctrine because of its views on capitalism. Protestantism sees hard work as a way to get to heaven; Catholicism doesn't denigrate hard work but it's not necessarily the path to heaven. As a businessman, he preferred the Protestant ethic: You have to work for your salvation.

He realized that if I stayed in Venezuela, I could be "tempted" to take a wrong turn. He thought, "Let's put his brain to use but in the United States." I think he was already planning his succession.

My mother didn't argue. She understood that he was a tornado and you don't try to obstruct a tornado. She let him go on his own path, while she stayed at home, nurturing the heart of the family. She knew the value of being the "*alma de la casa*" — "the soul of the house" — and we all recognized her value. My father consulted and cosseted her throughout their life together; we children did, too.

When I told my parents what Father Moreta had said, my father sprang into action. A week later, I was on a plane to the United States. After an intensive English-language course, I enrolled in junior high school at Nyack Boarding School just outside of New York City and later graduated from Suffield Academy, a preparatory school in Connecticut.

A quick aside: My brother Carlos, three years older than me, was already studying at Suffield Academy. Carlos had a valuable gift: He got along with everyone. He was handsome, a good athlete and sophisticated, all the elements necessary to be a big man on campus. And he was kind, too: He opened doors for me. I quickly became part of life at Suffield and felt right at home. My father was right: We could thrive in the Anglo-Saxon world. That was the point he wanted to make — to himself and to us.

I stayed in touch with my family through letters, phone calls and trips to Caracas during school vacations. My father also traveled to New York frequently on business and this was the period when I began to spend a lot of time with him and shadow him at his business meetings.

Like my father, I, too, became a cultural chameleon. He sowed the seeds of my own global mindset. What I've learned is that if you want to fit into a different country, it's not enough just to live there. You have to learn its language and respect its culture. As a student of history, I like to know what and whom I'm dealing with. So if I'm in Paris, I familiarize myself with the topics people care about. The same thing when I'm in Spain or Miami or New York.

I like to look at a country not just through the lens of local business dealings but through the lens of its art and artists. People in the art world are completely different from people in the business world. Art keeps your brain alive, refreshed and up to date. I have an advantage thanks to my wife Patty, who as the founder of the Colección Patricia Phelps de Cisneros, has dedicated her life to enhancing appreciation of the diversity and sophistication of art from Latin America. We have the privilege of meeting artists in their studios. Patty is a walking encyclopedia and is very good at explaining the nuances. It's like having my own personal professor.

Patty and I ensured that our kids would also be culturally adaptable. While the majority of their schooling was in Venezuela, all three received a completely bilingual education: Guillermo, the eldest, went to St. Paul's School in New Hampshire, then to Yale University and Columbia Business School; Carolina, our older daughter, went to the Chapin School in New York and Miss Porter's School in Connecticut, then to Georgetown University; and Adriana, our youngest, went to the Nightingale-Bamford School in New York, then Deerfield Academy, Columbia University and the New York University Journalism School. We had an apartment in New York and spent a lot of time there, as well as taking vacations and long weekends in Venezuela and the Dominican Republic so the kids wouldn't forget their Latin American heritage.

Like my father, I always offered the kids the opportunity to get to know my business: to be chameleons in different business settings. I invited them to join me on professional trips and shadow me in meetings. As I'll describe later, when Adriana was 14 and on spring break, she accompanied me on a tour of South America when we launched DirecTV, the direct broadcast satellite service provider. Twelve days, twelve countries. We'd arrive late at night, have a press conference in the morning, then sign the contract with our local partners. In the afternoon, Adriana would be a tourist, then we'd meet for dinner. It was fun for us both.

Like me with my father, she was intrigued by this taste of the business and wanted more. And like him, I was happy to provide it.

* * *

"Meet the customer's need"

My father started his first business venture when he was in his mid-teens to bring in extra money for the family. His initial idea was to make ice cream, using a hand-cranked freezer that functioned with ice and salt water.

Thinking back, I can imagine that my father quickly realized that the payoff for all that cranking wasn't worth the immense amount of effort. He shifted gears and soon came up with a sweeter idea: candy. And not just any candy. Port of Spain's large community of Venezuelan exiles pined for a taste of home: specifically, *papelón*, a treat made from sugar and molasses. Traditional *papelón* wasn't available on the island, since Trinidad didn't produce molasses. My father drew on his mother's candy-making expertise and together, they created a recipe and designed a wooden mold which produced something close in flavor and appearance to *papelón*. He hawked it on the street and it sold very well. My father recalled, "This was my first experience of making something to meet the customer's need."

In Caracas, my father and his brother Antonio decided to try their luck in the new and promising field of public bus transport to serve the steadily growing population of the city. They obtained a permit to operate a route in Catia, a developing working-class neighborhood west of the city, and converted their dump truck into a bus which they named "*El Expedito*," or "Prompt and Punctual." In the small city that Caracas then was, service was very personal. To ensure quality, they moved to a house in the Nueva Caracas district that had a garage, where they could park and service their bus.

Caracas' economy in the 1920s and 1930s was booming but many people were still so poor that they could not afford public transportation. My father recalled, "At first, we made our runs with hardly any passengers. Then we decided to lower the fare. By charging only a *locha* — twelve and a half *centavos* — the number of customers multiplied." The fare remained the same for the next 20-some years.[3]

The business grew, other vehicles joined "El Expedito" and by the mid-1930s, my father and Antonio had built up a syndicate of more than 200 buses, a gigantic number for a city of fewer than 250,000 inhabitants.[4]

The brothers made sure that the service was first-class. They hired people who wanted to be in the business; rather than taxi drivers who have to buy their own medallion, the bus drivers invested their own capital in "their" bus and were paid on commission. As a result, the buses were clean, well-kept and ran on time, because the drivers saw the direct rewards of maintaining a pleasant atmosphere and an efficient, reliable service. It also helped that my father stationed himself on street corners in Caracas to personally check that the drivers stayed on schedule.[5]

He taught me to be prompt, and it's something that I insist on. Latin America used to be infamous for a *mañana* mentality, but I always wanted people to value time — their own and others'. Once we moved into the television business, we were forced to be punctual. The news broadcast had to begin at 9 on the dot — not 9:03. The only way we could stay on schedule was by hiring people who could manage time efficiently. If delays occurred, we made sure we were caught up by the end of the day. It was tougher to be on time in our personal lives, but it was something Patty and I modeled and made sure the kids followed. We kept North American time. When an invitation called for a dinner or an event to start at 8, we arrived at 8 sharp. This habit stood us in good stead when the organization expanded into the United States and Europe. Being punctual was already engrained in our blood. Meetings began on time.

My father and Antonio got out of the bus business in 1939, when they learned that the municipal council of Caracas wanted to control the fares. Once prices can be set by the government, rather than the market, it's a recipe for disaster. They sold the buses to the drivers, many of whom formed their own cooperative. It was an efficient way to dispose of things and the public never noticed.

From bus transport, they moved into another promising market: selling spare parts for and servicing the increasing number of cars and other kinds of automotive vehicles. In 1940, he and Antonio launched D. Cisneros & Cia., which concentrated on dealerships for a variety of consumer goods, including Hamilton appliances and Reo trucks.

But these enterprises would be dwarfed by the founding of Pepsi-Cola of Venezuela. The process began by chance. In 1939, while Antonio was visiting New York on his honeymoon, he went to one of the main attractions of the time: the World's Fair. There he encountered Pepsi-Cola for the first time.

He fell in love with the taste and the spirit of the brand. Even though its perennial rival, Coca-Cola, was the official soft drink of the fair,[6] Pepsi was fighting back hard. Its 12-ounce bottles were twice as big — the labels advertised "Bigger drink. Better flavor" — but sold for the same price.[7]

Antonio saw an opening. He promptly contacted the company representatives and refused to budge from the office until he was assured that he and my father would have the right to negotiate for the concession to bottle and distribute Pepsi-Cola in Venezuela. It was the first wholly-owned concession granted by the company outside North America. This allowed the brothers to coordinate manufacturing, marketing, distribution and advertising with a combined, uniform strategy.

The deal was finalized on May 8, 1940 and the first Pepsi-Cola plant in Venezuela was opened in September 1940. The brothers initially estimated that they could supply the entire country with 1,300 cases a day for Caracas and 200 for the interior. A primitive machine, capable of filling 1,800 bottles an hour, was deemed sufficient. They were wrong.

Almost overnight, Pepsi-Cola was a huge hit. The taste was a perfect match for the Venezuelan palate and climate. As Venezuela grew — the population of Caracas *tripled* from 400,000 in 1945 to 1.2 million in 1954 — sales of Pepsi grew with it.[8] One bottling plant was constructed, then another and another. In 1944, the production of Pepsi-Cola in Venezuela equaled that of

LESSONS I LEARNED FROM MY FATHER

Coca-Cola; in 1948, it was twice as much and, by 1952, Pepsi controlled two-thirds of the national soft-drink market.[9] Thanks to Cisneros, Venezuela was one of the few countries in the world where sales of Pepsi-Cola surpassed Coca-Cola.

My father and his brother were a perfect partnership: They knew each other's strengths and complemented each other very well. My father was the ideas man; Antonio made the ideas happen. (As I'll describe later, my younger brother Ricardo and I and Antonio's son, my cousin Oswaldo, would follow their model.)

My father constantly strove to make Pepsi a drink that would please every sector of Venezuelan society. Pepsi was, the advertisements declared, "*un refresco de amistad*" — "a drink of friendship" — a product everyone could enjoy (I would have the same goal at Univision: to bring together a widely diverse audience under the common umbrella of speaking Spanish.) My father didn't just meet the customers' needs: He anticipated them and cultivated them.

Mass-market advertising was completely unknown in Venezuela then but my father had seen how it worked in the United States and immediately saw the potential for translation. "The message always has to be in the consumer's mind," he preached, and it was: billboards, neon signs, placards both inside *and* outside retail outlets where Pepsi was sold, the radio (and later television) and dozens of other channels of communication proclaimed, "Twice as good, twice as much."

My father relentlessly kept his finger on the consumer's pulse. Again applying American know-how in market research, he instituted regular and exhaustive surveys of the public's buying patterns and expectations. That knowledge led to the successful launch of the Hit line of soft drinks in local fruit flavors like pineapple, lemon, orange, and *frescolita* (red cola).[10]

My father viewed the *bodegas* — the little neighborhood shops — where Pepsi and Hit sodas were sold as customers in their own right, with needs to be satisfied. They wanted to boost their business? He could help them attract *their* customers: by providing advertising banners, cold storage, promotions and, of course, a quality, low-priced product.

The *bodegas* became our biggest ally. Profit margins in soft drinks are low, unlike beer, where the margins are high. You have to be very efficient. My father insisted on always being the lowest-cost producer, so that he had a margin for growth.

That idea percolated throughout all our companies: No matter what industry we were in, we always concentrated on enterprises where we could offer a mass market a quality service or product at affordable prices. That gave us a gigantic advantage.

It was a lesson I would apply throughout my own career.

Creating a colossus

Pepsi-Cola Venezuela was both a podium and a launch pad for Diego Cisneros. As Pepsi-Cola Venezuela began to generate more resources, Cisneros diversified its holdings into satellite businesses that revolved around and supported the core product.

There was no element in the supply chain that was not controlled by Cisneros or by companies in which Cisneros had an interest. Such integration was a way to ensure a steady supply of raw materials in a country where shortages could occur when least expected.[11]

Partnerships were an efficient way to introduce and leverage outside expertise. Diego Cisneros was a founding partner of the Venezuelan plant of Liquid Carbonic of Chicago, producer of the carbon dioxide that made soft drinks fizzy. Another essential ingredient was sugar; my father partnered with Don Jesús Azqueta, an experienced Cuban sugar producer, in the Central

Azucarero Portuguesa mills in Central Matilde, marking a decisive step in modernizing Venezuela's sugar industry. Tapas Corona was set up with the Zapata family in Mexico to supply bottle tops; an alliance with the Ferré factory built a plant for manufacturing the bottles.[12]

My father took the responsibility of partnership very seriously. He ensured his partners got their money's worth. However, if the partners didn't hold up their end by supplying quality products at low prices, then goodbye. He was unyielding, which was why he was so successful.

Early on, Diego realized that one key way to differentiate Pepsi from other soft drinks was to make sure it was truly refreshing: "If it's cold, it's sold," he preached. But there was a problem: Much of the country didn't have electricity to power refrigerators. Consequently, he founded a gigantic company to manufacture ice cubes — and that's how Venezuela got mass-market cold storage.

Diego Cisneros recognized that to grow the market, he had to offer other products in addition to Pepsi. He created Concentrados Nacionales to produce the flavors for the Hit line of soft drinks.[13] *Since Cisneros originated and manufactured the flavors, it didn't have to pay royalties as it did for the Pepsi-Cola formula. All the profits flowed right back into the business.*

He combined the growing expertise in ice-making, cold storage and flavor manufacturing to set up Tío Rico ice cream. Then he signed an agreement with Borden's to share their technical knowledge, with the result that Tío Rico became the #1 ice cream company in Venezuela. Later, he opened a completely different market with popsicles. My brother Carlos inherited our father's marketing genius and further revolutionized the ice cream business by inventing novelty ice cream products for kids — a totally different way of selling ice cream in those days. The children told their parents what they wanted and their parents bought what their kids dictated. As a child-driven company, Tío Rico expanded from a solid company to a very big company.

Diego Cisneros even added the Studebaker automotive franchise to the existing Reo truck distributorship, enabling him to supply stylish and sturdy Studebaker bodies for Pepsi-Cola trucks.

All the parts of the enterprise were symbiotic, creating a vertically integrated, diversified operation whose reach and efficiencies were hard to match. Early in his career, Roberto Goizueta, who became the chairman and CEO of Coca-Cola, was sent to Venezuela to try to expand Coke's beachhead. "We were outgunned and outsmarted," he recalled. "I swore we would get even someday." (In fact, he didn't just get even — he got something even better, as I'll describe in Part II.)

To manage the fast-growing enterprise, in the late 1950s, Diego Cisneros created the Central Office for the Socio-Technical Advice and Assistance, known by its Spanish acronym OCAAT. OCAAT was the nucleus, the center of operations coordinating and constantly refining the common functions of the different divisions, such as finances, advertising, human resources and legal services. That set up the model for "decentralized centralism," a balance between central control and broad operational autonomy within each entity's specific competence.

Putting all the management functions under one roof was a revolutionary idea in Venezuela at the time — not even the international oil companies did it. More than just a novelty, though, it was a huge improvement in streamlining the enterprise and would be the prevailing philosophy of the organization for years.

What kept the dynamo humming smoothly were my father's management precepts, which I saw played out all the time and everywhere, and which he shared with me in our customized seminars.

* * *

"If you find the right person, you can do any business"

All of the firms that comprised Cisneros were distinguished by cutting-edge technology, competitive pricing and, most of all, rigorous employee training to develop their operational know-how. Employees were expected to continuously improve their skills and were one of the essential sources of innovation for the enterprise.

Long before the phrase "our employees are our biggest asset" became a cliché, my father believed that his employees really *were* what gave Cisneros its competitive edge. "All these machines and buildings are only bricks and mortar," he liked to say. "What matters is the people who come here to work."

One of the principles he frequently repeated was, "The person comes first. If you find the right person, you can do any business." So who were "the right people?" In his opinion: immigrants — or the children of immigrants.

As an immigrant himself coming from Cuba to Trinidad, then Trinidad to Venezuela, my father knew in his bones the characteristics of someone who can survive and thrive in a new environment. He knew that immigrants shared a similar goal: to make a better life for themselves and their families. After all, that's why they left their home country.

In the workplace, that translated into a willingness to put in the long hours and work like hell. Immigrants will get the job done and, equally important, they will follow the rules 100% because they know they cannot afford to make a mistake (I know this first-hand: When I first came to the United States, I felt the same way. I didn't dare mess up. And if I did, I made sure to correct things immediately.)

Because they're used to dealing with so many challenges — a different language, a different culture, a different political system — immigrants are good at adapting to different circumstances. They have an international perspective, are fluent in at least two languages, and share similar middle-class values about family and education. You can bet that their children will have at least one college degree and often more. Consequently, they'll be successful in any area.

After World War II, Venezuela was flooded with immigrants from Europe. Between 1947 and 1951, it welcomed over 17,000 refugees and displaced persons through the International Refugee Organization (IRO), making it the tenth-largest receiving country of the IRO's resettlement program on a global scale and the third-largest in relation to its own population.[14]

Venezuela was a top choice of refugees for a simple reason: It was seen as a country of opportunity. Thanks to its boundless supply of oil, the nation enjoyed the highest standard of living in Latin America[15] and by 1950, was the world's fourth wealthiest nation per capita.[16] It became the training ground for all the major multinational corporations: consumer goods giants like Procter & Gamble and Palmolive, automobile manufacturers and, of course, all the oil companies sent their best people there to hone their skills and get a piece of the action. It was a multicultural fermentation tank for ideas and initiatives, both in business and in the arts.

The head of acquisitions for Cisneros was a man named Rafael Navarro, a Sephardic Jew whose family had emigrated from Morocco to Cuba, then to Venezuela. With all his gifts, why did he choose to come to Venezuela? He explained, "This is manna from Heaven."

In other words, my father had his pick of talent — and it paid off. I would follow his model. When I was running the company, almost all of our top executives were the children of immigrants.

* * *

"Hire the best and trust them"

My father always added that crucial corollary: Treat everyone with respect, as if they owned the business. Trust was the cornerstone of the company. We expected people to be honest and, in return, we gave them a lot of leeway. When your boss trusts you that much, you feel a lot of responsibility and you perform accordingly.

That was the key to our growth. Everyone worked as if they owned the company — because they felt that they *did* own the company. It didn't matter what their position was in the organization; they felt they had a direct line to the top. They felt their opinions mattered and they did. The layers of management were very thin and very dispersed, so you always knew whom you were working for. It was a true family business.

That's why I've always relied more on people than on systems. The more systems you put in place, the stronger the signal that you don't trust somebody. And when you grow very fast, systems can kill you. People are much more adaptable than systems.

* * *

"If the chief has the capacity to learn, the employee also has the capacity to learn"

Curiosity was a strength my father honed constantly and encouraged in others. He believed that curiosity opened your eyes to opportunities; in turn, opening your eyes to opportunities enabled you to spot and get ahead of changing circumstances. If you were ahead of the curve, you had less fear of what might be around the corner.

To increase his capacity to learn, my father was a literal fire-hose of questions. When he inspected a bottling plant, for example, he would interrogate the manager: What was the degree of carbonation? What was the result of the Brix test for density? Some questions about quality control tests were so detailed that the managers had to carry them out themselves in order to feel secure with their answers. It was an excellent way to force them to expand their own capacity to learn.

He didn't just ask questions; he consumed information like a starving man at a feast. I think there's an important distinction between nitpicking versus asking questions because you're genuinely interested. My father wasn't just interested: He was fascinated. He might engulf you in a maelstrom of questions, but his energy was so positive that you couldn't help diving in.

Curiosity is a virtuous circle: The more you learn, the more you *want* to learn. I know, because I'm the same way. You have to cultivate your curiosity. If you're not curious, I can guarantee that's going to stop your career.

* * *

"If you miss by an inch, you miss by a mile"

My father's insatiable curiosity and insistence on creative thinking was matched by an irrepressible desire to excel, both as an individual and an entrepreneur. He was always searching out new possibilities and progressive solutions. When I first learned about the Japanese concept of kaizen, or continuous improvement, it seemed old hat: My father had been preaching it for years. His mantra was: "It can always be done better."

He was relentless in his pursuit of quality in the business: the quality of the product, the factories where it was produced,

38

the bottling plants where it was packaged, the trucks that delivered it, the distribution network that made it available to anyone who wanted a refreshing drink, the advertisements that marketed it and so on, through every step of the supply chain.

For example, one of the hurdles in the company's growth was transporting its products. The bottles were initially moved in wooden crates that broke easily, causing losses in merchandise. My older brother Diego noticed that plastic crates were used in Europe and suggested that they be used at the Cisneros facilities in Venezuela. My father and Diego traveled to Germany, where they obtained a patent; they secured funding, bought the equipment and set up a factory with three machines. As demand soared, Gaveplast — "Gaveras Plásticas Venezolanas," as the new enterprise was called — worked 24-7, halting production only on public holidays.[17]

He sought out experts from anywhere and everywhere. He regularly hired American consulting companies for help in corporate planning and long-term strategies. My father was recruiting talent in Cuba even before the Castro revolution unleashed a flood of well-trained, English-speaking exiles. We snatched up executives and technicians galore. Colombia offered its people a high degree of education and good training; it was another talent pool for us to fish in.

In his obsession with continuous improvement and quality control, my father often said, "If you miss by an inch, you miss by a mile." He was determined not to miss by a millimeter.

* * *

"Anyone who stops, stagnates. And anyone who stagnates is lost"

My father broke the mold in his personal life as much as he did in his business. He loved to spend time in California. "You see things differently in California," he used to tell me. "You become new and fresh."

Once we got into the television business through Venevisión, as I'll describe below, we spent a lot of time in the Golden State. Together, we met the people at Paramount, Disney, Twentieth Century Fox, and ABC who supplied the programming that we aired. My father and I could both see that they were a different breed of people doing different things. They had a different mentality: Anything goes, anything can happen.

My father enjoyed and maybe even envied California's creativity. We both tried to inculcate and nurture it in ourselves. As my father said, "California has to be in your *mind*."

One of the ways he cultivated his inner Californian was through yoga. He loved yoga and practiced it a lot. This was in the 1950s, when most people thought "down dog" was a command to unruly canines. He regularly visited Rancho La Puerta, a spa in California — I attended all his classes — and brought Indra Devi, a star teacher at Rancho La Puerta who was known as "the first lady of yoga," to live with us in Venezuela and give him private lessons.

As we all know now, yoga is not just a series of physical exercises but a never-ending path to enlightenment. It was the perfect practice for my father, who liked to say, "Anyone who stops, stagnates. And anyone who stagnates is lost."

* * *

"Money is like manure: If you spread it around, everything grows"

My father may have started from almost nothing but he was no cheapskate. He was relentless about investing in the organization. If he decided that a business was worth acquiring, then he would acquire it without trying to buy it at a discount. When we bought the CADA supermarket chain from the Rockefellers, for example, people said that we were crazy to pay the price we did. We soon proved that we hadn't overpaid; if anything, as I'll describe in Part II, we underpaid.

He also believed in investing in people: paying them decent salaries and offering incentives and bonuses in recognition of work well done, one of the first organizations in Venezuela to do that.

At the time, the best jobs, i.e., the ones that offered stability and a good salary, were with the foreign oil companies. My father wanted Cisneros to become a talent magnet: He wanted to offer smart kids a real choice. If they wanted steady, if conventional, work, they opted for oil. If they wanted excitement and growth opportunities and the chance to do something for their country, they came to us. We became the Google of the day.

We paid our people a lot and they repaid us with their loyalty. Many would stay with us for decades.

* * *

My father also had specific advice for me personally. Following it helped me to focus my energy, identify and hone skills that were essential for what I was doing and not waste time on extraneous activities. I think that made me a better leader — and a better person.

"Park your ego in the closet."

I was an arrogant kid but my father was a tough taskmaster. Every time I made a mistake, I was told it was a mistake. Every time he thought I was too big for my boots, he cut me down to size. He was my harshest critic but he offered more than just criticism. He had the patience to teach me that there was another way.

"Gustavo, you have to park your ego in the closet," he would say. "You have to have humility. You're not born with it, but you can teach yourself. "Everyone has something to contribute," he emphasized. "You must pay more attention to what is said than to the person who says it. If you are not open to others, if you insist on enclosing yourself inside a narrow circle of relationships and ideas, then problems simply move around you and there is no hope for a solution. To get out of the trap, you have to open yourself to new ideas and listen to other people's opinions carefully."[18]

I trained myself to have more patience. It wasn't natural because, of course, I have an ego — an immense ego. But I soon discovered that there were great rewards in not insisting on being the last man standing in a conversation. Specifically, I learned to be a better listener.

My father always insisted that I first listen before opening my mouth. If I gave an opinion out of place, he would give me a look so that I knew exactly what I did wrong. "Think before talking," he would admonish me. "Don't just make decisions; think for solutions." (I still try to do that today!)

He also always asked for summaries of meetings, immediately, to debrief. That helped me to learn how to focus and to take good notes. It was great training. Over time, it became clear that the more we grew, the more I needed to listen and the less I should speak. There was so much information that it was overwhelming; jumping into a discussion would have been like diving into Class 4 rapids. Staying on the sidelines was the only way for me to get a good perspective.

I soon saw the advantages of listening rather than acting or spouting off whatever I had in my mind. I began to understand that everyone had something interesting to say, if you just took the time to listen for it. And the people who surrounded my father always had something interesting to say: They were bright, they were original and they often saw a different way of doing things. I didn't have to agree; I just had to listen. That's how I got —and still get — ideas: by listening to people.

I think everyone has something to add to a conversation, whether they're a politician, intellectual, businessperson or fisherman. What they have to say may be completely different from what I think but I like to have that mix of information. You waste time by being snobbish — and maybe waste opportunities.

You have to be open to being convinced. And the only way to do that is to listen. For example, I had a good relationship with Carlos Fuentes, a great Latin American writer. Along with other businessmen, politicians and intellectuals, we founded the Foro Iberoamericano (which I'll talk about in Part III). He had a completely different take on life from me — he's a man of the Left but he was open to everyone: businesspeople, intellectuals, politicians. His gift was that he could attract the best minds to focus on problems. We didn't agree on many things but I learned to respect him and sometimes he convinced me to change my opinion.

Fuentes introduced me to Gabriel García Márquez, another great writer. Because I came through Fuentes, García Márquez and I had many chats and he opened the door to his soul. García Márquez was a devoted Leftist. I'm a confirmed capitalist and a deep believer in democracy. Once we were able to bridge that chasm, I would join García Márquez on his evening rambles around Cartagena. He'd go from bar to bar, inventing songs and poems, gathering an ever-growing train of people until we'd end up at a *taberna* at dawn for breakfast. He had a real people's touch, and I learned more about human nature from him during these outings than I could have learned from anyone.

In the process, I learned to understand and work with someone completely different from me. It was an immense lesson I could apply to business. If I could get along with García Márquez and Fuentes, I could get along with anyone. That gave me an advantage to this day that I can talk to anyone.

I also found out very quickly that if I put my ego away, it was easier to ask other people to put *their* egos away. When I was running the company, we had a group of executives who were very smart and naturally had very big egos. They needed an example of when to put their ego in the closet and how to do it; as their boss, I was a strong role model. As a result, they became a group of talented people who knew how to step back, and be ambitious without grandstanding.

It's something I still work on — maybe not enough. Every day, I remind myself, "You have to check, check, check your ego." It all starts by learning to keep your mouth shut and listen.

* * *

"Don't waste time being an accountant. Get the best accountant"

And the best administrators, the top finance people, the smartest creative types and so on. Long before Donald Clifton and Marcus Buckingham enjoined us to "discover your strengths," my father was telling me the same thing. (I'll discuss what I think my strengths and responsibilities as a leader are in Part II.)

"Don't waste time doing what others can do better," he would say. "You don't have to learn everything. Smart people can do anything. If you hire smart people, you save a lot of time." In many ways, he was preaching to the choir. I have dyslexia for numbers. Thanks to my father, I didn't waste time struggling with numbers. Instead, I always hired the best numbers of people. And then when computers came along, we backed them up with computers.

(We went into the business of computers very early, representing Fujitsu, NCR and even Apple in Venezuela. I wanted to learn how to sell them, which meant learning how they worked and how we could use them. What my father did to Coca-Cola, I was able to do to IBM. Venezuela was IBM's biggest market in Latin America until we beat them. It was the first time IBM had ever lost the top spot. Knowing that a giant like IBM could be beaten would give me a lot of confidence to grow outside of Venezuela.)

Similarly, as my father pointed out, I'm a very bad administrator. I like to say that I inherited that from my father, too. But he already knew that about himself, which was why he had very strong administrators and top finance people working for him. And he engrained that discipline in me: to hire people who were better than me.

* * *

"Don't just criticize. Bring me a solution"

My father reserved his harshest criticism for me when I raised issues without suggesting a solution. He would refuse to listen to an argument unless it was presented with a smart "out." "Don't just criticize," he would say. "Bring me a solution."

It took a long time for me to organize my mind that way. But it's a drill that has stayed with me.

Focus on the solution, not on the personalities. Meet everyone with an open mind. Look for the best in people, not the worst. Have trust in them and they, in turn, will have trust in you.

My father was a very positive person and now, thanks to that discipline, I'm a very positive person. My father taught me the benefits of being positive: "If you bring a solution, you'll feel better," he would add. "It's good to be a critic. But it's better to be a builder."

* * *

"Build on commonalities. Don't divide on differences"

My father always told me, "You cannot judge people. You need to know what they're doing and whom they do it with, what they like and what they hate, where they go to school, where they party. You need to get drunk with them once in a while. "And don't be snobbish," he'd add. "You have to touch people and be inspired by them, small or big. Build on commonalities, don't divide on differences."

* * *

"You only need one visionary at a time"

My father surrounded himself with people who were smarter than him: He made sure he had a good executive team and that they hired good assistants. That was part of his determination to learn as well as to ensure that the various divisions of the enterprise ran smoothly on their own without needing his constant supervision. But when he was in the room, he had a hands-on approach and was a fantastic presence. Everyone was inspired by him and looked to him for direction.

As I began to become more involved in the organization, I, of course, suggested changes. One day, he pulled me aside and told me to cool my jets. "The vision is already set," he said. "Yes, we can improve on it. But not now. It's working now. Wait your turn. We can have only one visionary at a time." That was a humbling experience. Young people in their 20s think they know everything. They say, "I could do that and I could do it better." He gently corrected me and pointed out that I had to earn my spurs first.

* * *

"Challenges are our main business"

For more than a century since declaring independence first from Spain in 1811 and then in 1830 from La Gran Colombia, a remnant of the Spanish empire, Venezuela was shaped by political turmoil and autocracy, its government a constantly shifting kaleidoscope of dictatorships, juntas, regional caudillos (military strongmen) wrestling for power, coups d'état and, occasionally, outright civil war, such as the one that drove my father's mother's family into exile from Venezuela.

My father doubtless heard stories of upheaval from his relatives, as well as from others in Trinidad's large Venezuelan community. He personally experienced the repression and capriciousness of the authoritarian system twice soon after he returned to Venezuela. His first confrontation took place when a gathering of "Dos

Caminos," an amateur soccer team he had joined, was broken up by the police, because the regime was suspicious of groups of young people congregating in public.

His second experience was more serious. My father had applied for the permits necessary to launch his public bus transport business and, after a long wait, had finally secured an appointment with the secretary of the governor, General Rafael María Velasco. When he arrived at General Velasco's office, however, a police officer refused to let him enter. My father showed him the notification verifying his appointment. The officer responded to this seeming affront to his authority by arresting my father and having him taken to the headquarters of the Caracas Police, where he was held incommunicado. Finally, after five long days, he was released, as inexplicably as he had been arrested.

These demonstrations of arbitrary power made a lasting impression on my father, strengthening his desire to promote and later support democracy in Venezuela.

In December 1935, General Juan Vicente Gómez, the dictator who had ruled the country for 27 years. Although still a poor, rural and mostly illiterate country, Venezuela was evolving: The oil boom brought migration to urban centers from the countryside, there were radio networks in all the important cities and the country began to be linked by a network of roads and highways. The social divide between rich and poor was, if anything, deeper than before, but an incipient middle class had emerged.[19] Gómez' successors restored some civil liberties, allowing the reappearance of political parties, trade unions and professional organizations, and the return of political exiles.

One of those exiles was Rómulo Betancourt, who became known as "the father of Venezuelan democracy." My father met him in 1937, a year after Betancourt's return. Their warm friendship endured throughout their lifetimes. Although I haven't played *an active role in politics, my father once said, "I've always identi-fied with democratic values."[20]*

In 1958, after another series of coups and exile, Betancourt became president in the first free elections to be held in Venezuela in a decade. The new government was on shaky ground, though, with the most serious threat coming from Fidel Castro, whose dic-tatorship had taken over Cuba in February 1959.

The climate of insecurity caused many businesses to go bank-rupt, among them the company that operated Caracas' Channel 4 television station, then called Televisa. The country's television and radio industry were dominated by the Phelps family, which had launched Radio Caracas, the first radio station in Venezuela, then expanded into the new medium of television. William H. Phelps, Sr., the son of a high-society New York family who had first come to Venezuela in the late 19th century on a bird-watching expedition, was as much of a wizard in business as he was gifted in ornithology. Even as other television licenses were granted, none could match Radio Caracas Television (RCTV) broadcasting on Channel 2.

These were difficult times in Venezuela. When Channel 4 went bankrupt, the unions were owed a great deal of money by the former owner and took control of the station. Amid an atmos-phere of confusion, conflict and confrontation, Channel 4 stayed on the air but began to turn into a forum that favored extremist sectors — especially the extreme Left, which supported Castro. Its growing influence was of great concern to the democratic leaders.

Betancourt knew that a state bailout or shutdown of Televisa might be interpreted as an authoritarian action muzzling the free speech he had worked so hard to instill. He proposed that my father buy the station with the aim of achieving two goals: turn it into a profitable independent business and, even more important, use it to shape public opinion to support and strengthen the new democracy. *"We don't want to close Televisa,"* he told my father. *He offered a deal: "If you can solve the problem through capitalism, we will help with the bureaucracy."*

My mother, Albertina Cisneros, played a crucial role in my father's thinking. She, more than he, was a devoted television viewer: She was his eyes and ears for this new medium — and she didn't like the political views broadcast on Televisa. (Remember, the Catholic Church was fiercely opposed to Communism and my mother was not only a devout Catholic but had a sister who was a nun.) She told my father, "If Channel 4 continues to grow, they'll be spreading godless Communism. Do we want to become a Communist country? You cannot allow this to happen." Nor was she willing to cede the playing field to the Phelps family without a fight, because why should one allow the Protestants to win?

Between being lobbied by Betancourt and my mother — and once she sank her teeth into something, she wouldn't let go — my father began to watch TV. He soon became fascinated with the opportunities to communicate in such a dynamic field. And it was a platform to promote democracy. In addition, I'm sure my father thought, "If everyone is so interested in television, maybe I should be interested, too. I don't want to miss out."

Yes, there would be significant challenges. He would have to obtain the support of the trade unions, invest an enormous amount of money and learn to manage an entirely new business. Television was, he later wrote, "a permanent theater that one cannot leave, and where one cannot lose the public's interest. It is a daily, constant challenge." But, as he liked to say, "Challenges are our main business."[21] The bidding for Channel 4 took place in June 1959, and my father's bid was accepted. Venevisión was officially launched in July 1960.

* * *

"The entertainment business is a great school for life"

Television may have been an entirely new industry for my father but he applied the precepts that had served him so well in building the Pepsi-Cola empire. He knew he needed a partner with expertise. He found one in Leonard Goldenson, the president of the American Broadcasting Company (ABC). Like my father, Goldenson was a businessman who migrated to television when he acquired the then-struggling ABC for $24 million in 1953.[22] Goldenson advised my father about the purchase of rights to syndicated programs and Hollywood movies, as well as a mix of programming guaranteed to keep viewers glued to the screen. Equally important, he helped my father adapt to a management model better suited to nurturing actors and screenwriters than salespeople and numbers-crunchers.

For creative talent, my father could thank Fidel Castro. In the 1950s, the powerhouses in Spanish-speaking television were Cuba and Mexico, where Emilio Azcárraga's Televisa was topping the charts. (Azcárraga and I would become partners in Univisión, the premier Spanish-language network in the U.S., as I'll describe in Part II.) When Castro nationalized Cuban TV, most of the Cuban talent fled to the U.S. or Latin America. My father was brilliant at attracting those emigrants.

Choosing the right mix of programs to be aired was a fantasy come true for someone attuned to customer satisfaction. Venevisión's programming appealed to both adults and children and reflected uniquely Venezuelan attributes of hard work and the pursuit of excellence. It played an important role in boosting middle-class values.

For adults, it offered a balance of information and entertainment: perceptive news broadcasts (one host said she used

Walter Cronkite as a model);[23] thoughtful talk shows with analysts who became known for their intellect and honesty; raffles and contests such as *El Batazo de la Suerte* ("The Lucky Hit"); comedy and variety shows; dubbed versions of American series like *Cheyenne* and *Maverick;* local productions like *Casos y Cosas de Casa;* and, of course, wildly popular *telenovelas*, such as *La Cruz del Diablo*. For children, there was *My Friend Flicka* and *Los Amiguitos de Gioia*, a hugely popular program.[24] Practically the entire country tuned in to *Sábado Sensacional*, a five-hour programming marathon that ran every Saturday from 4 to 9, whose guests included Frank Sinatra, Celia Cruz, Miriam Makeba, John Travolta, Julio Iglesias, the Jackson Five, Roger Moore (aka "James Bond"), Christopher Reeve (aka "Superman") and other celebrities. Venevisión was a resounding success.

Managing the talent at Venevisión was a challenge that forced my father — and then me — to up our game. *Any* other business would have been easier. There were lots of diverse personalities with only one thing in common: They were the *crème de la crème* of talent — and they knew it. The guy who connected the cables thought he was the *best* cable guy. The guy handling the camera thought he was the *best* camera guy. Ditto for the directors and the people who sold advertising space. And let's not even get started with the actors, the broadcasters, the interviewers and the hosts. Someone was constantly getting in a snit about someone else. Feathers were frequently ruffled. Temper tantrums were routine.

And such is the nature of television that everything happened very quickly, while the programs *had* to air on time. Getting everyone to work together took skill, drive and diplomacy. No wonder my father declared, "The entertainment business is a great school for life. You have to deal with different types of people, with big egos. If you can manage this, you can manage anything."

I was 15 years old when Venevisión began broadcasting. It was exhilarating and creative. I promptly fell in love with television. How could I not?

From the outset, Venevisión was a vocal defender of democracy. As the first fully democratic government, headed by Rómulo Betancourt, was coming to a close, Venevisión began broadcasting well-regarded interview and opinion programs featuring guests ranging from politicians to writers, musicians and artists, to stimulate debate and illustrate the freedom of speech that is the cornerstone of democracy.

The election of 1963 took place amid threats of violence and sabotage. Venevisión took its cameras to the street so that voters could see for themselves the long but peaceful lines at the polling booths throughout the country. On March 11, 1964, Venevisión broadcast the peaceful transfer of power from a democratically elected president to his legitimate successor. By 1965, Venevisión was the leading network in the country, broadcasting in 18 of Venezuela's then 20 states and with the largest audience in the country.[25] (Venevisión and Radio Caracas TV alternated first and second ratings positions for the next 40-odd years, until RCTV was closed in 2007. However, Venevisión occupied the top spot for longer periods than RCTV.) It was modern, fast-paced, responsive — thanks to my father's obsession with market research, we were constantly polling our audience — and exciting. It was *the* place to be.

My father recognized that I had an interest and special affinity for television. When I was in Venezuela, he insisted that I continue to accompany him on his daily rounds of the Pepsi-Cola plants — my working day usually began at five in the morning and ended at ten at night[26] — but it was clear to us both that my heart belonged to Venevisión. We both assumed that it would be my future.

* * *

"Be a positive agent for change"

Creating Venevisión was more than just a business decision for my father. It was a concrete illustration of a belief that he had been thinking about for some time: that an entrepreneur should not neglect the society supporting his enterprise.

Around the same time that he was considering acquiring Channel 4, my father joined the Mont Pèlerin Society. An international organization composed of economists, political scientists, historians, intellectuals and business leaders, the society was founded soon after the end of World War II with the aim of promoting free enterprise and healthy economic competition within a democratic and pluralistic form of government. It would become one of the world's most prominent think tanks, whose members included Presidents, Chancellors, Prime Ministers, finance ministers, plenty of thoughtful businesspeople and a large number of Nobel Prize winners in Economics. (A bit of Mont Pèlerin Society trivia: MPS actually helped create the Nobel Prize in Economics, specifically to legitimize free-market economic thinking.[27])

My father attended a meeting of the Mont Pèlerin Society in September 1959, accompanied by Nicomedes Zuloaga, a friend and fellow Venezuelan businessman who was also an MPS member. I like to imagine them having animated discussions deep into the night about the role and responsibility of business to shape and strengthen a viable vision of democratic government, one which guaranteed the rule of law for all while broadening the scope of opportunities and incentives for every member of society.

Corporate social responsibility was a natural outgrowth of that thinking. At the time, Venezuelan businessmen generally were not inclined to allocate capital to social and cultural programs, regarding such causes as expenses rather than investments.[28]

So, it made a big impact in 1968, when my father accepted the International Advertising Association's award for "Advertising Man of the Year" and publicly announced his plan to create the Fundación Diego Cisneros.

My father often said that a real, legitimate democracy "cannot exist and grow vigorously without the participation of the business community." His credo was summarized in a single sentence during his remarks at the Foundation's inaugural ceremonies: "There can be no political freedom without economic freedom."[29] As his friend Nelson Rockefeller put it, "It's hard to be a Communist on a full belly."[30]

Full bellies were part of the promise of Cisneros. Whenever and wherever my father set up soft drink plants in Venezuela, it would spark an immense change: There would be better jobs, better pay, clean water, quantities of ice and, most of all, plentiful opportunities for a better life. People knew that when they worked at a Cisneros-owned and -operated facility, they were working with the best. It was exhilarating, it inspired loyalty and it produced results.

My father would often exhort his business colleagues, "Gentleman, let us invest money in disseminating the best product known to mankind: the philosophy of freedom."[31] And he did: not just through the better-known charities like the Venezuelan Red Cross, the Venezuelan Cancer Society, the Hospital Ortopédico Infantil and the Children's Foundation,[32] but through programs like the Venevisión Cultural Foundation, which used television and radio (we acquired/created Radio- visión in 1974) campaigns to promote public service and civic excellence, and ACUDE (Asociación Cultural para el Desarollo), an innovative literacy initiative that used the latest technology to reach a mass audience. (ACUDE was realized and run by my wife Patty, as I'll describe in Part II.)

In these and so many other ways, he was laying the founda- tion for a new Venezuela. I was at his side, supporting him and soaking it all in. My father deeply believed that professional excellence had to be balanced by concern for humanity — and a dash of daring, enough to be able to do things differently. He often said, "You can't have a successful business if you don't have the three essentials: brains, heart and courage."

Of all the lessons he taught me, this was the most funda- mental and the most significant. It would be my compass throughout my career and my life.

* * *

In February 1970, I received a telephone call with the news no child ever wants to hear: "Gustavo, I'm calling because of your father." It was the regional vice president of the Pepsi-Cola plant in Maracaibo. My father had suffered a heart attack. The heart attack was followed by a stroke and he was unconscious by the time he was brought to the San Román Clinic in Caracas. The doctors held little hope.

Until then, I had expected that I would work at the company, concentrating in Venevisión. After I graduated from Suffield Academy, I had applied to and been accepted at the Wharton School of Business at the University of Pennsylvania. I deferred admission in order to return to Venezuela to study law at the Universidad Católica. (In the United States, if you request a deferral after being accepted, you're still guaranteed a place in whichever class you matriculate with. This gave me an exit route back to the U.S. if I didn't like Venezuela.) I completed the first year of law school, which was more than enough to show me that I didn't want to be a lawyer. But I obtained a Venezuelan baccalaureate diploma, which gave me credentials I knew would be helpful in setting me up in business in Venezuela.

I wanted a business education that focused, specifically, on the technical side: finance, accounting, all the tools you need to be a good manager. After my legal detour, I wanted it fast. Wharton, however, had other ideas: They insisted that I take liberal arts courses; furthermore, the curriculum requirements would take three years to complete.

I didn't want to wait that long. Fortunately, I found out about Babson College, which was just outside of Boston. Babson is strictly about business. Half of the students when I went there were the first generation of their family to go to college; they were ambitious and hard-working. Babson let me take classes in their night school, so I could get my degree six months earlier than I would have at Wharton. And another thing: They understood the power of networking long before the concept became popular and their network was amazing. I fell in love with the place. Nowadays, if you want to go into business, my advice is, "Go to Babson. Or Wharton or IESE (the graduate business school of the University of Navarra in Spain)."

In 1968, I graduated cum laude with a degree in economics and promptly started an internship at ABC to prepare for taking control at Venevisión. The timing couldn't have been better. ABC may have been the smallest of the big three major networks in the U.S. but it was the most innovative.[33] Its president, Leonard

Goldenson, had advised my father at Venevisión and became my mentor. Since the operation was relatively small, I was allowed to do whatever I wanted, from operating the camera and handling the cables to learning the nuts and bolts of the production and editing departments. I also studied the economic and financial aspects of a television company, and the income and expenditures of a highly competitive industry in a state of constant change. It was a fabulous learning opportunity.

As I moved around the network's offices in Detroit, Chicago, New York and Los Angeles, I met other people who were just as enthralled with the television business as I was. People like Michael Eisner, who would head the Walt Disney Company, and Barry Diller, who would build the USA and Fox networks, were starting their careers at the same time as me. We became colleagues and friends.

The actual internship lasted only a few months but the "permanent internship" continued for years. The doors were always open when I needed them. Leonard Goldenson would make people available to me, invite me to meetings and generally keep me in the loop. I returned the favor by selling 20% of Univision to ABC in 2007.

It was an exciting time in my personal life as well. Patricia Phelps was one of a group of Caracas kids attending prep schools and colleges on the East Coast of the United States. (She was at the Madeira School just outside Washington, D.C., then went to Wheaton College in Massachusetts.) We'd all meet up in New York on weekends; we'd attend 1 p.m. mass at St. Patrick's Cathedral to please our parents, then enjoy ourselves.

The Phelps and Cisneros families ran the two main private media networks in Venezuela, so of course Patty and I vaguely knew each other. But Patty was two years younger than I was, and, at that age, two years makes a big difference. Patty recalls the

*first time she saw me. It was at a Nat King Cole concert in Cara-
cas. She says, "I was about 15, wearing a dress with a little Peter
Pan collar and no make-up. He drove a sporty blue convertible
with two soap opera stars in the back seat, all decked out with
glamorous clothes and stylish hair. Later, when we met at St. Patrick's, I found him arrogant. If anyone had said that we'd be married, I would have said, "No way!"*

Fast-forward to 1969. Patty had graduated from Wheaton
and was teaching at the newly founded Simón Bolívar University
in Caracas, where she established the department of foreign languages. I ran into her at a concert — she was with someone else —
then, a few weeks later, at a nightclub, with yet another date. I
began talking to her. She was smart, self-sufficient and had such
sparkle. I wanted to be with her all the time. I thought, "I need to
get this woman in my life!"

As Patty remembers, my father had offered her a job and she
came to our house for lunch a few times, so she had already met
my family. Our first real date was in December. Once I set my
sights on her, I invited her to New Year's Eve dinner with my family. My mother brought the silver candelabra out of storage — a
sure sign of her approval. I proposed 11 days later and we were formally engaged three weeks after that.

Then my father had his stroke. I had spoken to my father
many times about going out on my own and we had planned my
path together. I wanted to be a business tycoon like him but in
other industries. I saw an opportunity in what we were doing with
Venevisión, especially the opportunity to expand our reach outside of Venezuela to other Spanish-speaking countries and Spanish-speaking audiences in the United States. All of these things I
had discussed with my father and he had agreed.

When he had his stroke, everything changed. When he could
speak, he said to me, "You have to concentrate on saving the

family and saving me." I knew he meant, "Save the businesses" — not just Pepsi but also Venevisión. The most important thing was to preserve his vision of the future and our ability to realize that vision.

I concentrated first on saving him. He needed special care and equipment which weren't available in Venezuela. I contacted my father's doctor in New York, who was connected with the world-famous Rusk Institute there. "It's going to take a year or more," he said. (Actually, it would take less.) "I recommend you move to New York."

The Venezuelan doctors were against it: "Gustavo, he may die on the plane," they warned me. I said that I'd rather he died trying than not trying and dying in Venezuela. My mother agreed, and then we consulted the rest of the family. They gave their permission to transfer him to Rusk. The Venezuelan doctors refused to sign the release forms; they didn't want their names on a "death certificate." We knew it was an immense risk but our feeling was, if he died, that's better than letting him just wilt away.

Rehabilitation at the Rusk Institute was a full-time job for both my father and me. We began at 5 a.m. with physical therapy and ended at night. My mother, brothers and sisters came often, but I was managing his care. When he was ready to leave Rusk and become an outpatient, I found an apartment for him at the Waldorf Towers and set up a system of nurses and medical assistants, who later accompanied him to Venezuela to train local caregivers and helped set up a complete rehab operation in our house.

Patty's father was in failing health, so it became imperative to get married while he was able to walk her down the aisle. We were married on June 10, 1970, in a simple ceremony in the Lady Chapel of St. Patrick's Cathedral. We were both so busy looking after our respective fathers that Patty bought her wedding dress off the rack at Bergdorf's while I ordered a cake by phone from a local bakery. Our wedding occurred not a moment too soon. Patty's father died a week later.

That's how our marriage began — in the middle of chaos. The foundations of my world had shifted. My family didn't know how to react to this man who, in the blink of an eye, went from a force of nature, a tornado, to being bed-bound and unable to speak.

Because I had spent so much time with him, I was the child who understood him and knew what he wanted. People — including my siblings — began to turn to me with their questions. What everyone — in the family and the company — wanted to know was: Who is going to protect us? Who is going to take care of us? Who is going to be in charge?

I forced a difficult conversation. Thanks to the Rusk Institute, we had access to very good psychiatrists. (Dr. Howard Rusk knew that a key part of helping the patient was helping the family.) I hired two: one for my mother and one for the rest of the family. They explained the changes we could expect to happen to my father and how those would affect my mother and the rest of us. They became close advisers, ready to step in and spend time with family members whenever they visited.

The psychiatrists helped manage the knowledge vacuum in the family. In addition, I read everything I could get my hands on about my father's condition. (My father had made me take a speed-reading course, which now came in handy.) With more knowledge there was less tension. Somehow, I was able to answer most of the questions. And fortunately, I gave the right answers.

Thankfully, my father was more physically than mentally impaired. It took three months for him to learn to speak again but he could always understand fully. He would recover about 80% of his capacities.

Still, it was clear early on that he wouldn't be able to return to his former responsibilities at the company. We would have to *adapt. I spoke to my mother and all my siblings about the organization's financial situation and how to best express our father's wishes. I said, "Anyone can run the business. But right now, with your permission, I'll continue doing it until our father recovers or we change direction."*

At a certain point, my father said, "Why don't you run the business full-time until I recover?" It evolved that everyone agreed that I was the guy to do it. It just came naturally. I had wanted to be an independent entrepreneur, but I agreed to hold the helm until my father could resume his place. In my heart, though, I think I knew that it would be permanent.

My older siblings were already involved in the business. Diego, who was six years older than I, was brilliant but suffered from health issues. The condition had shown up when he was in his late teens, and at that time, in the mid-1950s, there was no effective treatment. (He eventually found very good doctors in Spain.) Diego was always the smartest person in the family in terms of IQ and was very creative, always thinking out of the box. He had been instrumental in coming up with the idea for Gaveplast, which became the largest plastics company in Venezuela. He had the idea for Pentacom, which I'll discuss later. He worked closely with me as a sounding board, brainstorming partner and adviser, and could be relied on to bring a different perspective to company board meetings. He was a very happy brother and, even though he was older, there was never any issue of rivalry. (Diego was the first of our family to cash out of the firm; he retired and moved to the United States in the mid-1990s. We were still talking and brainstorming right up to his death in October 2017.)

My sister Marión, who was five years older than I, was a talented architect with a business of her own. In addition, she oversaw the design of almost all of our real estate and infrastructure projects. Like our father, she was a good people connector. Her ability to build relationships made her extremely helpful on the board of directors.

Next in line was my brother Carlos, three years older than I. He was a brilliant and charming guy. He'd graduated from UCLA with a degree in marketing, married and returned with his wife Shahla to Venezuela, where he worked first for Philip Morris and then for Cisneros, where he took charge of our expansion into Brazil. He already had plenty on his plate.

My brother Ricardo, who is two years younger, had graduated from Babson College a year earlier, in June 1969, and came to work at Cisneros. He was always more comfortable with details and numbers, while I was a big-picture guy. My father had once told a close collaborator at Pepsi-Cola, "Gustavo will open new paths for the group, and Ricardo will take care of consolidating them."[34]

A month after my father's stroke, we made it official: Ricardo became the COO of Cisneros and the following month, I became the Chairman and CEO.

Notes

1. For more information, see Rodríguez, José Ángel, *Cisneros: A Family History*, Fundación Cisneros, 2017, pp. 73, 55.

2. Quoted in *Gustavo Cisneros: Pioneer*, p. 28.

3. *Diego Cisneros: A Life for Venezuela*, p. 55.

4. https://en.wikipedia.org/wiki/Timeline_of_Caracas#20th_century

5. *Cisneros: A Family History*, p. 92.

6. https://www.1939nyworldsfair.com/worlds_fair/wf_tour/zone-3/zone-3.htm

7. https://www.britannica.com/topic/PepsiCo-Inc

8. *Diego Cisneros: A Life for Venezuela*, p. 107.

9. *Ibidem*, p. 109.

10. *Gustavo Cisneros: Pioneer*, p. 31.

11. *Diego Cisneros: A Life for Venezuela*, p. 146.

12. *Cisneros: A Family History*, p. 106.

13. *Gustavo Cisneros: Pioneer*, p. 31.

14. *Processes of Spatialization in the Americas*, edited by Gabriele Pisarz-Ramirez and Hannes Warnecke-Berger, p. 244. https://www.peterlang.com/view/9783631772089/html/ch22.xhtml

15. https://en.wikipedia.org/wiki/Economy_of_Venezuela

16. *Ibid.*

17. *Cisneros: A Family History*, p. 105.

18. *Diego Cisneros: A Life for Venezuela*, p. 158.

19. https://en.wikipedia.org/wiki/History_of_Venezuela_(1908%E2%80%931958)

20. *Diego Cisneros: A Life for Venezuela*, p.169.

21. *Ibidem*, p.176.

22. *Gustavo Cisneros: Pioneer*, p. 24.

23. Interview with Beatrice Rangel. August 3, 2021.

24. *Cisneros: A Family History*, p. 110.

25. *Diego Cisneros: A Life for Venezuela*, p. 179.

26. *Cisneros: A Family History*, p. 117.

27. Maxton, Graeme, and Randers, Jorgen, *Reinventing Prosperity: Managing Economic Growth to Reduce Unemployment, Inequality and Climate Change,* Greystone Books, 2016, p. 77.

28. *Cisneros: A Family History*, p. 113.

29. *Diego Cisneros: A Life for Venezuela*, p. 205.

30. https://agrarianstudies.macmillan.yale.edu/sites/default/files/files/colloqpapers/09hamilton.pdf

31. *Diego Cisneros: A Life for Venezuela*, p. 206.

32. *Cisneros: A Family History*, p. 114.

33. *Gustavo Cisneros: Pioneer*, p. 34.

34. *Ibid.*

Part II

TRANSFORMATION: 1970s

There's never a good time for someone to suffer a severe stroke but my father was felled at a particularly inopportune moment. My father was on the verge of taking the next steps to make Cisneros a larger organization. I believe he was considering going public, so that he would have the financial resources to buy out his partners' shares. He had been uncharacteristically slow to move ahead on this — maybe because he didn't want to tackle head-on an issue that would be sure to exacerbate tensions among long-time partners, maybe because he was an optimist and thought he could convince them to go along.

In any case, when he got sick, the knives came out — and now they were pointed at me. There was a lot of resistance and hostility from the shareholders, some hidden and some right out in the open. Their message was, "We like you, but you're 24 years old and too young to run the business. We want to do it our way. Otherwise, we're leaving you." Even our banks were wavering. It was an impossible situation.

To everyone, I said, "Diego Cisneros is alive. If he were dead, I would, of course, consider changing the leadership. But I think he's going to be fine and will make a very effective chairman." To myself, I said, "We're in trouble. We have all the issues we had before he got sick and now we have even more. We need to make the extra push to settle our debts and pay off our partners. If not, we'll lose everything he accomplished."

I knew the partners just wanted a regular check. We wanted to expand the business — a lot. They were happy with the size of the business as it was. With partners like that, it's better to part ways. If they don't want to join you, do it alone. When I asked my father if he would agree to let me buy out his partners, he said, "Yes. You will do me a favor. I knew I should have done it but I just didn't."

I thought we had the wrong bankers and the wrong lawyers to accomplish such a complicated task. I asked him, "Who is the best lawyer in town?" He said, "Pedro Tinoco." At the time, Tinoco was the Minister of Finance, as well as the legal representative for all the Rockefeller family interests in Venezuela, which included the oil companies and Chase Manhattan Bank. He was also a good friend of my father. My father added, "He's both the #1 lawyer and a top financier, so we'll get two experts for one. And he has the best Rolodex, so we'll have access to the best people in Venezuela and the United States." I gave all our legal business to him.

Another ally was George Moore. Moore was the President of Citibank (the predecessor to Citigroup). During his tenure, he oversaw the bank's expansion into Latin America, and then became its chairman. When my father got sick, Moore was one of the first people he turned to.

Pedro was the best advisor we could have inside Venezuela and George was the best outside. They got along very well because, as is often the case, the best people understand each other. They backed me and Ricardo, and together they told people, "Give these kids a chance. They will pay their debts."

Remember, the soft drink business has fantastic cash flow. People could see that we wanted to continue on my father's path and make immense combinations of businesses, which would, in turn, provide an immense payback. Thanks to Pedro Tinoco and George Moore, we lined up more than adequate lines of credit with the top banks in Venezuela and the U.S.

My father controlled all of his holdings in eastern Venezuela. With our new financial backing, we were able to buy out the partners who controlled Caracas and central Venezuela. That left a few hold-outs in the Maracaibo region in the west of the country, but we had the necessary majority. We came to an understanding and they eventually agreed to be bought out. I knew that whatever price we gave them, once we had full control, it would be a drop in the bucket.

We also had a big operation with Pepsi-Cola and other soft drinks in Brazil, which my father and my brother Carlos had started. Carlos had done extremely well there. He was charming and handsome, his wife was elegant, and they quickly became the "it" couple in Sao Paolo. My father began to see that Carlos had gigantic gifts for advertising and marketing, so we had the right person doing the right things.

We dreamed of replicating our vertically integrated "empire" in Brazil. But Brazil was always a complicated place — it still is. The great Brazilian musician Antonio Carlos Jobim had a phrase: "Brazil is not for amateurs." In Brazil, you always need to follow *o jeitinho* — "the little way" — to make a deal or resolve a problem. It's never A to B; it's A to B, via Z and K.

My brother Carlos said to our father, "Every time you turn around in Brazil, it's a different situation. We don't have the money and talent to be #1 in Brazil *and* expand into the United States. I'd rather have us be in the U.S. long-term."

My father had long dreamed of establishing a foothold in the United States, particularly in California, and I agreed. The business and banking system in Venezuela was beginning to shift; it was becoming more welcoming to a younger generation. My father was still very weak but he told people to support the plan. He made it clear that he was behind me 100%, which helped persuade the older "establishment" to trust me.

We sold our bottling operations in Brazil. The proceeds of the sale kicked off a period of very fast growth, first in Venezuela and, eventually, in the U.S. When we sold our Brazil operations, Carlos had the opportunity to start something new in the United States. Instead, he returned to Caracas and focused on our Tío Rico ice cream company. He had a knack for marketing and such a good head for business. He copied the Pepsi system of distribution and installed cold storage everywhere. He realized that children were the driving force behind impulse buying and tapped our expertise in flavor concentrates to put out a new product every week. The company became very successful. He then took charge of public relations for Cisneros overall in Venezuela, working with municipal councils and chambers of commerce. He was perfect for that but it was clear he had bigger ambitions. He started to get involved in politics and was a natural: He got along with everyone. He had ideas about how to make the country bigger and better. I could imagine him as a fantastic President. He drowned in Canaima National Park in 1983, rescuing his son from river rapids. It was a tragedy for our family and for the country.

When my father got sick, everything could have gone to pieces. He was totally inactive for one full year. But we had Pedro Tinoco and George Moore organizing money and connections for us. We were doing so many projects — especially with Venevisión — that the business world gave us the benefit of the doubt. They didn't jump in and collaborate, but they were willing to be put on standby: "Let's wait and see what these kids can do."

Then they began to call other people and say, "Hey, these guys are serious. They will do what needs to be done. Don't jump to conclusions." That meant Ricardo and I were doing many things correctly. One of my father's lessons was, "From crises, bigger and better opportunities emerge." His illness could have been a death knell for the organization. Instead, it was a launch pad.

A period of promise

In the 1970s, Venezuela was bursting with potential. As Ariana Neumann wrote in her memoir When Time Stopped, *"There were serious problems — social disparity, corruption and poverty — but there was also a sense that such issues were being addressed. Social and educational programs were being implemented; government housing, schools and hospitals were being built. [The country] had a stable democracy, a rising literacy rate, a flourishing art scene and, thanks to oil, a well-funded government intent on developing further industries, infrastructure and education. Businesses, both local and international, were keen to invest. Migrants were attracted by the quality of life, relative safety, climate and opportunities. [Caracas] was a bustling, modern metropolis. There were daily flights to New York, Miami, London, Frankfurt, Rome and Madrid. Even the Concorde made regular flights from Paris to the Maiquetía airport."[1]*

William Luers, a U.S. diplomat who arrived in Venezuela in 1969 and later became the U.S. Ambassador, described Venezuela as "the star of Latin America." It was a time of hope and promise — and we intended to help fulfill those hopes and realize that promise.

The common thread linking the businesses in the Cisneros conglomerate was simple: a determination to provide quality products and services to mass-market consumers at an affordable price. We had a vision that all of our businesses — both the

present ones and any future acquisitions — would contribute to
making life better for the average family.

After we consolidated our ownership of companies in the soft
drink industry, we turned our sights to the television business, so
that we could control our destiny there, too. We knew we would
outgrow Venezuela, very likely sooner rather than later. I said, "I'm
going to be very opportunistic. I'm going to buy anything that has
good cash flow, that could do even better with improved manage-
ment and marketing and advertising, that could grow worldwide."

All the steps we made were based on optimism. Optimism was
part of our DNA. Our father taught us that when you approach
every decision with a constructive attitude, you will not see only
obstacles: You will see possibilities.

My family backed me up, for which I was and am eternally
grateful. They all agreed with our father that I should be the head
of the Cisneros organization. I was able to communicate my opti-
mism and they believed in me, as they had believed in him.

But first, we had to get our act together in Venezuela.

* * *

"Build a brain trust you can trust"

I grew up with the idea that you need to be able to call on the best
brains. My father had an informal brain trust composed of Don
Kendall, the CEO of Pepsi-Cola who became a personal friend;
Pierre Lavedain, a Canadian businessman who became one of
his partners; and Luis Beltrán González, the owner of CORPA, the
best advertising agency in Latin America at the time.

They'd meet periodically in New York City or in Curaçao,
which was close to Venezuela and where they could trust that
the telephones wouldn't be tapped (phone tapping was a national

hobby in Venezuela. My father never knew whether his phones were tapped by the government or the competition. The only phones in the region he could trust were in Curaçao or Aruba; as Dutch constituencies, they offered safe communications.)

I had two main problem-solvers who served as my private advisors and wise counselors. (Once his health permitted, my father also became part of this brain trust.) One was Pedro Tinoco, who was nicknamed "Buddha," for his unwavering calmness and uncanny ability to parse human nature and power. He was instrumental in opening financial channels for us. Because he was the lawyer for the Rockefeller interests in Venezuela, he knew the inner workings of Chase Manhattan better than anyone. When I needed money, he knew which levers of power to pull. Things that would have taken three months, we could accomplish in one week, because he had the institutional knowledge and we had his reputation.

George Moore was my other close advisor. He had recently retired from the presidency of Citibank but wanted to stay active, so he signed on as my full-time consultant. His comprehensive mastery of the U.S. market, his prestige in both New York and Washington, D.C. and his international network of connections — he also consulted for the Onassis and Niarchos families — were invaluable for us. When in 1984 we bought Galerias Preciados, a bankrupt chain of Spanish department stores that no one else was willing to bail out, he reassured the Spanish banks that we knew what we were doing. He was instrumental in giving them confidence.

I consulted with Pedro Tinoco at 6:30 every morning, either in his office or over the phone. Similarly, I called George Moore every day, no matter where I was. Together, they were a formidable combination. I needed mature people, people with experience, who could hold me down. They were good at saying,

"Gustavo, let's think about it a little more. Let's see if we can do this without betting the whole company."

In addition to reining me in, they were tremendously helpful at advising Ricardo. He was a very tough partner. He was a rebel in his private life. He had simply walked away from Hotchkiss, the elite prep school in Connecticut, despite having amassed more academic awards than anyone in his class. We shared a house when we both attended Babson and after I woke him up in the morning and left for class, he'd sneak back into bed and skive off for the day.

Despite his rebellious streak, he was fiscally much more conservative than I. I always had to convince him that a business idea was going to work. If it didn't pass his exam, it was back to the drawing board. Between Ricardo, George and Pedro, I had one "Mr. No" and two "Mr. No But Possibly Yes." (By the way, I now fill both these roles for my daughter Adriana.) That turned out to be exactly the right ratio.

Moore and Tinoco put us in touch with banks that wanted to invest in Venezuela; we also began to connect with American banks that would give us credit. We were always either receiving visits or making presentations, whether we needed to make a deal or not. Our goal was to develop relationships so that they would cover us when we needed it. It took a while for things to gel but that was the beginning of our relationships with Chase Manhattan, Citibank, Goldman Sachs and Salomon Brothers.

You have to be very careful whom you choose for your wise counselors. People can have their own agenda; they can talk very confidently about stuff they don't know about. That's why you need people from outside your normal life. They don't have a vested interest in the organization.

You also want someone who is more important than you, so the advice stays honest. Tinoco and Moore both held more senior positions than I did. I may have been the CEO of Cisneros but they had far more influence in their spheres than I ever would.

If the people you trust give you honest advice and are wise, not only can they be a good sounding board but they can provide other ways of approaching or solving a problem. You need that. After all, to build a business, you must be relentless in your search for the best approaches and solutions to the toughest problems.

Expanding our reach

Just as my father and his brother Antonio complemented each other as they built the organization, my brother Ricardo and I also developed roles that best suited our skills and personalities. As CEO, I set the strategy for our growth and expansion. As COO, Ricardo served as the financial filter and ensured the strategy was backed up by solid tactics. One person described our partnership in this way: "Gustavo was the architect who designed the property, organized its spaces and designated the builders, while Ricardo made certain that the edifice had no structural faults and kept within budgets and established timetables."[2]

Speaking of organization, I felt it was time to update and modernize OCAAT, the Oficina Central that my father had created to bring together smart people from completely different backgrounds and expertise. While the Oficina Central was humming along nicely, I wanted to duplicate the brain quality in a separate organization with separate offices and a different name to signal a new beginning.

That was the seed for our move to the Paseo Las Mercedes in Caracas. Designed by the renowned Venezuelan architect Jimmy Alcock, the building was a fresh way to look at an office: It was in a new upscale shopping mall, where one could stroll and have a cup of coffee — a precursor to the campuses of Google and Apple that were designed to bring people from different areas together and spark ideas. We wanted to say, "We have a new way of managing things. And we're open for business — new business." It would be our headquarters for the next 30 years.

At the time, Venezuela was celebrating the recent completion of the Simón Bolívar Hydroelectric Plant, which came online in 1969. The Guri Dam, as it was known, was an engineering marvel, whose hydroelectric power station was the largest in the world at the time.[3] It would transform Venezuela by providing affordable electricity for nearly the entire country.[4]

Coincidentally, when you combined the first two letters of Ricardo's and my names, the result was "GURI." GURI was what we called our new approach. We would leave intact the Oficina Central, including the executives my father had hand-picked to manage "legacy" businesses like Pepsi-Cola and its related operations (soft drinks, sugar production, bottling, etc.) but the control center for an exciting future would be in GURI.

GURI was a fitting symbol of the transformational dreams I had for Cisneros.

* * *

"If it's worth $20 million, it's worth $22 million"

We had been thinking about what to do next. Pepsi was in very good shape: We managed all the stages from the carbonation to the bottle caps and every step of the process was in the hands of good operators, under the leadership of our cousin Oswaldo Cisneros. We thought we'd done enough there. It was time for us to grow.

I want to say a word here about Oswaldo Cisneros. When my uncle Antonio died in 1951, Oswaldo was just 10 years old. My father stepped in and brought Oswaldo up as another son, including him in our family activities and training him to join the family business. Like Ricardo and me, Oswaldo attended Babson College and, like us, returned to Venezuela and started working for Cisneros, becoming the head of operations. The three of us complemented each other in personality and know-how, forming a tight nucleus at the center of the organization. Together, we constituted a collective brain. Oswaldo was an extremely adept manager, whether he was in charge of soft-drink manufacturing and distribution or, later, the largest cell phone company in Venezuela. In my mind, there was no one better. With Ricardo at my side and Oswaldo at my back, I felt we could shoot for the stars.

Right now, though, I had my sights set on CADA short for Compañía Anónima Distribudora de Alimentos — a chain of supermarkets. But it was not just any supermarket chain. It was one of the brightest stars in the Rockefeller constellation in Venezuela. To set the context: The Rockefellers had been involved in Venezuela since the early days of commercial oil production. Creole Petroleum Company, the world's top oil producer until 1951,[5] was a subsidiary of Standard Oil of New Jersey. Nelson Rockefeller first visited Venezuela in 1935, a visit which he claimed caused him to fall in love with the country. He founded the International Basic Economy Corporation (IBEC) as a vehicle to strengthen relations between North and South America, drawing on the Rockefeller Foundation model of using American know-how to improve everyday life in developing countries and to promote American democracy against the threat of Communism.[6] Supermarkets seemed an ideal vehicle.

Most Venezuelans purchased their food from tiny *bodegas* that were really more like stalls in open-air markets. With little transportation or distribution infrastructure to connect farms and consumers, the offerings were limited and sold at high markups.[7] A Rockefeller study estimated that Venezuela produced "probably less than one half" of its own basic food commodities.[8]

CADA opened its first stores in the summer of 1947. They were modeled on American supermarkets: clean, bright and well-stocked with a large array of goods priced, on average, 10% lower than the competition.[9]

By the mid-1960s, IBEC had established more than two dozen thriving supermarkets, including CADA and another chain called TODOS. It was the largest retailer in the country, outperforming Sears Roebuck, another American import, by more than $1 million in annual sales.[10]

CADA was a cash cow. It made its money by appealing to mass-market consumers. In other words, it was our kind of business. But, as far as I knew, it wasn't for sale. That didn't stop me from running numerous scenarios to either buy CADA or compete with it. It was a public company, so we studied it relentlessly, until we knew the balance sheet backward and forward. We knew its weaknesses and strengths. We *loved* that company. We concluded that competing would be impossible — they had the best brand and the lowest costs. Instead, we decided, if the company were ever available, we would attempt to buy it.

Then, one day, Pedro Tinoco called me. "I'm speaking to you as a representative of the Rockefeller family," he said. In 1973, Venezuela joined the Andean Pact, a treaty that promoted the nationalization of foreign investments. The writing was on the wall. Soon thereafter, Venezuela passed a law requiring all fuel distribution companies to sell 80% of their holdings in the country. That was what prompted Pedro's telephone call: The Rockefellers were quietly considering putting CADA up for sale and were offering us first refusal. The answer to my prayers!

I believed no one else in Venezuela had the combination of the expertise or the financial backing to do this. My father was an expert at hiring and developing good people, so we had the managers in place. We didn't lack for gumption. We just needed the funding. I said to Tinoco, "I want exclusivity. This is serious. We don't have the money but if you help us get the money, it's a done deal." Easier said than done.

Local partners in Venezuela were unable to raise the money and we couldn't ask Tinoco to ask Chase Manhattan to participate directly, because Chase was a Rockefeller company. Tinoco and George Moore went to Citibank Venezuela in tandem. Moore provided the connection; Tinoco provided the credibility. Citibank Venezuela didn't have the money to do a long-term transaction but it was willing to give us a short-term bridge loan — at an exorbitant interest rate.

We were willing to pay it because Tinoco had a brilliant idea: Have Chase lend the money that we needed to cover Citibank's loan to *another* bank, which would then lend it to us long-term at much more favorable rates. The director of the bank Tinoco had in mind had worked with him at Banco Mercantil, so there was a personal rapport. Essentially, we would borrow from Peter to pay Paul.

We were very open with everyone about our plans because it's always a good idea to stay on good terms with your finance partners. With the promise of money secured, Tinoco, Ricardo and I flew to New York to negotiate with Rodman Rockefeller, Nelson's son, who now ran IBEC. The negotiations themselves were very complicated but, ironically, one of the final stumbling blocks came from Ricardo. The Rockefellers wanted $22 million, which was on the low end of what we had expected to pay.

Ricardo was adamant that he didn't want to pay more than $20 million. ($22 million sounds like peanuts today but at the time, it was an enormous amount of money, equal to over $111 million today. It was the largest commercial transaction outside of the oil sector in the history of Venezuela.[11]) We were at an impasse. I called my father in Caracas. I started to describe the situation but he cut me right off. He barked, "If it's worth $20 million, it's worth $22 million!"

My father often said, "You have to be daring in order to do things differently." But he never leaped before taking a good look: He was exhaustive in gathering information. He followed the Rockefeller model in reaching out to experts. Like them, we hired brains all the time. My father had consultants on call on every subject you could think of; he used them as professors. Since his preferred method of learning was by listening, there was always an oral presentation going on — sort of like a personalized precursor to a TED talk. (This was such an enjoyable way to learn that I would continue that habit.)

He was able to make decisions that could seem daring or even revolutionary to outsiders but, in fact, were safe because he was so well-informed. And if a decision was wrong, he could quickly pivot because he had already thought through all the permutations.

I learned to imitate his process: to study every aspect of a possible acquisition, evaluate the risks, anticipate challenges and propose solutions before we made a move. The CADA deal looked complicated but it was a safe decision for me. We knew how to move the pieces and we were inheriting a very good manager. People thought I was diving into an empty pool but in my mind, it was full of water and inviting me to jump in and swim.

Thanks to my father's insistence on not pinching pennies, we acquired a package that included 48 CADA supermarkets, 15 soda fountain diners, a coffee-processing plant, a bread factory — the first of its kind in Latin America — a cattle ranch called Mata de Bárbara (more about which later) and 20% of IBEC, as well as some legacy businesses in Argentina, Central America and Brazil. In a few strokes of the pen, we became the largest private employer in Venezuela.[12]

It was the first major step in our vision to further diversify and grow the Cisneros organization. A world of possibilities began to take shape before us. My father was so pleased. His grand idea was finally being realized and in just the way he had hoped. He said to me, "I see what you're doing and where you're going. Now I can relax." I really believe that the CADA/IBEC acquisition gave him another five years of life.

The deal changed our lives in so many ways. When we bought CADA, no one wanted to give a dime for the 20% of IBEC. But I thought, "This is my ticket! Do a deal with the Rockefeller family and they will remember you." And they did. As you can imagine, that opened doors I'd never even dreamed existed, let alone imagined I could step through.

The deal gave me exposure outside Venezuela. It put us on the map of the major New York banks, which would have international ramifications in our ability to expand in the United States, Europe and Latin America.

Yet it was all done essentially under the radar, without anyone knowing. No one could snatch the deal away from us because no one knew CADA was even for sale. When we made the announcement in 1975, it was a gigantic surprise for everyone in Venezuela. "What??? How??? Where did these guys come from???"

That sent a strong signal: There were new kids on the block and they would do things their own way. I learned a valuable lesson: Always arrive before the competition.

* * *

"Always look for combinations"

My dream was to do with CADA what my father had done with Pepsi-Cola: Use it as the nucleus of a vertically integrated organization with the potential for endless expansion while staying relentlessly focused on satisfying consumer needs.

CADA was much, *much* bigger than Pepsi but there were lots of similarities. We benefited immeasurably from my father's know-how in satisfying consumers. "Of course, a supermarket chain is very close to people," says Miguel Dvorak, who started working at Cisneros in 1976 as a junior accountant and is now the Chief Operating Officer. "You understand the brands and how they're trying to better their position, and the needs of the general public and their desires. And it's really, really fascinating."

We needed to move fast to make our mark, and we did. In 1975, when we took over CADA, there were 55 supermarkets in Venezuela. Within five years, there were over 100.[13] We were opening up a new supermarket every month. Within five years, sales had doubled and the chain was serving over one million customers *every month*.[14] Illustrating our belief in building up Venezuela's economy, CADA also enthusiastically promoted local enterprises: Between 80% and 85% of our products were marked "*Hecho en Venezuela*"— "Made in Venezuela."[15]

CADA became our model and our means for acquiring large-scale businesses. We looked to buy companies whose products we could sell in our supermarkets and advertise on Venevisión. From meat to mustard to women's make-up, we were always looking for combinations.

We followed a straightforward five-point formula when considering whether to purchase a company. It must:

- Be a leader in its market. If it wasn't #1, then it had to be #2 with the potential for us to make it #1 through smarter management and better merchandising.
- Offer products that were simple to manufacture.
- Maintain a positive cash flow. I learned that from my father. The cash flow from the soft drink business enabled us to become very big. We continued that formula with CADA. We wouldn't buy any business unless we could see our way to positive cash flow in a few years. If it didn't have a strong cash flow, I had doubts about its survival.
- Have good managers. If the company ticked off the first three boxes, this was pretty much a given. But thanks to Pepsi and Venevisión, we had plenty of executives with skills in marketing, advertising and distribution. We simply shifted them over. Their talent was portable and they were smart enough to learn how to apply it in a new arena. Job transfers became a hallmark of working at Cisneros, as I'll describe in the next section.
- Be relentlessly focused on mass consumption. Always — *always* — give consumers what they want.

* * *

It was the perfect time to be in a consumer-focused business in Venezuela. Driven by petrodollars, by 1975, Venezuela's per capita purchasing power was equal to that of Japan; by the end of the decade, per capita income was higher than that of any other Latin American country.[16] Oil wealth had spread enough that even middle-class Venezuelans routinely took shopping trips to Miami and loaded up. Their rallying cry: "Dame dos" — "I'll take two!"

Of course, not everyone participated in this boom. Poverty was a real and widespread problem. The oil business had caused people to migrate from the countryside to the cities, because that's where the money and jobs were. At the same time, Venezuela's perceived wealth was a magnet for immigrants from Haiti, Ecuador and Colombia, which was experiencing an economic downturn. Many of these people were illiterate and, in the case of the Haitians, didn't speak Spanish. But in Caracas, for example, street vendors sold ice cream from little carts with a bell. They didn't need to speak Spanish to advertise their presence and, like hard-working immigrants everywhere, they were willing to push that cart for longer hours and less money.

There were plenty of petrodollars but there was an enormous disparity in their distribution. In the slums and shantytowns ringing the cities, quality healthcare was essentially nonexistent. Teachers in the public schools were always on strike. This was the tinder that would fuel the conflagration when the economy collapsed in 1983. But for now, for those able to tap the oil wealth, everything was golden.

Our acquisition of CADA kicked off a shopping spree of our own as we bought licenses and companies whose products would stock the shelves: from Cherry Blossom shoe polish to Helene Curtis cosmetics to French's mustard. This was further bolstered by the purchase in 1983 of the Sears Roebuck department store chain in Venezuela; renamed Maxy's, it became the country's largest retail chain store. Now we could further bolster our inventory with Spalding tennis balls, Evenflo baby products, Apple computers and luxury international beauty brands like Estée Lauder. (Leonard Lauder said Maxy's was one of his best customers worldwide!) Totally new brands were launched, like the Cotton Candy line of children's clothing.

84

As superb our managers were, that doesn't mean that they could simply shift from one industry to another without any training. To teach them about the supermarket business, in 1976, we sent 25 executives to the annual Food Market Institute trade show. Just as my father had partnered with companies that explained the nuts and bolts of the soft drinks business, we found an ally in the Florida-based Publix supermarket chain. They took our people on as apprentices and taught them everything from how to remodel a store without disrupting customers, to operating fundamentals.[17]

The supermarket business is sustained by sales volume. Higher sales volume, in turn, gives you the ability to demand greater discounts from suppliers. Everything depends on a streamlined inventory system. In 1976, we formed Castor Trading, which, under the able leadership of my college friend Johnny Fanjul, served as the centralized purchasing agent for CADA and, later, Maxy's.[18] In 1980, we opened a single center for buying, warehousing and distribution; named for my brother, Antonio José Cisneros, ALTRAN — Centro de Almacenamiento y Distribución Antonio José Cisneros, was one of the largest consumer products warehouses in Latin America.[19]

Although Antonio was eight years younger than I, we were very close. He was fantastic at marketing and advertising, and focused those talents on our Burger King franchise and the supermarket business, both in Venezuela and elsewhere. Hard-working and competent, he was in charge of ALTRAN. We expected him to be the best CADA general manager and discussed how he could head our expansion into the United States. Antonio had a pilot's license but we made a rule: We'll give you a plane but you cannot fly by yourself. You always have to have a pilot next to you. In 1981, he went for a short vacation over Valentine's Day and grounded the pilot. The plane disappeared near Bonaire and was *never found. I was devastated. His death was a huge shock to me and a tremendous loss to our family.*

The CADA *package included 15 soda fountain diners attached to the supermarkets. As the number of markets increased, so did the number of diners. However, by the late 1970s, soda fountain eateries were going out of style: Consumers no longer wanted to sit at a table, choose from an ornate menu and wait for their order to be delivered. They wanted grab-and-go service — no table service, no tips. Cisneros switched to fast-food brands, opening the first Burger King, Taco Bell and Pizza Hut franchises in Venezuela in the soda fountain space.*

Our business planning became so skilled that we could reliably predict that if a new or newly acquired enterprise met its goals in the first quarter, it almost always did so for the next three quarters as well.[20]

An entrepreneurial spirit pervaded the organization. At one point, we even had a small operation to bring Christmas trees to Venezuela for the holidays. A manager had discovered that refrigerated trains that shipped oranges and grapefruit from Florida to Canada returned empty. We took advantage of this unused capacity to fill the cold cars with Canadian pines for the return trip; upon reaching Miami, the trees were loaded onto planes and flown to Caracas, to be sold in CADA *stores for $5 to $20.*[21] CADA's *scale made it worthwhile.*

Venevisión was a key element in the equation. Consider this: Cisneros owned the largest supermarket chain in Venezuela, as well as a major television channel. The combination provided a platform for the mass-marketing of brands that no competitor could match. As one of our suppliers later said, "They own the media and a large part of the distribution. How can you lose in that position?"

In fact, we were facing a paradox: Where Venevisión was concerned, we were almost too successful.

* * *

"Don't think of frontiers. Think of commonalities"

From my first day at Venevisión, I knew I wanted to transform the channel into something different, something international. Following the pattern my father set with Pepsi-Cola and I aimed to do with CADA, I envisioned Venevisión as a model of vertical integration, producing both the content and the means of distributing it.

By the mid-1960s, Venevisión was the leading network in Venezuela. It was broadcasting in 18 of Venezuela's 20 states[22] and had cornered two-thirds of the viewership. There was no more room to grow in Venezuela. If we wanted to grow, we had to expand into other countries.

Our strategy was based on *telenovelas*. Soap operas were a cornerstone of television programming in Latin America, but they were mostly broadcast only within the countries in which they were produced. Pan-regional soap operas had not yet been born.

That would change in 1970. Johnny Fanjul still remembers my excited telephone call to him in Costa Rica. "Juanito, turn on the television! We just sold our first *telenovela!*" *Esmeralda* marked Venevisión's debut on the international TV soap opera stage.

From Costa Rica, we started exporting our *telenovelas* to Spanish-speaking markets all over the world. We plowed the money we made right back into the business. We analyzed the scripts of Mexican and Cuban *telenovelas* with an eye towards how we could improve them. We recruited top writers and directors from the Cuban diaspora — Delia Fiallo, the writer of *Esmeralda* and many of our other hit series in the 1970s and 1980s, was Cuban — and the best actors and directors. The Venezuelan accent was an additional plus: It's a neutral Spanish, like Mexican Spanish, but "sweeter" and more melodious. Our efforts paid off: By 1975, we were #1 in audience share in Puerto Rico and Spain.

Telenovelas were a fantastic calling card and our ticket to become known outside of Venezuela; eventually, we sold dubbed versions of our *telenovelas* in Greece, Turkey and even Indonesia. Meanwhile, Venevisión telenovelas became a model for soap operas in other countries. (Venevision International has the most extensive library of original programming in Latin America; its soap operas, comedies and other programs are viewed in more than 100 countries across five continents.[23]) Their success proved one of my father's lessons: "Don't think of frontiers. Think of commonalities."

I began to dream of reaching the millions of Spanish-speaking homes in the United States. It would take nearly 20 years, but the dream would eventually come true in the 1990s with the acquisition of Univision.

* * *

"Treat mavericks like cat"
Television requires a balance between iron administrative discipline and a high degree of creativity. It's a world in which everyone is a diva: the writers, the directors, the producers, even the camera operators and, of course, the actors. It often seems like its own version of a telenovela.

Creative people have very different ideas about how to break an egg. The creative process is often noisy and messy, yet it is vital to give people the support they need to make the shows a success. If a channel loses favor with its public and its advertisers, repositioning it is a herculean task.

Show business is a complicated, dynamic business but it can be run successfully once you understand it. I learned to handle the noise and the executives making and managing the noise. I had to learn how to handle people who think completely differently from each other. And I became much more accepting of mavericks.

I learned that the best way to manage mavericks is to treat them like cats: Let them perform, don't give them too many rules and dole out praise and treats when appropriate. If you tell them exactly what to do every minute of the day, they're going to hate you. They already know what they need to do. My father had a knack for managing mavericks. He told me, "Your role is to provide challenge and meaning: Find out what their dreams are and make their dreams come true."

When I took control of Venevisión, one of the most valuable mavericks was Enrique Cuscó. Enrique had no other interests (beyond his family); he worked 24/7 and slept in the office. He was opinionated, aggressive, irreverent and challenging — a "take it or leave it" person who was very hard to manage. People asked why I put up with him, but I supported him 100% because he attracted the best scriptwriters, the best producers and the best actors. Venevisión was losing money but we turned it around because we had the best talent. I had to have a lot of patience, but I learned a lot about programming, which was Cuscó's forte. We fought every day, but I said, "So what?" We raised the ratings for Venevisión across the board. He remained as the head of Venevisión Venezuela for two decades.

Once I saw what Cuscó and his ménage of mavericks could do, I learned to search for mavericks: for different points of view, different ideas, people who weren't part of the norm.

* * *

From television, we wanted to expand our media reach by making radio an extension of Venevisión. Radio is an old-fashioned mode of communication, but it had a huge niche in Venezuela as a source of news and entertainment, although it tended to be small and localized. For example, the largest station in the country was Radio Caracas, which had been established by the Phelps family in 1930; some 30 years later, it was still just one station. I thought, Let's change this. I saw the potential for a nationwide network, like the way ABC radio broadcasts all over the United States.

We bought as many local stations as we legally could; when we couldn't buy them, we rented them. We made the signal available — sometimes for free — to anyone who wanted to partner with us, whether they were in the most remote areas of the country or in the biggest cities. In 1974, Radiovisión began operations as Venezuela's first national radio network.

We already knew a lot about radio because Pepsi-Cola was the largest advertiser in Venezuela. Radio advertising is cheaper than television advertising and it attracts a different type of advertiser: smaller, more local clients, like the guy who wants to publicize his chain of shoe stores or a resort in a vacation region.

Now, we combined local and national news and advertising, with a hefty dose of sophistication and technical ingenuity. Radiovisión was the counterpart to Venevisión: We used each to promote the other. Drawing on the best news and entertainment from Venevisión, Radiovisión was a winner from the get-go.

And then there was music. In 1978, Rodolfo Rodríguez, the son of Venevisión's executive vice president, presented me with an idea: We should build a factory to produce vinyl records. He offered to front half the capital and suggested that Cisneros provide the other half. Rodven pressed its first records in 1981.

*The money in music has never been in selling records or tapes;
the real gold mine is owning the rights and producing the music.
Rodríguez bought the rights to some popular music classics, which
he compiled into one album, called* Momentos. *It is still among
the top-selling albums in Venezuela. Then, in exchange for the
promise of airtime on Radiovisión and advertising space on Venevisión, we negotiated a contract with music powerhouse Warner
Elektra Atlantic for the rights to some of their artists. (It helped
that I was good friends with Ahmet Ertegun, the co-founder and
president of Atlantic Records, and his brother Nesuhi, also an
Atlantic executive.)*

*Soon, Rodven began producing home-grown artists and sell-
ing their licenses outside Venezuela. One of our first successes was
Guillermo Dávila, who had been a stage actor of limited prominence until he starred in the Venevisión telenovela* Ligia Elena
*and crooned its soulful theme song, "Solo pienso en ti" ("I think
only of you"). The record was a smash hit, selling 300,000 copies
in Venezuela alone; it would be popular in Puerto Rico as well and
wherever* Ligia Elena *aired.[24] Other best-selling albums leveraging the Rodven-Venevisión partnership followed.*

The most beautiful alliance was yet to come.

* * *

"Promote a good image to the world"

There's a reason that during the 1980s, much of the world
believed that Venezuela's major export, in addition to oil, was
beautiful women: the Miss Venezuela pageant. Cisneros
acquired the pageant in 1980. I wanted to have a good image of
Venezuela to export to the world — and a way to promote our
telenovelas and beauty products locally.

We knew Osmel Sousa from his work as a society reporter for a local newspaper; he was also well-known for advising previous pageant contestants, many of whom won the Miss Venezuela crown. We hired him to run the entire organization.

He used a model similar to that of a major-league baseball team's talent development system. He scheduled castings in the largest cities in the country and put would-be contestants through an arduous selection process. Thousands of young women applied, but only 28 were accepted every year.[25]

We prepared the contestants carefully. Like contestants anywhere, they were taught how to parade, to develop their diction and to improve their etiquette. In addition, though, they were trained by teams of stylists and designers, instructors in languages and culture, and sports coaches. They worked hard — and they produced results. Miss Venezuela contestants won over 70 beauty pageants, including, as of 2021, seven Miss Universe, six Miss World and eight Miss International titles.[26]

We wanted the pageant to make compelling viewing, a sort of live *telenovela* before the invention of reality TV, and a calling card for Venezuela in the world. Osmel Sousa, together with Joaquín Rivera, a renowned choreographer, put together an unforgettable Broadway-caliber production that we sold worldwide. The four-hour event was rebroadcast in 100 countries, bringing in advertising revenues that more than covered the pageant organization's hefty budget.

As always, we had aspirations that went beyond profit and promotion. We were change agents. The contestants were ambitious young women who wanted to improve their lives. Becoming a Miss Distrito Capital or a Miss Venezuela — let alone a Miss World or a Miss Universe — was a passport to a new life. Many became models or went into the entertainment industry — the selection and training program was a goldmine of local talent.

Many went to university on scholarships and became accomplished professionals: dentists, doctors and teachers. Some became successful businesswomen. One, Irene Sáez, winner of Miss Universe 1981, became mayor of Chacao (one of the five municipalities of Caracas), and governor of Nueva Esparta state.

Smart mistakes

Within the Cisneros organization during the 1970s, there was a sense that nothing was impossible. But that didn't mean we didn't make mistakes. Nobody's perfect. What's important is to learn from your missteps — and not repeat them. Here are three experiences that taught me particularly useful lessons.

* * *

"Switch tactics to succeed"

Early on, when I was still my father's assistant, he made a big investment in a new lemon-lime soft drink flavor that we called Twin Top. (It tasted sort of like 7Up.) No matter how much we promoted it, it didn't do well. In desperation, I suggested, "Why don't we buy another brand that's already successful, like Chinotto, and then add a lemon-lime flavor to its line-up?"

My father agreed, and the lemon-lime Chinotto was an immense success. I have no idea why. Maybe it was due to the switch from an American-sounding name to one that sounded Italian — there were a lot of Italians in Venezuela. Who knows? Some things work out and some don't.

The main takeaway was that I learned early to switch tactics when initially thwarted. Stay open-minded and try a different tack, even if it's incrementally different. Rather than give up, improve on what you have. You never know.

Now we even have a phrase that encapsulates that approach: *huir hacia adelante* or "flee forward." If the business is stuck, look for another way forward: fix it, reinvent it, take the things that work and see what we can do with them. If you're still stuck, sell it. This would be our guiding principle during our massive restructuring in the 1990s.

The point is, maybe you'll flunk the test but you don't have to flunk the class. You don't have to get a zero. You can always salvage something from defeat.

* * *

"Right product, wrong market"

Soft drinks were a springboard into other beverages. The petroleum boom had increased the demand for all consumer goods, and that included fine wines and liquors. In 1974, we launched O'Caña, a distributor of international wines and liquors. (The name is actually a pun. "Caña" is slang for "a drink," so the company's name means, "Oh, drink!") Thanks to the Cisneros reputation as the only Pepsi-Cola bottler in the world that could outsell Coca-Cola, we soon acquired the rights to brands like Dimple whiskey, Mumm champagne and Paternina wines. An advertising campaign on Venevisión and Radiovisión boosted sales; by the early 1980s, O'Caña was selling as many as 120,000 cases of Scotch a year.[27]

My father — and I — had also long considered getting into beer. The beer business isn't all that much different from soft drinks. In 1992, Cisneros acquired Cervecería Regional, the second-largest brewery and beer distributor in Venezuela; it would be an especially good pairing with Los Leones del Caracas, one of the most successful baseball franchises in Venezuela, which

94

we bought in 2001. A year later, we bought a 20% stake in Backus and Johnston, the largest brewery in Peru and the sixth-largest in Latin America. I suppose I assumed that we had an unbeatable formula. I forgot that my father had warned me against being too full of myself.

I set up a business with Bacardi, the most important rum company in the world. José "Pepin" Bosch, Bacardi's major shareholder, was a genius at marketing. One of his successes was white rum. White rum is cheaper to produce than aged rum and is of a lesser quality. But at the time, most consumers in Venezuela had not been exposed to aged rum, so they didn't have a taste for it. Bacardi marketed white rum as a mixer — think rum and Coke — and it was a blockbuster everywhere from the U.S. to Brazil. (It tastes like *cachaça*, a popular clear Brazilian spirit that's a key ingredient in *caipirinhas*.)

Why shouldn't it do just as well in Venezuela? I was wrong. Being the best rum maker in the world was not the same as selling a best-selling rum in Venezuela. Venezuela's national taste is for dark rum, because that's what Venezuela produces. Thanks to catchy ads and enticing promotions, we could persuade people to drink white rum once or maybe twice — but not three times.

We failed miserably. I called on Mr. Bosch and said, "I made a mistake." He said, "I know. You should have come to me before you bought in. I would have told you not to do it. You had the right product but the wrong market." He offered to buy us out and, in return, sold us part of a Venezuelan brand of dark rum called Cacique, which was the best-selling rum in Venezuela and a leading export to Latin America and Spain. From a bad situation, we went to a better situation. (We eventually sold Cacique to Seagram for a very good return.)

I learned an important lesson: Marketing and advertising will take you only so far. You cannot change people's tastes. Even though it was a good product, it was the wrong product for that market.

* * *

"Don't be Joan of Arc. You might get burned"

Throughout much of Venezuela's history, its economy was driven by the extraction of its natural resources: from the pearls that drew Christopher Columbus' attention on his third voyage to the New World,[28] to cocoa and coffee, to, ultimately, oil.

While I was growing up, oil was seen as a bottomless wellspring that would provide an endless source of riches for the country. In 1934, petroleum generated the equivalent of $42 of fiscal income for each Venezuelan. In 1973, that income had increased over 10 times to $583. A year later, thanks to the oil boom of the previous year, it had tripled *again* to $1,540.[29]

But there was a fly in this otherwise glorious ointment. Venezuela's Hydrocarbons Law of 1943 guaranteed a 16.6% royalty in exchange for allowing the world's biggest oil companies access to Venezuela's vast reserves for 40 years[30] — a gigantic amount of money pouring into the government coffers. It could have been more, however, except for the fact that the Venezuelan constitution forbade Venezuelan private enterprises from extracting oil. Only the state-run oil industry was allowed to drill and manage the wells and their derivatives. And, like many state-run organizations, IVP (Instituto Venezolano de Petroquímicas, or Venezuelan Petrochemical Institute) was characterized by stifling bureaucracy, poor management and operational inefficiency. Even President Carlos Andrés Pérez had criticized the IVP after a visit to one of its plants.[31]

Some people interpreted his open criticism as an invitation for the private sector to intervene. I already had an idea that could get Venezuelan private businesses into the petroleum industry through the back door: petrochemicals.

Venezuelan companies were already providing services to the industry and Venezuelan employees were doing the vast majority of the work. What if, instead of competing against the state and the foreign oil giants in extracting the oil, private investors created a company to refine it? Most of the foreign concessionaires transported Venezuelan crude oil to refineries in Texas and Louisiana to break down into gasoline, kerosene, naphtha and other chemicals.

Why not do it ourselves? The law was clear that private companies could invest in petrochemical refining. Refining Venezuelan oil on Venezuelan soil would be a huge boost to the overall economy and, in doing so, help strengthen our fledgling democracy. After all, a country without a private sector is only half a country: It's the Soviet Union.

My older brother Diego and I envisioned a public-private partnership of the government in participation with Cisneros, other Venezuela companies and some foreign partners in creating and operating three petrochemical plants that would produce 36 chemicals. The organization would be called Pentacomplejo Petroquímicos, or Pentacom.

I convinced a group of consultants and colleagues, including Pedro Tinoco, to contribute 10 million *bolívares* (about $3 million) to cover the costs of the technical studies for the project. Various foreign companies were interested. I described it to President Carlos Andrés Pérez and one of his ministers, explaining that the only way this could work politically would be if the government invested 50% of the costs. They seemed willing.

In February 1975, Pentacom made its public debut when an influential magazine in the region wrote an article describing the project as "the most powerful entrepreneurial association ever achieved in Venezuela."[32] I have to confess that I never imagined the political firestorm that erupted. One congressional deputy accused Pentacom of being "a vulgar maneuver by the bourgeoisie." Another claimed it was a façade for a secret pact between capitalists and Pérez to turn the country into an oligarchy.[33] The foreign oil and chemical companies started backing away.

I did everything I could to save Pentacom. I spoke in front of congressional subcommittees, I made statements to newspapers, and I gave speeches. Behind the scenes, I consulted my elders — Pedro Tinoco, George Moore, my father. I had already been talking to Rómulo Betancourt from the beginning. The first democratically elected president, he was still a powerful figure and a good friend of my father; you could count on him. Now I asked him, "Mr. President, what's going on?"

"Gustavo, you are in the middle of a great problem," he explained. "The private sector is on trial and you are the proxy for the private sector. We don't have the strength in Congress to defend you as we should. The democratic forces are afraid of the Left. They will tell you they will back you but they will not."

I'd already seen that when push came to shove, Carlos Andrés Pérez, who had privately endorsed me and given me permission to go ahead, would not be so supportive in public. I asked Betancourt, "What should I do?" He said, "You will lose if you continue pushing. Unless you want to be a politician — and I will help you if you do — you have to get out of this." I did not want to be a politician.

On May 2, 1975, I sent a formal letter to the Miraflores palace, Congress and the newspaper *El Nacional* announcing my decision to give up the project. Betancourt wrote it for me. Everyone knew that the language came from him; I signed it so that people would stay away from me. Even so, he warned me, "After this, they'll go after you big time. They need to destroy you." It was a full retreat, both in public and in private. (I did, however, pay back all of the partners.) I said to myself, "I'm no Joan of Arc. I don't want to be burned. I'd rather regroup and live to fight another battle another day."

It was a good eye-opener for me to do things completely differently. For one thing, we would not be part of the petrochemical industry. But more than that, I realized that we'd better solidify our plans to invest outside of Venezuela because we couldn't count on the government to defend the private sector. From that moment on, we devoted ourselves to going international — emotionally and mentally.

Just in case I needed confirmation of that, a little over three months later, on August 29, 1975, Carlos Andrés Pérez signed into law a bill ordering the nationalization of the country's petroleum industry, effective January 1, 1976.[34]

Philanthropy with a purpose
After a breathless decade, by the late 1970s, we — my father, my family and our business — reached a point where we could exhale. 1978 would be CADA's thirtieth anniversary; the following year would mark the 50th anniversary of the founding of Cisneros.

It was a good time for reflection — and for action.

Philanthropy has always been a part of our family's ideals. To us, social responsibility and successful business practices go hand in hand. It's not just that we believe that businesses have an obligation to invest in society. We take an entrepreneurial approach to philanthropy. We expect our "investment" to pay off in

99

education; in exposure to and participation in music, arts and culture; in learning to be a good citizen of your country; in living a better life.

That was the essence of my father's dream when he founded the Fundación Diego Cisneros in 1968. However, his stroke and the need to focus ferociously on protecting and then growing the Cisneros organization put the Foundation's development on the back burner.

We relaunched the Fundación Cisneros with a mission of promoting "free enterprise, private initiative and democratic values" in areas of impact such as education, art and music. The idea was that education and culture could be used as critical instruments of positive change and to teach democratic values.

My father often said that the cornerstone of a stable, democratic government where everyone could prosper — not just a few — was an educated citizenry. He was always on a campaign about education: Once people had enough money for food and shelter, he believed, their next goal would be to educate themselves.

Today, we know that's true but at the time, this was a fresh idea. My father treated the topic like an ongoing campaign, talking about it all the time. He brought in people from the United States to give lectures and spread ideas. If one idea out of ten stuck with someone, he was happy. He loved hearing that "ping" when the lightbulb went off in someone's brain. (It certainly resonated with Patty and me, and was the seed that grew into ACUDE, which I'll describe below and in Part II.)

We began by hosting an international symposium in 1978 on "Autocracy, Democracy and Totalitarianism." Among the Venezuelan and foreign guests who attended were prominent figures from the academic and political world: former Venezuelan presidents Rómulo Betancourt and Rafael Caldera; economist John Kenneth Galbraith; Harvard University historian Arthur M.

Schlesinger; Richard N. Goodwin, former speechwriter and adviser to the U.S. presidents John F. Kennedy and Lyndon Johnson; his wife, Doris Kearns Goodwin, already making a name for herself with her best-selling biography, Lyndon Johnson and the American Dream, *and who would win the Pulitzer Prize for her examination of Franklin and Eleanor Roosevelt's marriage and extraordinary partnership during World War II; Jean-François Revel, a philosopher and journalist with the French weekly* L'Express; *and Felipe González, then leader of the Spanish Socialist Workers' Party, who would serve as Spain's prime minister from 1982 to 1996.*

Also, there was the recently appointed American ambassador to Venezuela, William Luers. "It was my first taste of Gustavo's approach to his work," Luers recalls. "There were so many military governments in Latin America in those days. He wanted to associate himself with the idea of democracy in Venezuela and the model of democracy that Venezuela offered the Latin American world."

As we began to think more deeply about philanthropy, we sharpened our focus and our mission. There's charity — like giving alms — and then there's strategic philanthropy. Patty and I have never been interested in simply writing a check. Like our business dealings, we want our philanthropic efforts to be transformational.

* * *

"Make every program transformational"

Education and poverty are closely related. There's a deadly relationship between low levels of education and high levels of poverty. Carlos Slim, the Mexican business magnate and philanthropist, would later say, "Poverty does not create markets. To take people out of poverty is good for the economy, for the country, for society and for business. It is the best investment."[35]

I couldn't agree more.

Patty and I knew about the work of Monsignor José Joaquín Salcedo, whose innovative program of long-distance learning had been producing good results in Colombia since 1947. We asked him for advice on combating illiteracy in Venezuela, where it was also rife, and visited Colombia five or six times to examine the effects of his work. We'd go into a village and stop by a house where people participated in Salcedo's program. It would have a vegetable garden and painted walls, all bright and neat. Ten yards down the street would be another house that wasn't part of the program, and you could tell immediately.

The difference that literacy made was obvious.

We had just acquired the Mata de Bárbara cattle ranch in southern Venezuela as part of the Rockefeller deal that brought us CADA. There were about 60 cowboys working there, most in their late teens and early twenties, as well as their wives and girlfriends. None of them knew how to read or write or even how to hold a pencil. Being isolated out in the countryside made the ranch a perfect laboratory.

We called our experiment ACUDE, short for the *Asociación Cultural Para el Desarrollo* — the Cultural Association for Development. It launched in 1979.

Patty had founded the language department at the University Simón Bolivar, where she created a whole new method of teaching languages. She was the perfect choice to head ACUDE.

ACUDE's teaching methods were unorthodox but in keeping with our experience in entertainment. The working tools consisted of a record player, vinyl records and written materials (which could be obtained inexpensively, thanks to subsidies from Cisneros companies). The program identified potential community leaders who were eager to take responsibility for encouraging their neighbors to participate. As one neighbor reached out to his or her companion, this created a ripple effect.

Learning to read and write was just the first step. The entire philosophy of ACUDE was not just promoting literacy: It was to teach values and self-esteem, for both men and women. So, in the kit teaching the alphabet, "A" wasn't for "aunt" or "apple," but for "admirable." Then the students would be asked to describe what it means for something or someone to be admirable.

"The struggle against poverty demands, first of all, respect for individuals, for their dignity and their potential," Patty says. "Rescuing self-esteem is a first step. Developing aptitudes and creating the conditions for material prosperity are also essential. The process should move forward on all fronts simultaneously."[36]

Once the students learned how to read and write, we followed up for two years with five booklets, sent every four months, to reinforce and complement their new knowledge.

The books covered subjects like self-improvement, hygiene and respect for women. In many communities, women tended to be treated as less important than men. We were determined to help change that.

We analyzed ACUDE the way we would analyze any business: If we couldn't measure success, we'd pull the plug. But we could see results happening before our eyes.

The day we introduced chess, almost everyone learned to play. They realized that chess is more than a game: It involves thinking and planning ahead. Then we got two big poles and put-up goal posts for soccer, so that on their days off, the *campesinos* could play soccer or chess, instead of sitting around and drinking beer. And the purchase of beer on the farm went down 45%.[37]

One of the booklets was on the subject of health and nutrition. It encouraged men to value vegetables. Up until then, men ate only fresh meat and processed meat, like Spam; greens were considered unmanly. The book encouraged them to help women create vegetable gardens, which they did, and provided recipes for women to cook, which *they* did. And the men started eating vegetables.

We were constantly measuring the program's efficiency with an eye toward scaling it up. With the success of the pilot program at Mata de Bárbara, ACUDE was rolled out throughout Venezuela. The nationwide Pepsi infrastructure took charge of distributing learning materials and transporting staff, while our media enterprises promoted the benefits of the program. I rarely promoted ACUDE personally, so that it wouldn't be seen as a public relations instrument for Cisneros. We didn't want that impression.

ACUDE reached more than 300,000 people during the first half of the 1980s, in a country with a population at the time of about 15 million. In the early 1990s, the kit was revised, and the updated version was distributed to more than 800,000 Venezuelans. Unfortunately, changing political circumstances ultimately led to its retirement.

ACUDE led to *Cl@se*, a television channel created when we founded DirecTV Latin America satellite broadcasting. DirecTV was the first pan-regional television platform in Latin America and *Cl@se* was the first pan-regional, Spanish-language free educational channel. I'll describe it in more detail when we discuss our partnership with DirecTV.

Cl@se, in turn, led to AME, *Actualización de Maestros en Educación* (Training Teachers in Education). Launched in 2003, AME took advantage of the latest technology to advance the development of schoolteachers in Latin America and the Caribbean through the internet.

* * *

"Fund the music"

One day, sometime during the early 1970s, I got a call from Pedro Tinoco. He told me that there was a problem with a partner of ours, an economist named José Antonio Abreu whose accountancy consulting firm was the best in Venezuela. "Abreu wants to give up economics and do music," Tinoco said.

"What should we do?" I asked.

"We have to fund the music," Tinoco said.

Abreu had the idea of promoting social justice through music. His program, called El Sistema, brought free classical music lessons to children in some of Venezuela's poorest areas. Thanks to Abreu, orchestras sprang up all over the country; classical music infused everyone's education and an awareness of classical music became part of Venezuela's cultural identity. We supported El Sistema heavily through Venevisión. Tinoco was also very helpful in using his political know-how and connections to access public budgets to support the program.

But then we discovered that although the kids were learning to play Mozart and Beethoven, they didn't have the opportunity to *hear* great live performances of the music. When the top artists and orchestras toured South America, they went to Brazil and Argentina — and skipped right over Venezuela. Patty decided this was unacceptable.

In 1985, she founded the Fundación Mozarteum Venezuela (FMV) in 1985 with the goal of bringing the world's finest orchestras, ballets, musicians and singers to Venezuela for the benefit of people unable to afford international travel. (A partner organization already existed in Argentina.) The first concert was in September of that year: Lorin Maazel lef the Vienna

Philharmonic. She became an arts impresario, presenting the New York Philharmonic, the Berlin Philharmonic and the Israel Philharmonic. Conductors like Zubin Mehta, Daniel Barenboim and Lorin Maazel stayed at our guesthouse and became family friends. And Mozarteum became the most successful provider of classical music programming in Venezuela.

If El Sistema had one shortcoming, it was that it taught a common denominator: There was no encouragement to excel. We wondered how many kids were as gifted as Gustavo Dudamel, an El Sistema alumnus who became the conductor of the Los Angeles Philharmonic and the Paris Opera, but weren't recognized and encouraged.

We set up the Escuela Mozarteum to find out. It included a program to identify kids with outstanding talent and match them with existing scholarships to study at prestigious music academies in the United States and Europe. We helped them fill out the applications; if they won, we helped them get a passport and subsidized their travel. We even bought them necessary clothing, like shoes and warm coats. We sent about 350 young musicians abroad. (When the program was going to end, José Alvarez Stelling, his daughter Violeta and I chipped in to keep it going as long as possible.)

We also established a scholarship, awarded annually, for an outstanding pupil to study for two months at the Aspen Music Festival in Colorado. I'm proud to say that the Venezuelan scholarship winners were among the first Latin American musicians to perform in Aspen.[38]

* * *

The more widely Patty and I traveled for work and for leisure, the more we saw how culture — music, art, literature, etc. — is the life-blood of free thought. I could see that my father was right when he said that private enterprise has an important role to play in nurturing and protecting people's ability to speak openly and share ideas. Since businessess rely on the constant bubbling up and inter-mixing of ideas, it makes sense for them to support the cultural world.

That's what my father taught me and it's what I believe: Culture is more important than business. You need culture to do business. It was just one more lesson in his enduring legacy. My father died on July 15, 1980.

After my father recovered from his stroke and returned to Venezuela, I visited him every day for breakfast or dinner when we were in Caracas. If I were traveling, I'd call him to tell him everything we were doing. We assembled a management model that enabled him to take part in every decision and play a functional role in the organization. Right up until the end of his life, he was a dynamic force in the business and the family. He knew it and we knew it. That made him deeply happy.

Paradoxically, for a man with such an enormous list of accomplishments, my father saw himself as a dreamer. Or, rather, I should say, he believed in the power of dreams: to inspire you, to imagine goals so compelling that you couldn't help but want to work hard to realize them.

So I suppose it's not surprising that he often visits me in my dreams. And when he does, he always has some advice to share: "Gustavo, check your ego. Remember to listen. Everyone has something to contribute. Stay curious." And, of course, "Always — always — give consumers what they want."

Notes

1. Neumann, Ariana, *When Time Stopped*, Scribner, 2020, p. 9.

2. *Gustavo Cisneros: Pioneer*, p. 42.

3. https://en.wikipedia.org/wiki/Guri_Dam

4. https://www.power-technology.com/projects/gurihydroelectric/

5. https://en.wikipedia.org/wiki/Creole_Petroleum_Corporation

6. Hamilton, Shane, "From Bodega to Supermercado: Nelson A. Rockefeller's Agro-Industrial Counterrevolution in Venezuela, 1947-1969", in *Yale Agrarian Studies Workshop*, November 4, 2011, p. 5.

7. *Ibidem*, p. 12.

8. *Ibidem*, p. 16.

9. *Ibidem*, p. 28.

10. *Ibidem*, p. 30.

11. *Gustavo Cisneros: Pioneer*, p. 50.

12. *Ibid.*

13. *Cisneros: A Family History*, p. 121.

14. *Gustavo Cisneros: Pioneer*, p. 54.

15. *Cisneros: A Family History*, p. 123.

16. *Gustavo Cisneros: Pioneer*, p. 52.

17. *Ibidem*, p. 54.

18. *Cisneros: A Family History*, p. 164.

19. https://www.cisneros.com/ourhistory

20. *Gustavo Cisneros: Pioneer*, p. 57.

21. *Ibid.*

22. *Diego Cisneros: A Life for Venezuela*, p. 179.

23. KKirkman, Alexandra. "The visionary," in *Forbes Global*, November 26, 2001.

24. *Gustavo Cisneros: Pioneer*, p. 59.

25. *Ibidem*, p. 60.

26. *Cisneros: A Family History*, p. 170.

27. *Gustavo Cisneros: Pioneer*, p. 40.

28. http://countrystudies.us/venezuela/2.htm

29. *Gustavo Cisneros: Pioneer*, p. 45.

30. Rangel, Beatrice, "Of Stubborn History and Tectonic Faultlines: Learning from history to rebuilt Venezuela," 2015.

31. *Gustavo Cisneros: Pioneer*, p. 46.

32. *Ibidem,* p. 47.

33. *Ibid.*

34. "Venezuela Nationalizes Her Petroleum Industry," in *The New York Times,* August 30, 1975. https://www.nytimes.com/1975/08/30/archives/venezuela-nationalizes-her-petroleum-industry-venezuela.html

35. Dolan, Kerry, "The World According to Carlos Slim," in *Forbes*, March 14, 2012. https://www.forbes.com/global/2012/0326/billionaires-12-americas-carlos-telecommunications-world-according-to-slim.html?sh=5996da2f3d5e

36. Quoted in *Gustavo Cisneros: Pioneer*, p. 52.

37. As described by Patricia Phelps de Cisneros, interviewed in 2021.

38. *Cisneros: A Family History,* p. 139.

Part III

RETHINKING AND
REORGANIZING: 1980s

When my father suffered his stroke, I took charge of the business and the family. The family was at ease with my role. Thanks to Pedro Tinoco, we had put together legal documents that clearly explained everyone's responsibilities and rewards. We made sure that my mother's opinions were taken into consideration — she had very strong opinions, so I consulted her on everything — consequently, she felt safe and protected. (She died in 1988.)

I made sure the transition was peaceful but, emotionally, I was devastated. My father was everything to me: He was my world. We were true symbiotic partners: He understood me and my business ambitions, and I understood his.

I knew the dynamics of the family and firm would be different without him. How different? I couldn't begin to guess. All I knew was that we couldn't afford to rest on our laurels. After all, as my father frequently preached, "Anyone who stops, stagnates. And anyone who stagnates is lost." Change was inevitable and we needed to prepare for whatever form it might take.

By 1980, the Cisneros organization counted over 50 enterprises under our control. We had consolidated our ownership of the gigantic Pepsi-Cola franchise, buying all the companies that my father and his brother Antonio had started or partnered with: from the sugar mills to the carbonation production to Gaveplast, the company that constructed the plastic crates used to ship the soft drinks to the shops. We applied the same model of vertically integrating the supply chain to Venevisión, where we developed *telenovelas* for a global market, and to CADA, whose supermarkets were stocked with Cisneros-produced coffee, bread, meat and other products.

We had wanted a good Venezuelan base, and now we had it. We had created a virtuous circle, a dynamo humming along. But alarm bells were beginning to ring. They were faint but you could hear them if you paid attention.

It was clear to me that Venezuela was not moving forward at the pace I hoped for. The local investors' appetite for risk and growth just wasn't there. Our government would not help Venezuela achieve the global standards that I thought we should meet if we wanted to participate in the entire world economy, not just the part having to do with oil.

The market wasn't there either. Venezuela was a small country: Its population hovered around 15 million, a 30% increase over ten years but still almost half the size of Colombia.[1] Our organization had an appetite to grow but no room to expand.

If our ambitions were one problem, our size was another. We were a big fish in a small pond. That created a lot of friction with the government and a lot of envy and resentment from the private sector. There was talk that we were getting too big, that we should be forced to break up.

If we couldn't continue to grow within Venezuela, we would have to grow outside of Venezuela. I had had this conversation several times with my father and he approved it 100%. We didn't want to give up our holdings in Venezuela — we still wanted to be the biggest enterprise in the country — but we decided that our Venezuelan holdings should account for no more than 50%

of our total business. Committing to a goal like that would force us to focus on outside expansion in a big way.

We weren't interested in small wins anymore. We were interested in big wins.

The biggest market in the world was the United States. We were used to operating in a very different environment. Would our knowledge and expertise transfer?

In fact, we believed that our experience in various countries in South America was an advantage. The business environment is complicated, dynamic and totally unpredictable. You have to learn to adapt or you'll never survive. Nelson Rockefeller used to say, "If you can succeed in Latin America, you can succeed anywhere."

When I consulted him about the possibility of expanding into the United States, he told me, "In the U.S., you say you want something done and it's done. In Latin America, you have to give three orders, and then it *maybe* gets done. Being an American can limit you on the international stage, because you get used to a system that works and is in order. But with your adaptability and capacity to work hard, you'll do very well in the U.S. because, in the U.S., things get done."

However, before we could make a move — or even begin to consider making a move — we had to get in shape. The organization had become too unwieldy for the kind of meticulous, personalized management that had been the hallmark when my father was alive. My father's death left a big void but it also forced me to take some time to reflect. My conclusion: We would need to rethink and reorganize.

* * *

We already had all the management consultants we needed. Representatives from McKinsey and other top firms were on our payroll on a continuous basis. Instead, I wanted someone I could talk to one-on-one, someone who thought outside of the box, someone who was both brilliant and practical, someone who could help develop and transform the complex, entrepreneurial collection of companies that comprised Cisneros into a worldwide organization that I could manage without killing myself.

Through the recommendations of some very smart people, I found my way to Dr. Yehezkel Dror, an internationally known social scientist at Hebrew University in Jerusalem. Dror was more than an expert in international relations; he also analyzed methods by which governments organize and act effectively. I have always admired lean, mean efficiency and that was his hallmark. He had set up the model for the Dutch government and he had advised Royal Dutch Shell (one of the largest players in the petroleum industry in Venezuela). His most impressive achievement, in my opinion, was creating the fundamental structure for the Israeli cabinet. Israel is a place where every day brings a new emergency. Yet despite the apparent chaos and even as cabinets and prime ministers butt heads — and the Israeli government is full of very opinionated people — the government continues to operate and life goes on. Something like that isn't an accident.

Dror and I had to address this conundrum: When so many things are happening all around us, how can our executive core receive information so we are always up to date and can make decisions quickly?

We settled on the model of the Israeli cabinet. We'd have a center — that would be composed of me, Ricardo and a few other key executives — with spokes going out. All the spokes would be equally important but would connect in the center, so all the information would flow into and out of the center.

It was the perfect model for us. It was a living organism: It was infinitely flexible and would enable Cisneros to grow as much as we wanted. Best of all, I could work and stay plugged in from anywhere in the world. With a few modifications, this was the corporate structure we followed until 1993.

In this scheme of things, the jefe de gabinete — *my chief of staff — would be the key to ensuring everything functioned smoothly. We needed someone who could be my gatekeeper for all the information coming in and my representative for ideas and directives flowing out. That wasn't going to be an easy task.*

Dror recommended that we look for a seasoned executive with an international background, someone with solid business training, an enormous capacity for work to match my own and the people management skills of a seasoned diplomat. That person would serve as my eyes and ears, which meant being informed about everything, *even something as seemingly small as why* CADA's *quarterly financial report showed an increase in the number of canned tomatoes being sold. Another important attribute is that they should be more educated than I was. That way, Dror said, they wouldn't have an axe to grind.*

After a few experiments, I found José Antonio Ríos. (Patty had already met him and brought him to my attention.) Here's his recollection of our first encounter:

> *I first met Gustavo Cisneros at a benefit concert at Carnegie Hall in April 1972. I was running the Latin American arm of Up With People, a non-profit educational organization that teaches young adults about intercultural communication through involvement in the performing arts. He came backstage, introduced himself and said, "I hear you're from Venezuela. Here's my card. Whenever you're*

117

ready to come back to Venezuela, please come see me before you contact anyone else."

I told him that I was happy at Up With People and had no plans to return to Venezuela. He said, "At some point, you will want to come back. When that happens, please, before you speak with any-one else, call me."

Almost exactly ten years later, my wife and I were expecting our second child and decided to move back to Venezuela. I went to the Cisneros office at Paseo de las Mercedes to deliver my CV with a short note. To my surprise, I was invited to meet him.

We spent three hours together. He asked about my parents and my values. Most of all, he was interested in how I might react to moving from a U.S.-based, educational non-profit organization to a Venezuela-based organization that was very much for-profit.

At the end of our conversation, Gustavo said to me, "We can both succeed but obviously we don't know each other yet. I am offer-ing you a position working directly with me as Assistant to the Pres-ident. Your position is going to be one that means a lot or nothing, depending on what you do with it. In the next three to six months, we can both determine whether this interests you as a career, whether you think you're good at it, and whether I also think the same."

By September, I was appointed to the newly created position of Director of the President's office.

José Antonio Ríos served as my chief of staff for three years, before becoming the chief operating officer of Cisneros in Venezu-ela. All in all, he stayed at Cisneros for 13 years, before becoming the founding CEO of DirecTV, one of our major acquisitions.

In addition to Yehezkel Dror, we also benefited from Peter Gabriel's advice. The dean of the business school at Boston Uni-versity, Gabriel was familiar with Venezuela from his time as a McKinsey consultant for American oil companies there. Dror was

a genius at conceptual matters but didn't do practical details;
Gabriel came from Germany and was brilliant at implementing
the nuts and bolts of a transformation.

For example, both urged us to switch from Spanish to English
in all our business dealings. But it was Gabriel who said, "I can
make it happen" — and he did. That gave us a gigantic advantage
because now we were speaking the language of world business.

Our challenge was basic and bold: We could no longer be per-
ceived as a purely Venezuelan company. To do that, we had to trans-
form a regional company into an international organization.

Leadership strategy: "Know how to transform people"

I'd had over a decade to think about what it means to be a good
leader. I came to the conclusion that leadership is about making
a difference. That's the responsibility of every leader, whether
he or she is in charge of a team, a division, an entire organization or even "a company of one."

The fundamental distinction between one organization and
another is not just its financial or fixed assets but the talents of
its people. Leadership means setting a strategy so that everyone
can make a difference: for themselves, their colleagues and their
customers.

Where do you begin? With these five precepts:

* * *

"Give people a purpose"

I have long admired orchestra conductors, who I think have one
of the most difficult jobs in the world. Thanks to Mozarteum, I
became friends with Zubin Mehta, who visited Venezuela as the
leader of the Israel Philharmonic Orchestra and conductor of

119

the New York Philharmonic. We had frequent conversations about leadership. He told me, "My job is to inspire people to create something better."

When I accompanied him to rehearsals, I could see how he did it. He was tough and demanding and he never gave up. But it paid off. The performances truly lifted your heart.

There's always a better way of doing things and good people will respond to a call to do better. My father taught me that "good enough" is *not* good enough. I tried to pass that on. After every event — every meeting, presentation, cocktail party or dinner — I'd always gather the team and ask: "What could we have done better?" Everything is important. A curtain hook off-kilter or a soda can tossed into the shrubbery aren't just sloppy; they reflect how we do things and, therefore, are not acceptable.

People will say I worked them very hard. I did — and I do. But it's a two-way street. They work me very hard, too. I have to be a good role model to show them what to follow and what to be like. A leader has to be someone they look to in terms of how to connect with other people and other cultures.

It's a mutual understanding: They want quality in their life and work, and we give them quality. A leader gives people a goal that's worth working hard for. You give them a purpose. It's the difference between working *at* Cisneros and being a part of Cisneros.

* * *

"Inspire people to use their abilities to the fullest — and maybe more"

I always try to ask more of people than they think they can give.

They may not know they can give so much, but I have a sense when I meet them that they're hungry for something bigger. They may not be ready at that moment but they will be.

Once you identify those seeds of possibility, it's up to you as a leader to help people develop them, to challenge and help them transform themselves into something even bigger and better than they might have ever dreamed of.

José Antonio Ríos likes to tell the story of how working for Cisneros changed his life:

> One day, Gustavo and Ricardo asked me to meet with them formally. This was unusual, because we were almost constantly together from sunrise to sunset. They asked me to take the position of Chief Operating Officer for the organization in Venezuela, overseeing six operating divisions and over 20,000 employees, including many valuable and senior executives, some of whom had worked with Don Diego. I refused, telling them that I was not a financial expert and was still too inexperienced in commercial company operations in a difficult economic, political and competitive environment.
>
> Gustavo and Ricardo did not like my answer, but persuaded me to meet again that Sunday at Gustavo's home in Caracas. I had not changed my mind, but they had not changed theirs, either. Despite my many misgivings, they convinced me to accept the position and promised all their support. It was a huge level of trust, leadership and vision.
>
> No one in the organization believed that I was going to be able to succeed but Gustavo. He saw something in me — a young guy with only non-profit expertise — that I had never imagined. And he was right. What a ride!

Ask almost any of our managers and executives, and they'll tell you a similar story.

"Gustavo and Ricardo loved to challenge people, and people would step up to the challenge," explains Steven Bandel, who succeeded José Antonio Ríos as my right hand. "At most corporations, you're promoted when they are sure you can fill the shoes. But at Cisneros, you were given the chance, and because you were thankful and wanted to prove that their trust in you was valid, you were very motivated. It didn't work 100% of the time, but they weren't afraid to make mistakes and correct them. As a result, they got the best of everyone."

Bandel started working at Cisneros in October 1983 as what he describes as a "very low-level" financial analyst. He was with us for 32 years, eventually retiring as co-chairman and CEO.

It's often said that we know how to transform people. Transformation begins by inspiring people to use all their abilities to the fullest capacity — and maybe even more.

* * *

"If there's no chemistry, there's no future"
Early on, I said to myself, "If I have the right people, I'm going to make a difference."

Making a difference starts with hiring the right people. Of course, you want smart people because, as I've said before, smart people can do anything. But smarts and skills are just the start; you want people who have the right qualities.

I'm most interested in the chemistry I have with a person: how I feel with them and how they feel with me. Do they feel comfortable in their skin? Are they comfortable with me? When you're going to be working closely together, you both need to feel good — about yourself and about each other. If there's no chemistry, there's no future.

When I met José Antonio Ríos, I already knew he had an important job. Running Up With People was a very big to-do. I said to myself, "This guy must be a people person" — which he was. "He must be very good at logistics" — which he is. He spoke English beautifully. And he was Venezuelan, so he could move back to Venezuela without a problem. But what really clinched my decision was that we had similar values and got along with each other.

When I asked Steve Bandel about his parents, I learned that he was the son of a refugee who found a new home and success in Venezuela. As I described earlier, my father always looked to hire children of immigrants. These are people who were able to overcome a traumatic event and adapt to a new country and culture. They value education and raise their kids to have a strong work ethic and solid middle-class values.

Anyone who works with me knows I endorse those values and want to seed them throughout the organization. I tell them, "When you're hiring someone, look for people like yourself. If you like yourself, you'll ask the right questions." I don't want an organization of mini-mes. I mean that they should look for people with the same values, people who are comfortable in their skin, who will fit into the organization.

Frequently those people were women. I am proud to say that we had women filling senior positions early on, which was unusual at that time. I first met Beatrice Rangel when she was chief of staff for President Carlos Andrés Perez. She was — and is — an independent thinker, unafraid to voice tough opinions, which created friction in the cabinet. When she left, I promptly hired her and made her my personal advisor. She since set up her own company but she remains my consultant.

If I knew the job was traditionally a man's job, I wanted a woman to do it. I knew she would do it even better: They were less egotistical and harder working than most men. You gave them a job to do and you knew they'd do it. For example, Maracaibo is the Texas of Venezuela: It's where the oil is produced and it's a very macho place, where all the bosses are men. We put Alma de Beck in charge of our institutions in Maracaibo. Alma was a very strong woman and she did a fantastic job. Similarly, we had Cristina Pieretti running Cervecería Regional, our brewery business. And I can assure you that there was no nepotism involved in putting my sister Marión, a talented architect who was also a cultural chameleon, in charge of designing our real estate ventures in Venezuela and, later, Spain.

I gave these women all the power, even the power to make mistakes. I figured I could add to my IQ very fast with all these under-appreciated women with such great potential. And if I caught anyone bad-mouthing women, I'd get rid of them.

That became part of the Cisneros reputation: that it was a haven for women. We'd train them, promote them and place them throughout the company, not restrict them to "pink-collar ghettos." We created a prototype of Venezuelan women who were smart, professional and successful.

If the chemistry and brains are there, the skills will follow.

* * *

"Bring everyone into your vision"

It's important to have a vision and know where you want to go. But you cannot be a dreamer only. You have to be a dreamer who can execute.

To do that, you have to bring *everyone* into your vision. People aren't always ready to follow you unthinkingly. It's better to wait to have everyone on board, to listen to other people's doubts and address their questions about areas where we could make mistakes before giving an order.

That can require immense patience. But even if the time doesn't seem right, there will always be another opportunity; things will always come around again. For example, when a group of Venevisión executives whom my father had hired from the outside decamped for one of our competitors (as I'll describe below), it set us back five years. But during those five years, I developed a new team the way I wanted to: from the inside. Those executives were so good that Venevisión became #1 in Venezuela and we were the hottest company in town. And the fun part was that my father was alive to see it.

The bottom line is: You have to have your sergeants and your generals on your side 100%. If you lose one or the other, you lose your army.

* * *

"I'd rather have a drink than a fight"

Most leaders are tough, tough and tough. I don't want to be on Fortune's list of "The 10 Toughest Bosses." I don't believe in it. I think you have to be a leader by example. If you're tough all the time, you end up surrounding yourself with people who are tough. They flex their muscles as a matter of course. They intimidate their employees, they don't tell you the truth if it might make them look weak and then you don't have all the information you need. They get you in trouble.

125

I've heard some people say, "The problem with Gustavo is that he isn't tough enough." I'd rather have that reputation than the opposite. I'd rather have understanding than conflict. I'd rather have a drink than a fight.

That's not to say that I can't be tough. I set high standards for myself and the organization. I'm especially tough when things are going well.

But when people need a reset, kindness goes a long way. I want to give that person a good chance — always. If people know that you will be kindly disposed when they make a mistake, they'll be willing to take a risk, knowing that they won't be fired. That makes them a better leader.

To limit mistakes, I spell out the rules very clearly. Some rules are explicit and some are tacit. You cannot codify everything. For example, loyalty can't be quantified; it has to be demonstrated. I'd rather be seen to be a little weak by being loyal to people.

I learned a good lesson about loyalty from other people's mistakes. My father had blind faith in a few people. You can be patient but you can't be blind. When he was making major changes at Venevisión, he hired outside executives and sent them to the United States for training. When they returned to Venezuela, one of our competitors — it happened to be the television station owned by Patty's family, the Phelps family — offered to pay them many times what we did, and they jumped ship, leaving my father completely alone.

This taught me that you need to have a loyalty that can't be bought. I immediately decided, "I will develop my own executives whose loyalty goes all the way to the bone." I found them by being extremely loyal to them; they followed my example and were, in turn, willing to back me all the way.

It's good for me to be seen to have a soft spot. Everyone needs to know that they can come to me, regardless of what they have done.

I've never fired someone for making a mistake — not the first time and maybe not the second time. At three times, though, I can tell you that person isn't going to be around me for one more minute.

Management tactics: Making things happen

If leadership is about strategy and style, management is about tactics: It's about the nitty-gritty actions that move you forward in the direction set by your strategy. Leadership sets the cultural context in which management takes place.

Every organization has its own culture: an idiosyncratic personality and set of values. It comes down to "how things work" at each company. Here are seven of the key tactics that make things work so well for us.

* * *

"Everyone is expected to have their own opinion"

I'm not afraid of other points of view. The more smart people there are in the room and the more they speak up, the better off we're going to be. Sometimes it gets noisy — but it should be noisy, when you encourage independent thinking and people don't agree.

Most people are used to being managed. I don't want that. I want honest, straight-forward people with open minds.

Everyone is expected to have their own opinion. If there are 20 people in the meeting, they know I'm looking for 20 different opinions, so they make an effort. If I hold a meeting and there's only one opinion, I'm suspicious that *I'm* being managed. And if someone has no opinion or doesn't try to defend their position, they will not be invited to the next meeting — and everyone knows it. So you *have* to speak up. And you have to believe in what you are saying.

I like to work in multidisciplinary groups of people of different ages. I want to hear from everyone: from the vice president of a company to a systems analyst to a recently hired junior accountant. As I'll describe later, the best ideas can come from unexpected places. I'd hate to miss a good idea because of some narrow-minded notion of hierarchy.

I listen to everyone's opinion — always carefully and respectfully — to make sure I hear all the arguments. I admit that identifying the right argument is as much a sixth sense as anything else. And sometimes I make the wrong decisions.

It's always good to have chaos in the beginning. But I never let a meeting finish without a path forward. If the path isn't clear, I will call another meeting on the subject in a day or so. It's not good to leave people with a wishy-washy unresolved situation.

If we're still in the decision-making phase, everyone knows they can call me or write to me immediately to register an opinion. And they know I won't worry if their opinion differs from mine. I will check on it; it will be thoroughly looked at.

Once a decision is made, however, there's no second-guessing. No interference. Everyone is expected to close ranks and do their best to make things work. They know I'll be watching like a hawk. If someone still doesn't agree or doesn't support our strategy, it's understood that they're not a team player and will be taken out of the decision-making process.

There's a lot of trust in our business and not much hierarchy. That does not make for a lot of drama.

* * *

"Make friction work for you"

I believe some friction and fighting are good for creativity. But there's good friction that spurs different opinions and bad friction that results in disharmony and bad feelings. You need to understand friction and make it work for you in a positive way.

You can ask anyone who worked for me and they will confirm that they were never in a meeting where someone showed disrespect to a colleague. Different opinions were encouraged but not personal criticism. That would not be tolerated. If things started to get personal, either Ricardo or I would step in and say, "This is what we're going to do."

We'd hold town halls, where people from different departments were encouraged to speak. I never said anything. I wanted people to speak freely; if they thought I would punish them, it wouldn't work. Instead, I would sit and listen and take notes. And I would learn. Afterward, I would meet separately with the ones who didn't agree with our course of action. Sometimes they were right. Sometimes not. In any case, they learned that they were always welcome to have an opinion.

Sometimes, we'd have two people who were intellectual rivals. When you have good generals, they fight — always — for more credit or more money or more resources. They didn't have to agree with each other but I insisted that we all dedicate our resources to fighting the same battle according to the same strategy. To achieve that, sometimes it meant locking them in a room with me alone; sometimes, it meant having them sit with me separately. The end result was that they may not have liked each other, but they agreed to work together.

They usually agreed to bury the hatchet because we were offering something so compelling. The alternative to Cisneros was working for one of the oil companies, but we were more interesting. We offered something different and with us, they knew they had plenty of room to grow.

* * *

"Rotation prevents stagnation"

From the company's earliest days, a pattern was set: Few people stayed on the same position for more than a few years. Everyone was young and hungry for success. The organization was growing, the atmosphere crackling with energy and excitement, and opportunities for promotion abounded. That model became an intrinsic element of challenging and transforming people.

We divided our managers into two groups: specialists and generalists. Specialists could spend years enriching their experience at one company or in one function. Generalists were trained to be more versatile. It was quite clear that we preferred to promote generalists; if you were a generalist with specific skills, so much the better. Of course, if you wanted to stay in the same track, that was fine. But obviously, there were more perks and more money if you were rotated.

My feeling was that once you had been in the same position for two or three years, you had done most of the things you would do and would start to repeat yourself. So, we might move you to a different position: If you had been in marketing, you might be promoted to sales. And maybe that position would be in a different company.

You were never stuck in one position, so you never had time to be bored and you were always challenged. You always had to learn something new. By jumping to a different company — and those opportunities were plentiful as we acquired more and more businesses — or shifting to a different line of business or even a different country, you could implement the things you had done right in other places and seed the new place with our values. Since you came from another industry, you could try new things.

Of course, you had to comply with the budgets and get approval for major moves but you were given plenty of leeway to show what you could do. Every three months, you met with Ricardo and me to report what you did, what went wrong and what went right. It was very easy to get approval for ideas, because you didn't have to make a formal presentation in front of a board of directors. You simply called Ricardo and me, and we'd say yes or no. In fact, this autonomy was something we counted on: We wanted to see how you balanced prudence and daring.

Take Miguel Dvorak. He started working for Cisneros in 1977 as a junior accountant in O'Caña, our liquor distribution business. After we sold O'Caña in 1985, he shifted to the main office. Because he had helped research the financial side of things when we acquired CADA, he was next transferred to CADA, where he served as treasurer, then was promoted to purchasing manager, and eventually vice president of sales and marketing. When we bought the Pueblo supermarket chain in Puerto Rico, Miguel stayed in supermarkets but relocated to a different country. He returned to Venezuela in the early 1990s to work in the main office in finance, working with Ariel Prat as we built and financed a new brewery.

After boomeranging between finance and operations in the food retail business, he next transferred to a completely different industry as the finance guy for Venevisión. (He recalls, "For a square-headed guy like me, it was a whole new world.") He did so well there that he became the executive president of the company. In 2009, he moved to the United States to help with the leadership transition from me to Adriana. Today, he's the chief operating officer, overseeing the day-to-day operations of all companies at Cisneros.

As for Ariel Prat, he's a wizard at numbers and is presently Cisneros's CFO. But he, too, has a typically varied resumé, ranging from the corporate audit department to the finance manager of the food department to taking charge of our baseball team. Under his leadership, not surprisingly, Los Leones de Caracas won the championship.

A precursor to switching positions was the ad hoc teams we created for specific projects. These were a terrific tool for spotting and developing talent. For example, in order to evaluate a potential acquisition, we might bring together a person from Miami, another from Caracas and a third from New York to work together for the duration of the project. Having a static team doesn't work. We always wanted to be very enterprising. The way to do that is to put the best people together on a team, even if it subsequently disbands. It's like throwing seeds into different fields and seeing which will sprout.

Adriana does something similar. She saw the power of collaborative brainstorming when she first took over and was trying to clarify the direction of the media business. "We felt we were stuck, so I started grabbing ad hoc teams and giving them a problem to solve. Back then, these weren't called 'hackathons' but that's what they were. It was amazing to see the power of collaboration. We had young guys from our legal team talking with digital producers talking with scriptwriters. All of our new lines of business came from that."

What made everyone want to jump positions rather than jump ship was that you weren't penalized if you didn't succeed. If things didn't go well, we understood that maybe you weren't ready for a new position yet or maybe it wasn't the right position for you at the time. We reassured people that in a learning process, you're bound to make mistakes and we'd never punish someone for learning. It was *our* mistake, not *your* mistake, for putting you in the wrong place at the wrong time. We'd simply move you to a different position where you could succeed and regain your confidence. Since you knew you wouldn't lose your job, you would try your best and be willing to try again.

In every case, we'd give you training and a really good #2 person. We tried to set you up for success rather than failure. We didn't know *anything* about some of the businesses we got into. But we knew how to create a cracking good team and they, in turn, knew how to create a good team, all the way through each part of the organization. We applied the same formula to every business we acquired. And it worked.

That's why Cisneros was *the* place to work. Every day, there were opportunities to grow.

* * *

"Put your generals to do the work of sergeants"
I was once invited to a Chinese state dinner in Canada and, after the banquet concluded, some of the guests had the privilege of visiting the kitchen to express our appreciation to the cooks. To my surprise, I discovered that the chef was a general in the Chinese army. His sous-chef was a colonel. They had been plucked from different backgrounds to go to Canada.

Obviously, this piqued my curiosity and I started asking questions. They explained that they put the best people on the job because it was *extremely* important for them to learn. They said, "When we need people to learn how to do something very well, we put our generals to do the work of sergeants."

What a great way to ensure your top people have first-hand experience of the down-and-dirty details they demand of their people! My father used to enjoin me to put my ego in the closet. This was a practical example of doing so.

* * *

"If you don't recognize people, they won't recognize you"

I try to be considerate — most of the time. You get much more out of people if you're considerate.

That doesn't mean that you're an easy mark. No, you can be and you *need* to be a demanding boss: You have to demand quality and efficiency. But when I blow my top, I'm quick to ask forgiveness. If I make a mistake, I will own up to it. And if I criticize you, I'll also let you know what you did well. The unspoken message is that I was expecting more from you but I still trust you and I'm sure you'll be able to do better next time.

It's part of my responsibility as *jefe* to be kind and considerate: to pay attention to what people want, to make a call to wish them a happy birthday, to make an effort to go to the wedding of an employee or help out when a family member is ill. It's part of being a *camarada* — a comrade — a member of our team. If you don't recognize people, they won't recognize you. That's why people who come to work for us stay with us. They're confident that we will take care of them.

134

* * *

"Schedule time for bad news"

I'm a positive person. I don't like negative people and I try to avoid a drumbeat of gloom and doom. But every now and then, you have to talk about things that aren't sunny. I hate to be corralled when I'm walking down the corridor or ambushed when my mind is on something else. So, every Tuesday morning, from 10 to 12, was designated "bad news time."

Anyone could call me and I would be there to answer. Once people knew that there was a regularly scheduled "open mic," they became careful not to call me at the wrong time or catch me on the fly. I'd listen, we'd talk and then once we made a decision, it would be written down, so that there could be no guessing or interpretation.

Two hours is plenty of time for "office hours." I'm not programmed for long-winded conversations. This way, people are forced to think about what they want to say in advance and focus on what's most important. It's short and efficient.

* * *

"Know what not to respond to"

Operations is something I know how to do and I like it very much. But you can get bogged down in details that prevent you from thinking ahead. You're thinking about being the best today and not thinking about growth tomorrow. Leadership is like skiing off-piste: You need to look far ahead in order to choose the best line.

It's difficult to learn not to sweat the small stuff and know what *not* to respond to. You have to be extremely disciplined not to get involved; if you break the discipline, the whole system falls to pieces. So, you have to have absolute faith in your people. Ninety percent of the time, they'll do the right thing. The 10% when they don't, you get involved. But make sure you get involved only once — not twice. If the person can't learn, they shouldn't be there.

You have to trust that people will come to you with a problem. There are many ways to bring something to my attention: email, phone calls, WhatsApp, whatever you use. I trust that my people will save my business life. So, if they come to me with a problem, I know I have to get involved.

"Everything started moving super-fast"

A couple of the decisions we made in the 1970s provided the rocket fuel that launched us onto the international scene in the 1980s. Both of them happened thanks to George Moore.

After George retired from the chairmanship of Citibank, he became — among other things — the trustee for the Onassis family. In the late 1960s, Aristotle Onassis placed a bold bet on New York City: At a time when the city was facing bankruptcy, crime rates were soaring, residents were fleeing to the suburbs and once-grand stores on Fifth Avenue were becoming empty shells, Onassis built a 51-story gleaming tower with office space and luxurious condominium residences on Fifth Avenue between 51st and 52nd Streets. Its northern edge abutted Cartier and St. Patrick's Cathedral was reflected in the mirrored glass of its southern wall.[2]

George suggested that we establish a New York City base of operations there. The Olympic Tower was formally dedicated in September 1974; a year or so later, we took an apartment, set up a small office there and hired Robin Wilson to be our Managing Director. (We would subsequently open additional offices in Miami and Madrid.)

Robin Wilson had run the U.S. branch of Hambros Bank, a very well-regarded European private bank. Like George, Robin knew everyone in the financial world; if they had any interest in Latin America, he would arrange for me to meet them.

I spent a lot of time getting to know these people. Many days, there was a carousel of meals at New York's power restaurants: breakfast at the Regency, lunch at 21 Club, dinner at La Grenouille. Those had been my father's favorite restaurants, so the owners and maître d's knew me from when I was a teenager and had watched me grow up. I told them, "Listen, we're trying to raise money here, so please give us a good table." They had a sense of humor and they did. They treated Ricardo and me with the importance we didn't have. Our guests sensed that we were on to something and wanted to be part of it.

In 1977, George Moore proposed that we make a significant investment in the Tennessee Commerce Union Bank. I couldn't see the point. It was a small local bank headquartered in Nashville, far from the financial center of New York. Furthermore, at the time, banks were prohibited from being owned and operated across state lines.[3] But Moore was betting that the government would eventually lift the restriction and when that happened, the value of the shares would skyrocket.

That's exactly what happened. In the early 1980s, legislation was passed permitting small, local banks to merge and form larger, regional banks. The great banking consolidation in the U.S. began. We eventually sold our shares at a good price to North Carolina-based Nations Bank.

Our investment paid off in intangible ways, too. Tennessee Commerce Union Bank was our foot in the door to the U.S. banking sector; it enabled us to establish a network of alliances and relationships among its movers and shakers. These connections would be invaluable as we ramped up our acquisitions both in the United States and in Spain.

* * *

"The best ideas can come from unexpected places"

We may have been the largest employer in Venezuela and the pre-eminent Venezuelan group in Latin America, but I wanted to establish Cisneros as a bona fide U.S.-based business. Being a U.S. business would establish our credibility in the financial and business community; it would serve as a springboard for growth in the U.S. and abroad.

We began to search for a business to buy where we could best apply our talents. I served on the advisory board of Beatrice Foods International. At a meeting in Hawaii, I learned that one of its subsidiaries, a company called All-American Bottling Company, was being sold. I asked the chairman if my team could examine it. He said, "Of course."

AAB was the eighth-largest bottling company by sales volume in the United States. It employed 2,000 people and manufactured, distributed and bottled almost every carbonated beverage you could think of, from 7-Up to Royal Crown Cola to Schweppes. The only two major brands it didn't handle were Pepsi and Coca-Cola. That was perfect from my point of view, because we wouldn't need to get permission from Pepsi or Coke to buy it.

Bottling is in my family's blood. We had managers with expertise in the industry, including my cousin Oswaldo, who was the best I knew, and we knew we'd further expand our talent pool by acquiring AAB. Pepsi-Cola wouldn't allow us to buy any of their bottling plants in the U.S. because they were afraid of us becoming too big. Buying AAB would allow us to do an end run around Pepsi. "This is your big ticket, Gustavo," I said to myself. "Don't screw it up!" As always, a fundamental question was where the money would come from.

138

One of the few mistakes my father made was to let himself be convinced by Don Kendall, the CEO of Pepsi, *not* to expand into the United States but instead to turn his sights on Brazil. Kendall's argument was that my father would be the sole bottler, the big fish in a very big pond. Brazil *was* a big market and my father and my brother Carlos Enrique did a fantastic job setting up Pepsi and Perrier plants in Sao Paolo and Rio de Janeiro. True to form, Cisneros became the #1 bottler in Brazil and it became a very good, solid business. But Brazil wasn't the United States.

When I came in, I said to my father, "We don't have enough management expertise for both Brazil and the U.S. I want to grow in the U.S. How would you feel if we sell our operations in Brazil and put that money in the U.S.?" He immediately agreed — he had always dreamed of setting up a U.S.-based business. I was able to sell the Brazilian Pepsi and Perrier franchises at a very good price. That money would be used to help establish our beachhead in the U.S. But it wasn't enough. Beatrice wanted $105 million for AAB. It was a big check for us – too big for us to swing on our own.

At about the same time, I got a call from Derald Ruttenberg, a lawyer turned extremely successful financier. Although he was a good 30 years older than I, we were comrades from fishing and hunting trips, and had become close friends. Derald was also a behind-the-scenes deal-maker and people-connector. He was calling because there was someone he wanted me to meet.

Maybe because of his age, Derald was the last person I would have thought would introduce me to an innovative investment strategy. But, as I said earlier, the best ideas can come from the most unexpected places.

Derald said, "You have to meet Teddy Forstmann," one of the principals of the investment firm Forstmann Little. He warned me that Forstmann had a questionable reputation:

He was a gambler and was very disorganized. Disregard all that, Derald said. "He has this idea and I think he needs you to make this work."

The three of us had lunch at the Knickerbocker Club in New York. Forstmann was an aggressive, "my way or the highway" guy. It was clear he was a maverick. And I'm always intrigued by mavericks. Forstmann's idea was a new twist on an old idea. The old idea was OPM – "Other People's Money" – and the twist was what would come to be called a leveraged buyout, or LBO.

In a leveraged buyout, a company is purchased with a significant amount of borrowed money. The assets of the company being acquired are often used as collateral for the loans and the debt is repaid from funds generated from the company's cash flow or sales of assets. When carried to extremes, the debt financing for an LBO can equal the value of the company's assets, so that nothing is paid for with equity. Investors lend their money based on the reputation and expertise of the management and the company's potential for improvement and growth. Once the debt is reduced, the value of the investors' equity can soar and investors can realize that gain if the company is resold.

LBOs would acquire a very bad reputation – in fact, Forstmann coined the phrase "barbarians at the gate" for rivals who financed their buy-out bids with high-yield, high-risk "junk" bonds. But at the time, this was a fresh, new financial idea. I immediately thought of AAB. Bottling was an industry we knew inside and out. Pepsi might badmouth us but our credibility was rock-solid and would, I was convinced, easily persuade banks to give us a loan.

Teddy Forstmann, too, had heard that Beatrice Foods wanted to sell its bottling plants. He was intrigued but with no knowledge of the business, he had been looking for an organization with the experience to manage operations. It was the classic example of two people from two different worlds having the same idea at the same time. Fortunately, Derald Ruttenberg had a foot in both worlds.

I told Forstmann that I was game but that we'd have to do it as partners, from scratch. Now we had to raise the money. Some we could raise ourselves. We had $10 million on deposit in the Banque Worms. Their head of finance, Alejandro Rivera, had worked for Cisneros in our financial department and was one of Pedro Tinoco's protégés. Accessing that money was relatively simple. But it was nowhere near enough what we needed.

Teddy, his brother Anthony (who was his partner) and I went to Manufacturer's Hanover Bank, at the time one of the largest financial institutions in the United States,[4] to make the pitch. (Manny Hanny, as it was known, would merge with Chemical Bank in 1991; four years later, Chemical would itself merge with Chase Manhattan.) I was a complete neophyte about LBOs — this was the first one I had ever participated in — so I was glad to have Teddy do the heavy lifting and share his expertise and credibility with us.

Manny Hanny agreed to put up $90 million but only on the condition that Cisneros contribute $25 million of its own. We didn't have that kind of money. Ricardo and I turned to our connections at Chase Manhattan, which agreed to loan us $25 million using Cisneros shares in CADA as security.

In February 1982, we officially acquired AAB. The total cost was $125 million, of which the capital was, in reality, all debt.[5]

It was a risk: If things went badly with AAB, we could have lost a significant part of CADA.

People sometimes think when I take a risk that I'm jumping into an empty pool. But I'm not; I have a safety net. In this case, our safety net was our expertise in bottling. We knew what we were doing.

I also viewed the money as a tuition payment: We were investing in an education in leveraged buyouts. We were on the ground floor with LBOs. We got to learn the key elements: to get along with the banks, to demonstrate that we could pay our debts on time even with high-interest rates, and to prove our credibility. Fortunately, we had the best professors with Forstmann, Little.

AAB was a great lesson, showing that we could succeed with this new source of funding. We would apply the formula time and time and time again. Throughout the 1980s, LBOs would fund most of our major acquisitions: All-American Bottling Co., Spalding, Evenflo, Burger King and, in Spain, Galerías Preciados.

The acquisition of AAB marked a significant shift for Cisneros. It confirmed that we could participate in big deals in the U.S. market without major difficulties. It convinced the New York financial community that we weren't just another — albeit very successful — Latin American business group with multinational aspirations; we were one of *them*. We became insiders.

From that moment on, we were on the list when investment bankers were looking for a buyer or investor. AAB opened the doors and deals began to flow.

* * *

"A changing business needs to change its source of financing"

Our timing was perfect. The mammoth diversified conglomerates that had dominated the business universe in the 1950s and 1960s, conglomerates like Gulf + Western and ITT, were slimming down and divesting their assets in order to focus on their core businesses. Those assets on the auction block could be acquired through an LBO, increasingly organized by what would become the twin giants of debt financing: Forstmann, Little and Kohlberg, Kravis, Roberts & Co. (KKR). Teddy Forstmann and Henry Kravis were always on the edge — pushing, pushing, pushing. I stayed off the edge but I learned a lot from them. (By the way, Henry Kravis, would become a fishing buddy and he and his wife, Marie-Josée, would become good friends. We sold Spalding to him while I was fishing with him in Colorado.)

Private equity demanded a completely different way of doing business. I had always wanted to build and build and build. This was what my father had practiced and it had been the foundation of his business success. With an LBO, however, the formula for success is buy, improve and sell. It was painful for me. But I quickly realized that before the banks would loan us money, they would always ask, "What's your exit strategy?" And I was forced to accept that we would have to sell the company. (It was good training in putting aside emotions for the sake of the business. We would sell AAB four years later. In the 1990s, we would divest ourselves of many of the legacy businesses that were the foundations of our company. It wasn't easy — in fact, it was painful — but selling those businesses enabled our company to survive.)

Reputation is exponential. In the beginning, private equity was a small world based in New York. The banks knew everyone. I had the two best contacts: Teddy Forstmann and Henry Kravis. But if I wanted to do this again and again, in order to build Cisneros into a bigger and bigger organization, I had to establish my own credibility. That meant having a record of buying and selling at a profit. It was an immense change for me. But if we wanted to expand, we would have to adapt to a new model of financing. Expansion wasn't just a wish: It was a fundamental part of our strategy to build an exit route from Venezuela.

The conclusion was simple: We were evolving and a changing business needs to change its source of financing. Under my father's aegis and when we bought CADA, we worked with banks that made money according to a model dating back to the first Rothschilds, by exploiting the difference between what they paid for their deposits and what they charged for their loans. In the 1980s, we shifted to private equity.

If we had not changed our model, we'd be dead by now.

Overcoming challenges

Oil defined modern Venezuela. It was the engine that powered our economy, boosted our standard of living and shaped our democracy. But now the engine was beginning to sputter. In 1973, a five-month OPEC embargo on countries backing Israel during the Yom Kippur War had quadrupled global oil prices and made Venezuela the country with the highest per-capita income in Latin America.[6] In the course of just two years, the windfall added $10 billion to the state coffers.[7]

In 1976, at the height of the oil boom, President Carlos Andrés Pérez nationalized the oil industry, creating the state-owned Petróleos de Venezuela (PDVSA) to oversee all exploration, production, refining and exporting of oil. Foreign oil companies could partner with PDVSA as long as PDVSA held 60% equity in joint ventures.

There was so much oil money gushing into the state coffers and so little government oversight that it was practically an open invitation to mismanagement. But there were enough oil revenues to support both the legitimate and shadow economies. Certainly, there was little attempt to create a sovereign fund to shield against hard times.

Then the bubble burst. The 1979 Iranian Revolution and the resulting Iran-Iraq War caused a global energy crisis marked by panic buying and soaring prices. The price of crude oil skyrocketed *in international markets to more than $30 per barrel, compared with about $10 per barrel in 1974.*[8]

A swift backlash followed. Demand from industrialized economies diminished as economic activity hit the brakes; at the same time, high fuel prices spurred energy conservation. Meanwhile, efforts to break the OPEC's stranglehold were paying off: The Trans-Alaska Pipeline System began pumping in 1977 and North Sea oil fields reached peak production.[9]

In June 1981, The New York Times *announced that an "oil glut" had arrived.*[10] *Global oil prices plummeted and demand slumped. The FOB (Free on Board) price of a barrel of Venezuelan crude cost, which includes the cost of loading the oil onto a ship, was nearly $25 in 1980; six years later, it was less than $11.*[11] *Between 1981 and 1983, Venezuelan oil exports slumped 30%.*[12]

Oil provided more than 60% of Venezuela's revenues and accounted for more than 90% of its foreign exchange income. In 1982, expected revenue fell short by some 17%, leading to a balance of payments deficit of $2 billion.[13] *On Friday, February 18, 1983 — "Viernes Negro," or "Black Friday," as it became known — the Banco Central announced the devaluation of the bolívar and a series of currency controls. The currency controls slashed Venezuelan purchasing power by 75% in a matter of hours.*[14]

That day, I was hosting James Robinson, the CEO of American Express, and Edmond Safra, the founder of the Trade Development Bank, for lunch at the Four Seasons Restaurant in New York. (The Trade Development Bank was being sold to Amex but a legal battle had ensued; I was trying to patch things up.) When the bill came, I handed over my American Express card. The maître d' returned it with an embarrassed apology: My credit card had been cut off. I gave him a different credit card. It, too, was rejected. In fact, none of my credit cards could be accepted. They were all issued from Venezuelan banks and were now locked out.

145

Pedro Tinoco and George Moore had warned me of the possibility of a devaluation. Venezuela was, as the president, Luis Herrera Campíns said when he took office in 1979, "a mortgaged country."[15] Now, the bill had come due, and Venezuela couldn't pay it.

It was a financial earthquake, ending a decades-long period of both stability and reliability of the bolívar and kicking off a spiral of inflation and further devaluation. From an exchange rate of 4.3 bolívares to $1 in January 1980, the bolívar would fall to over 42 to $1 by December 1989.[16]

The country would never recover. I didn't know that then, of course, but it was clear that we could not depend on Venezuela's erratic fiscal policies. I thought, "I don't ever want this to happen again to me or my family or my business associates. We need to start separating ourselves from Venezuela."

* * *

"Unforeseen circumstances demand innovation"

I've always believed that if you're creative enough, you can overcome any challenge. Unforeseen circumstances demand innovation. The currency devaluation, however, was an especially demanding challenge, especially for our O'Caña liquor distribution business.

The prices of essential imported products were held at the original exchange rate of 4.3 *bolívares* to the dollar. Unfortunately for us, imported liquors, which were O'Caña's mainstay, didn't qualify as essential products — no matter how much people *really* needed a drink as they adjusted to life after devaluation. The exchange rate was allowed to float and prices more than doubled.[17] To make matters worse, our European suppliers, concerned about the access of foreign currency in Venezuela, denied us credit. Just when we needed a steady stream of cash, cash flow dried up.

Our solution was to manufacture more liquors locally to broaden O'Caña's product offerings. We already made Cacique rum and Sagrada Familia table wine. I particularly wanted to develop a deluxe Venezuelan whiskey to replace Dimple premium scotch.

We had warehoused large quantities of alcohol fermented from rice and aged in oak barrels. Someone had the smart idea of mixing one-third rice alcohol with two-thirds alcohol from imported malt whiskey. Bottled and labeled locally, Black Horse was our first made-in-Venezuela premium spirit. It would be followed by Korsakoff Vodka, Britannia Gin and Leclerc Liqueurs, all manufactured with aged rice alcohol. (This innovation brought in cash and helped tide us over, but when it became clear that the credit limitations were not going to be lifted, we decided to sell O'Caña — and made a nice profit.)

When a country goes into a tailspin, there can be a lot of opportunities. In January 1983, the month before the devaluation, we acquired the Venezuelan franchise rights to Pizza Hut. As I mentioned earlier, initially we didn't even need to scout out locations; we simply replaced the soda fountains that we had inherited when we bought CADA.

There may be a mystique to pizza but it's just cheese and bread — and we already owned Venezuela's largest bakery. Cisneros businesses were also already supplying our Burger King franchise with mustard, ketchup, mayonnaise, meat for the hamburgers, soft drinks, cash registers, coffee and even the machines for making milkshakes. It was easy to share the appropriate ingredients and expertise with Pizza Hut. And, of course, we could expand the market by broadcasting commercials on Venevisión and Radiovisión.

Pizza Hut grew very quickly. Most important, it was a way to bring in *bolívares*. I wanted the CADA supermarket chain to have more money in its coffers and this would help bolster that company's finances. I said to our team, "We can be local and expand our operations in *bolívares*."

Instead of crying about the currency situation, we decided to make all our companies independent in *bolívares*. It was a safe decision and good discipline to ask, "Can we pay in *bolívares*?" If there was something we could not finance in *bolívares*, we did not buy it.

* * *

"Some things are for buying, some things are for selling"

One acquisition that looked especially appealing was Sears Roebuck's chain of stores in Venezuela. Foreign companies like Sears wanted to get out of Venezuela fast and we could pick up their chain of multi-purpose department stores at a substantial discount. I have always been fascinated by the retail business and we were already doing very nicely with CADA. I thought, "We can manage the Venezuelan risk better than Sears. If we can control the risk and have no connection to foreign currency, we can do well with this, too."

A retail business is a retail business. We knew about marketing and advertising from CADA. We were in a good position to buy things — or sell them. I'd seen inflation in Brazil, where stores had to change prices two or three times a day. I knew we'd eventually have to sell this business or shut it down, but for the time being, we had a boom. We might as well profit. As the real estate magnate Alfred Taubman told me, "Some things are for buying, some things are for selling." Some things are both. It all depends on the timing.

I asked a member of the Sears management team why they were selling, especially because I thought we could turn it around. He said, "It's down there [in Venezuela], it's too small and it's in Spanish, so we can't bother with it. Also, our economists tell us there can be a gigantic screw-up down the road."

If I were in his shoes, I would have said, "Gustavo, would you become our partner?" In fact, I asked them to become partners. But they just wanted to wash their hands of Venezuela. I called my close friend Leonard Lauder, the CEO of Estée Lauder, to ask his opinion. Leonard always served as a wise and impartial sounding board. He said, "They're my best customer. Buy it!"

In February 1983, we bought Sears' Venezuela business for $5 million. It was a great price, since it would eventually be worth $100 million. Sears had insisted that its trademark could be used for only two years; after that, a fortune in royalties would have to be paid to continue using the name. After an exhaustive market study, the name Maxy's was chosen to replace Sears.

We revved up the Cisneros publicity machine. Participants in the Miss Venezuela pageant visited Maxy's to promote our products and the new name. Stories about Maxy's filled the media; advertisements blanketed Venevisión and Radiovisión. Only eight months after the acquisition, a survey showed that Maxy's brand name eclipsed that of Sears.

* * *

By 1984, even though the Venezuelan economy was still reeling, Cisneros had become the largest group of privately held companies in Latin America, with over 50 companies and

149

35,000 employees. The organization was on target to generate annual revenues of 11,500 million bolívares (about $927 million).

But it was clear that Venezuela was a house of cards waiting to collapse: The markets were artificially propped up and the government was both too big and too unwieldy — and increasingly hostile to the private sector. Because the private sector was so small and the wealth disparity in the country so large, "capitalists" were an easy target to blame for annual inflation rates fluctuating between 6% and 12% between 1982 and 1986.[18]

I saw this movie when it was set in Brazil. Why wait to see the rerun in Venezuela? As José Antonio Ríos noted, "Every day, it became more necessary to expand our business abroad."

* * *

"Always look several steps ahead"

Cisneros had become the go-to organization for advice about doing business in Latin America. We had the brand, the knowledge, the people and the reach. We were 100% pan-regional: We were in the television business in Colombia and Chile, and distributed television content from Mexico to Argentina. We owned a beer business in Peru and had stakes in other businesses throughout the continent. And, thanks to our acquisition of AAB, we were increasingly being invited to participate in deals in the U.S.

One of those calls came from Dan Lufkin, co-founder of the investment bank Donaldson, Lufkin & Jenrette and another friend of Derald Ruttenberg. Two years earlier, Lufkin had acquired a public company called Q Holdings; he had taken it private and was now planning to break it up and sell its divisions at a profit.

One of those divisions was Spalding, an iconic brand in the sporting goods industry. Founded by a pitcher for the Boston Red Sox, Spalding was, for years, the sole manufacturer of the balls used in major league baseball before it diversified into equipment and clothing for football, basketball and golf.[19] It also manufactured Top-Flite golf balls, a leading brand among average players in terms of price and quality.

Spalding was a good fit for Cisneros: It was oriented toward mass consumption and promised significant cash flow. I am always very interested in cash flow. If the cash flow is good, I'll buy the business. Cash flow can always expand, while profits can't.

I try to buy companies that can give me something. We weren't just buying a business; we were buying talent. When I bought a U.S. company, I was buying their management. If we didn't think the management would stay for the long-term, we wouldn't buy the company.

I saw the potential for Spalding to be reborn. We could take this old-school company and, using our knowledge of the U.S. and world markets, transform it into an international brand very quickly. This was a good opportunity to prove ourselves in an area other than soft drinks.

We wanted American management both for U.S. companies and for companies that would expand from the U.S. into the world. I've always believed that management is exportable but some managers are more exportable than others. Venezuelans, at the time, preferred to stay in Venezuela. In the U.S., people move around so much that they're open to the possibility of relocating.

Spalding was a very American product, so we aimed to keep much of the management American, with some Venezuelans upstairs. It was an intense partnership as we worked through the cultural glitches. They were macho, macho, macho — far more macho than we were. We had told them to recruit more Americans; we had more than enough to chew on in Venezuela and it was a great opportunity to build our roster of smart Americans. To my surprise, all their candidates were white men. I said, "This is an all-American company. Where are the women and minorities?"

It turned out that the Spalding executives were members of segregated country clubs. I said, "We want Spalding to grow and be bigger in all-American settings, so we have to mirror the market." Eventually, it worked out well.

We learned a lot from the American companies we acquired. They knew how to manage scale. They had lots of financial know-how. And they were very disciplined: They knew how to run friction-free meetings where everyone knew what they were supposed to do. We saw what they were doing right and used that to pollinate our own businesses. But first we had to actually acquire Spalding — and, as it turned out, another company.

There were plenty of other potential buyers but they were turned off by Lufkin's stipulation that they buy Spalding and Evenflo, a manufacturer of baby products, as a package deal. They saw Evenflo as an anomaly. However, we saw it as an advantage. We'd already had experience with Chicco baby products in Venezuela so we knew the market. Like Spalding, Evenflo had a good reputation, sold to a mass market and had good cash flow. It was our kind of company.

We agreed on a price of $350 million. It was a high price, made even more expensive by the double-digit interest rates on loans then in effect, which scared off many other buyers. But Dan Lufkin and I worked together to convince the banks that we'd have better management. Even so, Citibank balked at financing the entire deal, insisting that Cisneros contribute

$65 million in capital.[20] I thought, "We can last for five years with Spalding's current cash flow. But after five years, we won't be able to hold on."

I didn't need a consultant to tell me that for Spalding to survive, I'd need to sell their products in Walmart. In the mid-1980s, Walmart was an unstoppable juggernaut; in 1980, it had reached $1 billion in sales, the fastest company ever to do so, and by the end of the decade it would have stores in over half the states in the country.[21] If we could sell to Walmart, we would have the best "in" into the U.S. retail market. Once you got into Walmart, you almost automatically got into all the other retail stores.

But I also didn't need a consultant to tell me that Walmart demanded the lowest possible prices from its suppliers. I'd met Sam Walton and his brother on fishing expeditions; we'd talked and spent quality time together. I knew their philosophy and their determination. I knew we'd have to cut our price.

I went to see the Waltons and said, "We can give you exclusivity and a gigantic business. Can you give us the best price?" Their people came back with a price that meant one thing: We'd have to shut down almost all the U.S. factories and move production overseas. (We could continue manufacturing Top-Flite golf balls in the U.S., where we were competitive.)

The relocation of American manufacturing plants to Mexico and Asia had begun in earnest in the late 1970s;[22] by the 1980s, offshoring was a controversial but increasingly accepted way of cutting costs. Exacerbated by recessions in the early 1980s, between 1980 and 1983, manufacturers of durable goods lost nearly 17% of jobs and non-durable goods lost close to 7.5% of jobs.[23]

I knew we, too, would eventually end up in China. But moving manufacturing from Chicopee Falls, Massachusetts, to

China, in one step, was too much for Spalding's management. Instead, we landed on middle ground: Thailand. I knew it wouldn't be permanent and it wasn't: After a year in Thailand, the costs went up and we were forced to contemplate relocating again. By then, though, people were in the frame of mind that moving from Thailand to China was inevitable. (Fortunately, I had many Chinese connections through David Rockefeller and had been visiting China for years. When I sent the Spalding team, they weren't orphans. They knew whom to call and what to do.)

We took a risk that management would stay with us. They were already very good; the question was, how could we make them better? Closing the U.S. factories was a do-or-die decision: If we couldn't lower our production costs, we'd either have to sell the company or shut it down. By moving production overseas, we kept the company and its executives. And they began to understand that they could grow bigger and be more profitable. The Spalding story was like a game of chess. We always had to look several steps ahead.

Changing production to China paid off. It gave us a gigantic lever to pry open other markets. Walmart accounted for 30% of our sales, and sales in other stores began to rise exponentially, because our costs were very low and our quality very good. By the time we sold Spalding and Evenflo in 1996, we were #1 in basketball and golf balls in both the U.S. and worldwide — and we were able to sell a company we had bought for $350 million for nearly $1 billion.[24]

* * *

"If you see a diamond on the floor, pick it up"

We acquired Spalding and Evenflo in September 1984, barely a year and a half after the acquisition of Sears in Venezuela. It was a lot to digest in such a short period of time and everyone was working flat-out.

Steve Bandel remembers talking with me around that time about our strategy for acquiring companies: Shouldn't we have a specific focus for the kind of business we wanted to be in before we scooped up more companies? "Maybe you're right," I told him. "But if I see a diamond on the floor, should I pick it up or not?" We could never have guessed that within weeks, an enormous diamond was about to be hand-delivered to me on the proverbial platter.

I was skiing in Aspen when I got a call from Pedro Pablo Kuczynski, the co-chairman of First Boston, an international investment bank. I knew him well from financial dealings with his bank and from socializing with him in New York. He was calling to let me know that Galerías Preciados, a famous chain of Spanish department stores, was for sale.

"It's a challenge," he said. "It's been offered to all the big businesspeople in Spain and nobody wants it. It's been offered to principal department stores in Europe and nobody wants it. It's been offered to El Corte Inglés (Galerías Preciados' main competitor in Spain) and they don't want it. It's been offered to the major department store chains in the United States and department stores in Latin America and *they* don't want it. I've presented this 100 times to 100 different groups and they've all turned it down. I think there's only one person crazy enough to think it has value" he concluded. "And that's you."

I loved Spain and had often visited Corte Inglés. I was thinking of applying the Corte Inglés model in Venezuela — and using Galerías Preciados as a model of what *not* to do. Reeling from the Spanish recession in the 1970s, it had been taken over first by a bank, then by the Rumasa conglomerate. When Rumasa turned out to be a shell game, the Spanish government stepped in and asked First Boston to sell off the assets. With 15,000 employees in 29 stores around the country, Galerías Preciados reported losses of $50 million a year. The company was drowning in debt and rigid labor laws in Spain prevented a reduction in the payroll. *The Wall Street Journal* quoted one of the people in charge of the sale as declaring it a "lost cause," adding they couldn't get rid of it "even if we wanted to give it away."[25]

To top it off, there were doubts about the stability of Spain's fledgling democratic government and the economic agenda of its socialist prime minister, Felipe González. I was intrigued.

George Moore, one of my first "wise men" and a close friend, was living in Spain. His advice was reassuring. Spain had a strong and stable middle class, he told me, with a great deal to lose from a populist government or a return to a Franco-style dictatorship. Felipe González might have been the Secretary-General of the Spanish Socialist Workers Party but his government plan was market-friendly. (In fact, I had met González in 1978 at the "Autocracia, democracia y totalitarismo" symposium Cisneros hosted. He was one of the most brilliant politicians I had ever met. He would take a backward country, modernize it and strengthen its democracy, then advise Mario Soares on how to do the same in Portugal.)

I sent a team to Spain to check out the situation. They reported that the Galerías Preciados stores were shabby but their locations couldn't be beat. Their advertising was beyond bad and their marketing was worse, but we knew how to fix that. We ran a rigorous risk assessment of the business. We were early to use computer projections to calculate cash flow projections, profit and loss; thanks to the computer projections, we never took on anything we didn't know how to do.

We had a saying about taking risks: "Point, point and shoot." We did not just point and shoot or, heaven forbid, shoot without pointing. We were maniacal about numbers. We constantly ran scenario after scenario until we knew the business inside out. We calculated and analyzed every possible outcome. That helped us to predict and manage risk, so we could identify problematic issues and bet on the best possibilities. Because our risk assessments were based on reality, we refused to be intimidated by the inevitable challenges and uncertainties associated with venturing into the unknown.

The key issues with Galerías Preciados were financing and labor relations. George Moore put Ricardo and me in touch with the most important bankers in the country, starting with Alfonso Escámez, the president of Banco Central, the largest private bank in Spain. We met at the U.S. embassy, because it was neutral territory, with Thomas Enders, the American ambassador, hosting. Tom said, "Gustavo Cisneros is a friend of the United States. It's in the interest of the American government to facilitate this deal. It will be good for the Spanish government and the Spanish economy."

We explained our strategy: We would apply modern marketing techniques, as we had done so successfully in the United States and Venezuela; we would launch a massive advertising campaign on television, which was unusual in Spain at the time; and we would improve the variety of products in the stores.

Escámez had started his career in the mail room. He knew political power and business power, and he knew he was seeing a demonstration of political interest in the big picture. Escámez promised his support and opened other doors in the Spanish banking community. We returned from Spain with lines of credit totaling more than $400 million.[26]

Meanwhile, Felipe González gave me an introduction to the labor leaders. The unions were holding an illegal strike but the head of the labor unions agreed to meet me personally. It was a huge step for him: He had been taught to hate capitalists from the cradle and had never talked with a capitalist before.

The unions were especially concerned about their pension obligations: Would Cisneros pay them? I said, "I will fully fund the pensions but I'll need a little time to build back the business. To do that, though, there can be no strikes." I needed to send a strong signal that we were committed to staying in Spain. And after that, we had no trouble with the labor unions. The unions agreed to reduce the company's payroll in return for participating in the decisions about who would be affected by the cuts. (Working together, we laid off 4,000 of the 15,000 employees, which helped ease the running costs.) We were ready to make our move.

At the auction, there were only two bidders: the Colombian Roca Group, which owned the Sears Roebuck chain in that country, and Cisneros. The Spanish government weighed the options: Roca, which generated $75 million a year, versus Cisneros, with annual revenues topping $4 billion.[27] We won and the news was announced on December 6, 1984.[28]

The financial package was structured on the same model as an LBO: We put in $16 million of our capital to buy a $350 million-dollar company. That's private equity for you.

Private equity was such a new concept in Spain that there were rumors that the deal was a political favor. It was not. And we knew how to resolve the issue: by doing a good job. As

I often say, once the transaction is structured and completed, all that's left is to roll up your sleeves and go to work. Or as my father used to say, *El premio de un buen trabajo es más trabajo* — the reward for doing a good job is more work.

We sent in a crack team: Hector Beltrán was a wizard at marketing, Humberto González was our best distribution executive and my sister Marión redesigned and renovated the stores to make them fresh and modern. (This raised a lot of eyebrows in Spain, where women were usually relegated to secretarial roles.) We broadened the range of merchandise, including bringing in Spalding and Evenflo products, and upgraded the product displays. We launched an aggressive advertising campaign on television.

We were going to take the magic wand we had waved to transform CADA and Maxy's and bring it to Galerías Preciados.

It was exciting but not everyone on our Venezuelan team wanted to participate. At the time, living in Venezuela was more appealing than living in Spain. If you tried to send Venezuelan executives anywhere other than Venezuela, they didn't want to go. Despite the devaluation of the *bolívar*, they were still making plenty of money in Venezuela, their kids were going to the best schools and they were surrounded by family. People thought Venezuela could always come up with a solution to its dysfunctional political and financial situation. Meanwhile, Venezuela, for them, was a paradise, so why go elsewhere?

Then there was the fact that Spain had a different way of operating. It had a European mentality that was completely different from the U.S. and Venezuela. Things moved more slowly. I got together with people and I listened to their concerns. I didn't force the issue. I asked them to be patient with their new Spanish colleagues; I encouraged them to bring people along and reassured them that eventually they would come around to our way of thinking and doing things. I said, "Spain is like California. It's going to be a new world. This is an opportunity."

For me, Spain became part of our exit strategy. I'd been feeling like the canary in the coal mine ever since "*Viernes Negro*." Even though we were kings of the hill in Venezuela, I felt it was time to walk away from it — at least, mentally. It was a very tough decision — but it would prove to be the right one.

* * *

"When you get an offer to sell, you sell"
The magic worked — up to a point. By the end of 1987, three years after we acquired Galerías Preciados, we had reduced the annual negative cash flow from 20 billion pesetas ($114 million) to 3 billion pesetas ($23 million) and our projections for 1988 showed us moving into the black. Furthermore, our deal ignited the interest of British and German investors. Spain was indeed becoming "the California of Europe."

However, the operational success didn't necessarily translate into a financial turnaround. Our agreement with the banks allowed a four-year grace period to pay off the debt. At the end of that time, the banks could reschedule the liability but only if we cancelled 40% of the debt. In addition, we needed to further broaden the merchandise selection and offer our customers store credit cards, something our chief rival, El Corte Inglés, was already doing. All of that required more capital. It was a difficult situation.

And then a different kind of magic happened. Anthony Clegg, a successful British commodities trader turned real estate magnate, was interested in buying Galerías Preciados. Thanks to Felipe González's capitalism-friendly economic policies and

Spain's entry into the European Union in 1986, Spanish real estate values had skyrocketed. Galerías Preciados's 29 stores occupied some of the best locations in cities around the country and Clegg's Mountleigh Group was interested in buying all of them at 100 times more than our initial investment.[29]

I, too, had considered using Galerías Preciados as the basis for developing a Spanish/European real estate portfolio. But when you get an offer like that, you don't hang around. You sell. There was one potential stumbling block to the deal: Clegg insisted that the Galerías Preciados senior management team stay on. After all, they were responsible for the chain's transformation. I spoke with them and explained the situation: The Mountleigh offer was very good for Cisneros but whether we could accept it depended entirely on them.

The team all agreed to stay at Galerías Preciados and the deal was signed on September 29, 1987.

Three weeks later, on October 19, 1987, the Dow Jones Industrial Average dropped by 508 points, nearly 23%, the largest-ever percentage drop in one day up to that point.[30] As the crash reverberated around the world, the price of Mountleigh stock was sliced in half.[31]

Mountleigh could no longer afford the terms of the original negotiation. However, Tony Clegg came up with an alternative: Instead of paying £150 million in cash, he offered £30 million in cash, an IOU of £80 million to be paid in 24 months and the equivalent of £42 million in Mountleigh stock valued at its pre-Black Monday level, which amounted to 7.2% of the company.[32] We agreed.

As the months passed, however, it became clear that the once-glittering British real estate market had dimmed considerably. Mountleigh stock was still severely depressed. We began to doubt whether they could pay off the IOU.

Consequently, in October 1988, a year after the stock market crash, we signed a *third* agreement with Mountleigh: We returned the IOU as a down payment for 25% of the value of five properties Mountleigh owned in London. My real estate dream was still alive.

The crown jewel of the Mountleigh properties was a group of buildings around Paternoster Square, the neighborhood surrounding St. Paul's Cathedral. The area had been heavily bombed during World War II as the Germans attempted to destroy a monument as central to British identity as Paris' Nôtre Dame Cathedral is to France. St. Paul's miraculously survived intact but the surrounding buildings were obliterated. When they were rebuilt in the 1960s, the nicest description of them was "pedestrian" and "mediocre."[33]

Everyone agreed that Paternoster needed a massive renovation. An investment bank described it as "the most attractive project to appear on the English real estate market in the past 50 years."[34] Every architect wanted to grab the gold ring.

Bill Keon, who oversaw tax and legal matters for Cisneros outside Venezuela and supervised the finances for AAB, also had experience in the real estate sector. "Bad News Bill" — a nickname he earned for his straight-shooting approach — spent 14 months commuting to London every week to renegotiate the lease of every tenant in our properties in Paternoster Square, from the smallest kiosk to large corporations like Reuters and KPMG.

But the biggest obstacle didn't come from a tenant. Alfred Taubman had warned me about Paternoster Square. He said, "You have a problem in England. What is not written is what counts. Prince Charles has ideas about architecture and your project will interfere with his dream. He doesn't have the legal capacity to go against you but he has great informal influence.

You'll never know what hit you but you'll never get anything approved."

Prince Charles, who was dedicated to preserving Britain's architectural heritage, had a special place in his heart for St. Paul's — and personally reserved a special place in hell for those who desecrated its setting. In a December 1987 speech to architects and town planners, he compared their efforts in Paternoster Square to "a basketball team standing shoulder to shoulder between you and the Mona Lisa" and said, "You have to give this much to the Luftwaffe: When it knocked down our buildings, it didn't replace them with anything more offensive than rubble. We did that."[35] It was obvious that we were marching into a minefield, no matter which design we proposed. The question was how to limit the damage.

I met personally with Charles at the Caracas residence of the British Ambassador to Venezuela. (He wanted to visit the Amazon and I made it easy for him.) We had designed an enormous *maquette* in royal green, complete with cars, trees, people and, of course, the cathedral, all to scale. It was really beautiful. I brought a couple of brilliant people to describe what we had in mind. But I could see that, just as Alfred had predicted, he wasn't going to go for it. I asked for time and Charles agreed.

Fortunately, I had a Plan B. When we were considering the Paternoster Square deal, I had a long lunch with Alfred Taubman. He explained the real estate business to me: when to buy, when to sell, when to buy again, and when to double up. To illustrate his point, he asked, "Do you know the sardine story?"

Here it is: A man catches a beautiful bunch of sardines in Italy. They are packed into beautifully designed cans and sold to a broker, who sells them to a store in another country. When they don't sell there, they're sold again to another store in another country. This happens multiple times. Finally, someone opens a can. By that time, it's so old that it stinks and the sardines are no good. Now Alfred told me, "This property is like the can of sardines. There are a few businesses that are for selling and this is one of them because you have a strong position."

I had many advisors telling me to hold on, that Prince Charles would come around to our point of view. Alfred disagreed. "Don't fight the establishment," he said. "Sell it." Alfred even offered to make the sales presentation — an immense favor. He did such a convincing job that within a year, at the end of 1989, we sold a majority interest in Paternoster to Greycoat PLC and Park Tower Realty. In early 1990, Mitsubishi Estate, which had bought Rockefeller Center, joined the partnership with a one-third interest; five years later, it bought out the partners.[36]

I was able to get out of that gracefully, without scandal and with my money intact. That was the end of my real estate dream in the U.K. But, as I'll describe later, not necessarily the end of all my real estate dreams.

* * *

"Always have a clear exit strategy"

When people give you their money — whether it's a bank, private equity or, today, a SPAC — the expectation is clear that you will do well. Very well. That means having a clear exit strategy from the very beginning.

For example, when we bought Galerías Preciados, the exit strategy was clear: Galerías Preciados had a portfolio of the best real estate holdings in Spain. If worse came to worst, we could always sell the real estate piecemeal, building by building.

With AOL in Latin America, as I'll describe, our exit strategy was based on setting a hard limit on the amount of money we were willing to invest — and not a dollar more. Determining an exit strategy is a process I do by myself. Other leaders assign it to a special team skilled in scenario planning. Either way, it's a lonely process: No one likes to talk about failure because failure is frightening. But as the saying goes, hope is not a strategy.

My father was, at heart, a big romantic. I think he purposefully trained me to be unsentimental, to be realistic. When the time comes to pull the plug, you have to be ruthless. That means that you have to put your ego aside. Don't try to improve a bad situation. It is what it is.

Sometimes the best thing to do is to throw out the box of sardines. That's the thinking that would guide me at the end of the 1980s when I began to contemplate the unthinkable: exiting our business in Venezuela.

Behind the scenes

When my father yanked me out of San Ignacio school in Caracas and shipped me off to the United States, waiting to meet me at Idlewild Airport (as it was called before it was renamed John F. Kennedy International Airport) was the chauffeur for the Rockefeller family.

How did that come about? My father was a very important man in Venezuela and was recognized as an influential figure by the U.S. State Department. He was also a client of Banco Mercantil, which was 80% owned by Chase Manhattan, which was a Rockefeller business. In addition, he was a client of Chase in the U.S. And because the soft drink business had good cash flow, he was a valuable client.

The Rockefellers, of course, knew who was who in Venezuela. Nelson Rockefeller and my father were contemporaries — Nelson was just three years older than my father; his brother David was four years younger. They shared much of the same point of view

165

about business and the role of business in a democracy, so it wasn't surprising that they became not just acquaintances but good friends.

The Rockefellers took me under their wing and, as I grew up and followed my father into business, our connection deepened. Pedro Tinoco was the lawyer for all the Rockefeller interests in Venezuela; when he became my lawyer and counselor, that was another node in the network. (At his recommendation, we also established a relationship with Milbank Tweed, a very powerful law firm that was the firm that handled business for the Rockefellers.) Nelson was always looking for good clients for Chase Manhattan Bank and Cisneros was one. David was the chairman and CEO of Chase; although he wasn't as enamored of Venezuela as Nelson was, we got along well from early on.

In the course of buying CADA and 20% of IBEC, both Rockefeller businesses, I met J. Richardson Dilworth. Dicky Dilworth was the senior financial adviser to the Rockefeller family and its investments and philanthropic institutions; as the leading manager of Room 5600, the family office in Rockefeller Center, he also served as the family's chief consigliere. He was the most important connector of all: In a family organization that prided itself on its network, he was the ultimate networker.

As the number one Chase client in Latin America, I met with Dicky two or three times a month. We bonded over my desire to grow our business in the U.S. and their desire to be a part of that growth. Patty and I became good friends with Dicky and his wife, Bunny. He recommended that I be named to Chase Manhattan's international council, which was a strong signal of trust and introduced me to some very impressive people.

Philanthropy was a deep interest of the Rockefeller family, as it was with the Cisneros family: We all endorsed the value of joining philanthropy and business. Dicky offered to put Patty and me on the "right" boards: Patty was involved with the New York Botanical Garden and the Museum of Modern Art early on and I joined the Council of the Americas (which David Rockefeller founded as a "regional" version of the Council on Foreign Relations) and was made a trustee of Rockefeller University.

If you do your homework and take part in boards that have nothing to do with business and work pro bono, it shows that you're good at providing solutions for the community. The boards also provide a network of people whom you can call or who know to call you. They tell you what's going on in the world and open the door to unseen opportunities.

If you're not there, you have fewer ideas and your deal flow is limited to the proposals brought to you by your lawyers and bankers. We were in the right place at the right time with the right people. My father was the most influential teacher in my life but David Rockefeller ran a close second. He pounded, pounded, pounded one lesson in particular: It matters how you form connections, how you strengthen them and how you use them. It matters from the very beginning.

* * *

"Soft power begins with small things"

As George Moore and Pedro Tinoco and all the banks began to send us people who considered giving us credit or who wanted to invest in Venezuela, we were constantly making presentations: introducing ourselves, explaining who we were and what we wanted. All of this went on without the immediate possibility of a deal, but it was a valuable investment.

It was the beginning of how we built and nurtured relationships. It was the beginning of my understanding and use of soft power. Soft power begins with small things. If an important visitor was coming to Caracas, I would go to the airport myself to meet him or her. We had a helipad at one of our buildings, so we could whisk from the airport to downtown by helicopter and avoid Caracas' infamous traffic. That visitor would always remember afterward that I had taken the time to go to the airport to pick him or her up in person and make their arrival easier.

We set up an office at Venevisión — which was very close to the center of Caracas, where the presidential palace and government ministries were located — specifically to streamline appointments. I supervised it myself. Anyone who came — even on 24 hours' notice — could call us and we'd arrange an appointment. And we never interfered with their business.

When people came to Caracas, we became the place for them to call first — or, at least, check in. Eventually, they'd think, "If the Cisneros organization can help me get an appointment so quickly, maybe they're good to do business with." I'm sure other people were doing the same thing, but this guaranteed that we wouldn't be ignored.

We adapted our approach in New York but with the same goal of nurturing networks. In New York, it was different. New York is all business, just straight facts. It's such a tough town that with an extra smile, you come out ahead.

Helping someone out, finding a solution, making life easier or more pleasant — if a connection starts off on a friendly footing, it's better all around. And it creates an opening to do business. If people need me, they will call me. They'll say, "Gustavo could be good as a partner."

We didn't call it soft power then, but that's what it was. It starts with pro bono work and is nurtured with loyalty and patience. Things change, people come in and out of power but we never dropped them and we never lost track of them. Soft power enabled us to tap an enormous pipeline of ideas, influence and connections.

I asked William Luers, the former American Ambassador to Venezuela, to describe his impressions of how we nurtured our networks through soft power. Here's what he said:

> From my first meetings with Gustavo and Patty Cisneros in the fall of 1978 after arriving in Caracas as the new American Ambassador, I realized that they were on a mission: to influence the way North American political, business and intellectual leaders thought about Venezuela and Latin America.
>
> Their first objective was to create opportunities for prominent Americans who had never been to Venezuela or Latin America to experience Venezuela directly and learn firsthand from visits with cultural, intellectual and political leaders. The symposium organized by the Diego Cisneros Foundation on Autocracy, Democracy and Totalitarianism was a perfect example. The participants, who included many thought leaders who hitherto knew little or nothing about Venezuela, became more conversant on the issues of South American nations. They carried the word back to the U.S. and started the buzz which opened more doors to understanding.
>
> Gustavo had learned a great deal about American political and intellectual life. He spoke the American language of business and the private sector, which was an entrée. He became the go-to person on questions about Latin America for bankers, journalists, professors and senior American political leaders, including every American President and their principal advisors. No one I knew outside of Washington or New York had such an extensive rolodex of powerful people. Doors would open for Gustavo, which allowed him to learn and listen.
>
> Meanwhile, Patty was determined to make people aware that 20th-century "Latin American art" was broader and richer and more

influential than the work of the great Mexican muralists and the popular Frida Kahlo. Through an active philanthropic commitment to educating curators about Latin American art, she greatly expanded the capacity of major museums to learn about and display more knowledgeably the really ground-breaking works from South America.

I have not experienced in my entire diplomatic career such a successful commitment of one family in pursuit of educating the world. You never felt you were being sold a bill of goods on Venezuela. Instead, Gustavo and Patty opened doors and minds.

* * *

"Keep up with the people doing the important things"

I learned from David Rockefeller the business of maintaining active contacts. People tend to change jobs or positions every five to ten years: In fast-paced countries like the U.S., people change jobs even faster. People move in and out of philanthropic boards, too, albeit more slowly. In any case, you have to keep up with the people who are doing the important things.

I'm not talking about the people at the very top. But the people below them disappear — and those are the people in charge of the actual nuts and bolts of business deals, the people you hammer out the details with. You have to know them *and* who their replacement will be, and build a relationship with them both.

My father often counseled me to be patient, so I learned to play the long game. I'd talk to people, listen to them and learn about them: their strengths and weaknesses, what they like and don't like, what their sense of humor is. I knew that when a smart, ambitious person is in a fast-track career, they are likely

170

to be promoted by their current employer or jump to a better position elsewhere. Either option opens doors to new opportunities for you. So I'd always follow up a meeting with a letter to keep the communication channels open. That was David Rockefeller's advice: Follow up, follow up, follow up.

And keep a file. I always kept a file of people who might be good hires, become business associates or provide a path for philanthropic projects. The file contained public information: birthdays, anniversaries, records of meetings, descriptions of business relationships, gifts given and received, and family relations, as well as my own personal impressions. Also, I always look at what people do outside of business. I wanted a sense of the whole person; it gives me more context.

Thanks to the file, when I meet someone again after a period of time, I can refer to a personal detail to show that I *really* remember them. For closer connections, the file reminds me to send a card or a small gift.

Nurturing a network of relationships was a lesson both David Rockefeller and my father frequently emphasized. It was as much a natural law to them as Newton's First Law of Thermodynamics: Relationships must always be built and cultivated; they should never be destroyed.

* * *

"Give your brain a break"

The more important you are, the more important it is to take a break. My father gave me a good perspective on how to do things — and how not to do things. He didn't take care of his stress as he should have, and consequently, he suffered a gigantic stroke. That was a huge lesson for me.

171

My brain is never completely off but my best ideas come when I'm exercising or at rest. I relax by being active. I find sports are the best for me: paddle tennis, swimming, bicycling, working out in the gym. Physical activity releases endorphins and makes me think more sharply. I also deliberately build a pause in my daily schedule. I think of it as putting the brain on simmer, rather than keeping it on the boil.

I like to take 20-minute naps — usually each afternoon. Naps are important. They give you a fresh, new perspective every time you wake up. They're a natural way of recharging your batteries. And they don't cost a penny. The best naps in the world are in a hammock. (If you don't have a hammock, think about getting one.) But sometimes when I'm in New York and walking around, I'll step into a church for a snooze. I've even done it in St. Patrick's Cathedral.

Like any habit, you have to work at it. My father studied yoga with Indra Devi, a great yogi, and I attended many of their sessions. I've also meditated with the Dalai Lama. That led me to learn techniques to not obsess about problems. I close my eyes, breathe deeply, focus on my breathing and pretty soon I'm out.

* * *

"Run your business. Don't let your business run you"
Naps are an inexpensive quick break but you also need to take longer vacations to put your brain on a different plane altogether. Initially, Patty would be upset because we'd go on vacations which we couldn't afford. I'd say, "Patty, it's going to pay for itself in ideas." And it would.

One of her favorite stories comes from one of our earliest vacations. I'm going to let her tell it:

172

It was 1973. Gustavo's competitors were out to get him and I had just become pregnant. We hadn't taken any time off for over two years, since we got married and Diego had his stroke. Gustavo said, "Patty, we need a rest. We're going to take a cruise to New York."

Gustavo doesn't like little spaces, so we reserved a small suite on the *Queen Elizabeth*. When we opened the door to the "suite," we discovered it comprised one room with one porthole, one closet and two narrow beds. We were supposed to stay there for two-and-a-half weeks? No way!

Gustavo talked to the purser. The only thing available was the Queen Mary Suite. It had two floors with balconies — in those days, ships didn't have balconies — and a private butler. Gustavo said, "This is perfect!"

I happened to peek at the room rate posted behind the bathroom door and nearly flipped out. It was $50,000. We didn't have that kind of money. But Gustavo said, "No, no, no! We're staying here!" So we did.

And the fact is, he rested, he got his thoughts in order, and when we returned to Venezuela, he went on to do everything he did.

The punch line to the story is that when Gustavo went to pay, the Cunard folks apologized for having made a mistake and only charged us for the original room. I just wish they had told us before. I was suffering the whole time!

After my father died in 1980, I realized I needed to get better at relaxing. Don't get me wrong, I love my work. But I could easily work nonstop, and that's not healthy. I didn't want to have a stroke like my father. Derald Ruttenberg gave me an invaluable piece of advice: "Gustavo, you need some monkey business in your life." Initially, "monkey business" meant going on fishing or shooting trips — in Iceland, say, or Alaska or Scotland.

I became part of a circuit of people who, even though they were high-powered businesspeople, were not connected through business but through leisure: Alfred Taubman, Don Kendall from PepsiCo, Vernon Jordan, Jim Wolfensohn from the World Bank, the Walton brothers of Wal-Mart, Leonard Lauder, Henry Kravis, to name a few, as well as former U.S. Presidents Jimmy Carter and George H.W. Bush.

In the course of things, some gave me very sage business advice and I ended up doing deals with others. For example, the Walton brothers came to Venezuela to fish with me in the Amazon before we did business together. That's why when we bought Spalding and Evenflo, I knew I could talk with them. What they said confirmed that we had to close the U.S. production facilities and relocate them first to Thailand, then to China. That gave us a gigantic advantage and enabled us to become a world leader in sports products. And it was due to the connections formed by the "monkey business."

But business wasn't the point. We trusted and respected each other and were able to relax with each other. We became more than companions: We were *camaradas* — comrades.

I reciprocated by hosting them in Venezuela: in Los Roques for bone fishing and at the Manaka camp in the Venezuelan Amazon region to fish for *pavón* (peacock bass). I soon realized that if I was taking important people into the jungle, I needed to set up a professional organization with someone in charge whom I trusted completely. That person was Johnny Fanjul, a former classmate from Babson College. I literally put my life — and that of my guests — in his hands.

Johnny arranged the most incredible trips to the Orinoco. We'd fly in by helicopter, following the river because there was no satellite or radio beacon for navigation, and then we'd switch to dugout canoes. Our guides included Charles Brewer-Carías, a noted Venezuelan explorer and naturalist, Mark Moffett, a biologist specializing in the ecology of tropical forest canopies, and Napoleon Chagnon, an anthropologist and the foremost expert on the Yanomami tribes. We'd visit a tribe's *shabono* — the doughnut-shaped communal dwelling that was the heart of a village — and spend time with indigenous people whose way of life was threatened by extinction. Leaders of countries and multinational corporations would talk to the tribe's chief and compare the differences and similarities of their roles and responsibilities.

(These trips to the jungle helped seed the idea of the Orinoco Collection within the Colección Cisneros, now comprising more than 1,200 ethnographic objects and documentation from 12 distinct and different indigenous communities of the Venezuelan Orinoco River basin. The indigenous world was disappearing so quickly that we felt it was of critical importance to preserve artifacts of their culture. This is now one of the most comprehensive collections of Amazonas indigenous art in the world.)

One of the most fascinating trips was with David Rockefeller. In the middle of the jungle are flat-topped mesas called *tepuis*. Some soar hundreds of feet into the air and some have sinkholes that were formed millions of years ago. One *tepui*, the Cerro Sarisariñama, is over 300 meters high with a sinkhole twice the height of the Empire State Building. It is estimated to have sunk over two million years ago, before the separation of the continental plates. The helicopter pilot lowered us in a cargo basket, four people at a time, into the sinkhole, past walls studded with the nests of macaws, feathered in brilliant scarlet and sapphire.

These were unique and unforgettable experiences. As Derald Ruttenberg said of one of our trips, "I'm so excited to be here that I'm peeing my pants!" Originally, we called the trips "razzle-dazzle," but then, because of Derald, we dubbed them "monkey business." We even had a special pin made: It showed a monkey crouching on top of the globe with its tail curling around the equator. We distributed it to our guests, as a souvenir of these extraordinary adventures.

Sometimes a vacation is a rest. Sometimes it is an adventure. Either way, it gives your brain a break. That's why these trips are worth it.

*　*　*

On December 4, 1988, Venezuela re-elected Carlos Andrés Pérez as president. Pérez had presided over the country from 1974 to 1978, the years of its greatest petroleum boom. The situation was very different now. Despite price controls and currency restrictions, by 1988, inflation had soared to an annual rate of 35.5%.[37] Petroleum earnings plummeted to $8 billion a year between 1986 and 1988, 43% less than the amount of the previous three-year period.[38] When Pérez assumed the presidency on February 2, 1989, Venezuela had international reserves of just $300 million[39] and was staggering under nearly $35 billion in foreign debt.[40]

Pérez was forced to borrow money from the International Monetary Fund (IMF), which mandated drastic economic and fiscal reforms, especially in the reduction of public spending. Pérez's Plan de Ajuste Económico was meant to be a short-term shock to the system. It certainly was a shock. Instead of returning to the abundance of Pérez's previous term, which many voters had anticipated, "el Paquetazo" ("the big package") further devalued the bolívar, increased prices for electricity and public services, such as telephone, water and sanitation, and public transportation, and reduced state subsidies for gasoline.[41]

The economic adjustment program was announced on February 16. Within a week, gasoline prices doubled. Public bus fares were set to rise by 30% on March 1, but bus companies decided to apply the price hike on February 27, a Monday and the day before payday in Venezuela.[42] *It was the spark in the powder keg.*

On February 27, 1989, a frenzy of riots, looting and shootings broke out in Guarenas, 20 miles east of Caracas, then spread to Caracas and throughout the country in what became known as "el Caracazo" ("the Caracas smash"). The government called out the army to restore order. In the resulting crackdown, at least 200 — and some estimate as many as 2,000 — people were killed, mostly at the hands of government forces.

Rumors flew that President Pérez was dead or taken prisoner, and that the military was taking over. Pérez asked to make a speech on Venevisión, something we supported because our democracy was at stake. We didn't realize that people felt so angry and disillusioned with Pérez that we would be tarred with the same brush. In what seemed like a blink of an eye, we went from being one of Venezuela's most admired companies to being its most reviled.

In the weeks after "el Caracazo," the entire country suffered from food shortages. Our company had the biggest warehouse in South America and the most extensive distribution system for our hundreds of stores, but people were hoarding goods and the shelves were often empty. All the supermarket chains were affected, but public opinion, fanned by the press, focused its attacks on CADA. We had a very hard time: Three of our big 18-wheeler trucks were hijacked and one driver was beaten so badly that he had to be hospitalized. We had to have the National Guard accompany our trucks.

Calm was eventually restored and the company bounced back. But the foundations of the country had been shaken at their core. The political establishment and los notables — a group of high-profile figures, including businesspeople, journalists, opin-ion-makers and intellectual thought-leaders — called for Pérez to resign. It was clear that they saw the opportunity to take him out as more important than the opportunity to save our country's democracy.

I had a bad feeling about the future of my country and its pol-iticians. I thought, "If this is the crème de la crème of Venezuela, quite frankly, the cream has gone sour." I felt things were out of control, that we had lost our compass. Everything that my father and I had been striving for, everything that we had built, was crumbling in front of my eyes.

I knew we were going to be in trouble in Venezuela. I com-pletely gave up on the commitment of the Venezuelan government to enable the private economy to change and grow. This was a real test — and our politicians had failed.

I said to Steve Bandel, who by then was the president of Cis-neros, "We can't wait any longer. We have to reduce our size in Venezuela — starting now."

Notes

1. https://countryeconomy.com/demography/population/venezuela?year=1980

2. https://en.wikipedia.org/wiki/Olympic_Tower#History

3. https://www.investopedia.com/terms/i/interstate-banking.asp

4. https://www.upi.com/Archives/1991/12/31/Chemical-Bank-Manufacturers-Hanover-officiallymerge/3446694155600/

5. *Gustavo Cisneros: Pioneer*, p. 83.

6. "Venezuela: The Rise and Fall of a Petrostate." Council on Foreign Relations, January 22, 2021. https://www.cfr.org/backgrounder/venezuela-crisis

7. *Ibid.*

8. Tarver, H., Micheal, *The History of Venezuela*. ABC-CLIO, 2018, p. 139. *See also* Statista: "Average Annual OPEC Crude Oil Price From 1960 - 2022." https://www.statista.com/statistics/262858/change-in-opec-crude-oil-prices-since-1960/

9. https://en.wikipedia.org/wiki/1980s_oil_glut

10. Hershey, Jr., Robert, D., "How the Oil Glut Is Changing Business," in *The New York Times*, June 21, 1981. https://www.nytimes.com/1981/06/21/business/how-the-oil-glut-is-changing-business.html?pagewanted=all

11. https://www.eia.gov/dnav/pet/hist/LeafHandler.ashx?n=PET&s=IVE0000004&f=A

12. *The History of Venezuela*, p. 141.

13. De Cordoba, José, "Venezuela Announced Partial Devaluation of Bolivar," in *The Washington Post*, March 1, 1983. https://www.washingtonpost.com/archive/politics/1983/03/01/venezuela-announces-partial-devaluation-of-bolivar-6/4accb36b-a9e9-4e44-b933-2e9e5e5ba827/

14. https://en.wikipedia.org/wiki/Viernes_Negro

15. Gunson, Phil, "Luis Herrera Campíns: Former President of Venezuela Forever Linked to 'Black Friday,'" in *The Guardian*, November 12, 2007. https://www.theguardian.com/news/2007/nov/13/guardianobituaries.venezuela

16. *The History of Venezuela*, p. 141.

17. *Gustavo Cisneros: Pioneer*, pp. 87-88.

18. https://en.wikipedia.org/wiki/Hyperinflation_in_Venezuela#Devaluation_of_the_bol%C3%ADvar

19. https://www.spalding.com/about-spalding.html

20. *Gustavo Cisneros: Pioneer*, p. 93.

21. Goldman, Leah, "The Incredible Story of Walmart's Expansion from Five& Dime to Global Megacorp," in *Business Insider*, July 20, 2011. https://www.businessinsider.com/the-incredible-story-of-walmarts-expansion-from-five-and-dime-toglobal-megacorp-2011-7

22. "Where America's Jobs Went," in *The Week*, January 11, 2015. https://theweek.com/articles/486362/where-americas-jobs-went.

23. Harris, Katelynn, "Forty Years of Falling Manufacturing Employment," in *Beyond the Numbers,* U.S. Bureau of Labor Statistics. November 2020; Volume 9, Number 16. https://www.bls.gov/opub/btn/volume-9/forty-years-of-falling-manufacturing-employment.htm

24. Barba, John, "History's Mysteries: Spalding Golf 's Final Countdown," in MyGolfSpy, October 19, 2021. https://mygolfspy.com/historys-mysteries-spalding-golfs-final-countdown/.

25. *Gustavo Cisneros: Pioneer,* p. 94.

26. *Ibidem*, p. 97..

27. *Ibidem*, p. 98.

28. "El precio de Galerías Preciados se ha multiplicado por 100 en cuatro años," in *El País,* November 15, 1988. https://elpais.com/diario/1988/11/16/economia/595638010_850215.html

29. *Ibid.*

30. https://www.investopedia.com/terms/s/stock-market-crash-1987.asp

31. *Gustavo Cisneros: Pioneer,* p. 102.

32. *Ibid.*

33. https://www.architectsjournal.co.uk/archive/why-paternoster-square-was-a-60s-disaster

34. *Ibidem*, p. 103.

35. Eliason, Marcus, "Prince Says Architects Damage London More Than the Luftwaffe Did," in *Associated Press,* December 2, 1987. https://apnews.com/article/bf42693c76c706633bca816401ffa73f

36. Rubin, Dana, "Mitsubishi Banks on St. Paul's Project," in *The Independent.* October 22, 2011. https://www.independent.co.uk/news/business/mitsubishi-banks-on-st-paul-s-project-1295680.html

37. *Gustavo Cisneros: Pioneer,* p. 110.

38. *Ibid.*

39. https://en.wikipedia.org/wiki/Caracazo

40. *The History of Venezuela,* p. 149.

41. *Ibid.*

42. https://en.wikipedia.org/wiki/Caracazo

Part IV

FLEE FORWARD: 1990s

Being in business — and the more businesses, the better — gives you a good seat in the theater. I could see what was happening on stage after "el Caracazo." There wasn't much I could do from the audience to affect the story, but I could make sure there was a clear path to the exits for our businesses and our people.

We celebrated our 60th anniversary in 1989. Our organization was bigger and stronger than ever. But our successes underscored the vital need to stay aware of changing circumstances and to prepare to respond to them.

Even before the events of February 1989, we had been considering reducing our operations in Venezuela. Twenty years earlier, when I picked up the reins from my father, our aim had been to diversify our business holdings, both to broaden the income base and to give more stability to our organization. We had done it first in Venezuela, by adding enterprises like CADA and O'Caña to our traditional strongholds of Pepsi-Cola and Venevisión. Then we expanded into the United States with our acquisitions of All-American Bottling, Spalding and Evenflo. Lastly, we moved into Europe when we bought Galerías Preciados.

Our goal of deriving half of all sales from international sources had been achieved. At the same time, we had built a solid buffer against the financial upheaval in Venezuela with our strategy of building businesses that brought in *bolívares*: Maxy's's, Pizza Hut, Burger King and Yukery, which produced baby products, juices, ketchup, pasteurized milk, chocolate and other products.

But the world was changing, not just inside Venezuela but outside it as well. Globalization was not a new concept but political, economic and technological developments accelerated the trend. The major multinational companies were extending their interests in Venezuela. Cisneros brands like Tío Rico Ice Cream, Yukery and Helene Curtis beauty products now had to compete against the local affiliates of Unilever, Nestlé, Kraft and P&G. CADA and Maxy's's were squaring off against Carrefour and Walmart. We simply didn't have their resources.

There's a saying in Spanish: *Huir hacia adelante para no reconocer los errores del pasado.* In English, that roughly means: "Flee forward, so that you don't repeat errors of the past." Once again, it was time to change paths and refocus the direction of our organization. Once again, we would experience a metamorphosis in our business and financial model. Once again, we would not just adapt to changing circumstances but reinvent ourselves.

As the decade unfolded, I didn't realize how much the phrase "flee forward" would apply to us. Nor could I have imagined how much we would leave behind.

* * *

"Shift when you need to shift and change when you need to change."

Throughout 1989 and 1990, Ricardo and I held many meetings with our smartest executives to brainstorm how we would evolve. Reducing our footprint in Venezuela would require an immense amount of effort. We had over 6,000 employees to protect, many living in a country facing an uncertain political future. My gut was calling for immediate action but my head slammed on the brakes. The last thing we needed was to give the perception that we were panicking. And, in truth, we weren't panicking. We were, however, extremely determined to create and implement a smart exit strategy.

In December 1990, we invited more than 600 Cisneros managers to the Hotel Macuto-Sheraton, a lovely beach resort close to Caracas, for a "strategic encounter." After the chaos of the past two years, we wanted — we *needed* — to assure our people, our partners and the institutions we dealt with that we had a clear, exciting and radically different vision for our future. We wanted — again, we *needed* — to galvanize them into action to help transform the organization and make that vision into a reality.

The first and most fundamental shift we announced was that no business could be dependent on a single country. It was no longer enough: In a small country like Venezuela, for example, we had already maxed out certain markets; there was no room for further growth. And it was no longer safe: Imagine if 35 out of the 50 largest companies in Venezuela were all owned by Cisneros? Just think of the negative energy we would attract.

From then on, we decided that every Cisneros business had to be international and based out of the United States. It could grow both in the U.S. and outside of the U.S., or it could be an international business that we could bring into the U.S. However, a company that could not internationalize could no longer justify its existence in our organization.

"All of you are accustomed to managing companies that generate *bolívares*," I said. "Now we'll learn to generate dollars."

That was a change with radical implications. It had already been very expensive to make dollars in Venezuela; after "el Caracazo," it had become impossible.

Our organization had been founded on the formula that "cash is king." With the exception of Venevisión, all of our companies had been founded or acquired because they could generate a reliable and abundant flow of cash. Cash flow had been a key indicator when deciding on a new acquisition; our financial analysis centered specifically on cash flow to the point that we always told bankers that we would buy a company only if its earnings were enough to finance its own growth and amortize all its loans within five to ten years. That was the essence of our LBO model. That would have to change, too.

I had seen in Europe and the U.S. how multinational consumer products juggernauts like Carrefour, Kraft, Unilever and Walmart leveraged their size to erode competitors' cash flow margins. I knew what would happen if we kept our consumer products businesses: They were so much smaller that they would be crushed like a mouse by a python.

Some of our Venezuelan-based enterprises could stand on their own. These included the Pizza Hut and Burger King franchises and Summa Sistemas, the distributor of computer brands like NCR, Apple and Fujitsu, which was the purview of my younger brother Gerardo. Gerardo, who was 11 years younger than I, had attended Stanford University when computers were taking off and had become fascinated by their potential. Like our brother Carlos, he was a whiz at marketing and distribution. Under his leadership, Summa beat IBM at its own game in Venezuela and became the most important computer distributor in the country.

Many of our other businesses could not. Atlantis, the company that made mustard, shoe polish and household cleaners was transferred in its entirety to Yukery and the Atlantis distribution center was shut down. Tío Rico ice cream would be sold to Unilever.

This wasn't a fire sale. The idea was to reduce our footprint gradually without a financial penalty and get the terms we wanted: a good price and protection for our employees. We made sure that our employees could stay with the new owner, otherwise we would find them another job. That was a mandate: Don't hurt anyone.

All in all, 15 companies would be sold over the next four years, including Yukery and even our beloved CADA. It would be extremely difficult to abandon such a key part of our identity but we couldn't afford sentimentality or nostalgia.

So what would Cisneros become known for? Instead of manufacturing and selling perishable goods for mass consumption, we would have a new identity: mass-market media entertainment on a pan-regional level. Venevisión and Radiovisión would be our launch pad for new growth. Nor would the concept of "entertainment" be limited to creating content for a television channel or a radio station: It would comprise a universe of products that supported entertainment, such as soft drinks, beer and even baseball.

This identity shift also meant rethinking our sources of financing. Our reputation with banks had been based on our expertise in generating cash flow. In the communications industry, however, companies are valued not so much on the basis of monthly income from subscribers as on their potential to create value: through expanding distribution networks across multiple geographies and filling those pipelines with compelling content. Banks had been happy to fund an expansion of a juice-processing plant, but that was a relatively modest investment compared to creating a new television network. To generate enthusiasm from banks, we would need to establish our credentials on a much larger scale.

We had been very good at tapping private equity markets and we intended to maintain and increase that investment stream. In addition, the sale of All-American Bottling and Galerías Preciados had given us a hefty financial cushion; we were ready to take on another opportunity.

But we were also investigating a new source of financing: new partners. This was not just a question of inviting partners to participate as passive investors. We would need experienced operators who could share their brain power as well as open their wallets and loan us dollars.

A dollar-based business meant relocating our base of operations to the U.S. For what we intended to accomplish, we would need access to bigger markets and bigger financing. That would be very difficult to do in Latin America. So it made sense to think in terms of U.S. dollars and, hence, in being a U.S.-based company.

That, too, was an immense shift for us. But we had made up our minds. We were going to be a U.S.-based company, with U.S. balance sheets, U.S. business customs and U.S.-based executives who met U.S. management standards. In fact, much of that was already in place. What changed would be the scale.

Because Venezuela was a limited market, we had to be involved in 50 different small things to grow — and even then, we always eventually hit a wall. The U.S. market was so enormous that we could concentrate on fewer areas and do more with less. And, as Nelson Rockefeller had advised me, it's much easier to grow in the U.S. because there's a much bigger pool of top talent, the operating systems work and the government is stable.

Our new base of operations would be Miami, Florida. (The company headquarters would remain in Caracas and our investment office would stay in New York City for the time being.) Venevision International had had offices in Coral Gables since 1972, so we were already familiar with the business climate in South Florida. It had also been a central location for various real estate deals we'd been involved with.

There was a joke in Latin America at the time: "Miami is so close to the United States." Thanks to its significant population of Cuban emigres and immigrants from Latin America and the Caribbean, Miami was a place where Spanish was widely spoken and the culture was familiar. At the same time, it had all the reassuring and reliable institutions of the U.S., with U.S. laws and regulations and, the "Miami Vice" television series and Carl Hiaasen books notwithstanding, a sense of order. For Venezuelans still reeling from "el Caracazo," Miami offered the best of the U.S. combined with a sense that they could feel comfortable and fit right in.

From a business perspective, Miami's location was a big advantage. We could reach out to the world while keeping a close eye on Latin American business. Caracas was just three hours away by plane and every major foreign capital was reachable by a nonstop overnight flight, connections that didn't exist in many Latin American countries. As a very large metropolitan area, it provided access to an international, bilingual staff accustomed to global hiring practices and standards. And Miami was neutral territory: There were none of the usual distinctions between Venezuelans and Colombians, Argentinians and Brazilians, or Mexicans and everyone else. Everyone could work together. Miami would be both our bridge to the United States and a bridge to Latin America. We felt certain we could compete from there in almost any arena we chose.

You shift when you need to shift and change when you need to change. In a time of turmoil, our people were given hope.

This could have been trauma with no solution. The change would still be traumatic, but it was trauma *with* a solution.

* * *

Early in the morning of Wednesday, February 5, 1992, I was flying to Madrid from the World Economic Forum in Davos when the pilot notified me of an urgent message from my personal assistant: There had been an attempted coup d'état the night before in Venezuela.

In the three years since "el Caracazo," on February 27, 1989, Venezuela had boomeranged between strikes, demonstrations and student protests. In May 1989, a general strike was called to protest President Carlos Andrés Pérez's drastic economic belt-tightening. In June 1990, there were violent demonstrations against rising gasoline prices. The following March, police killed two students in Caracas during demonstrations against the high cost of living; in November 1991, three more people were killed during a demonstration; and in December 1991, high school and university classes were suspended as a result of protests that left another at least 10 demonstrators dead at the hands of the police. By January 1992, demonstrations were taking place across the country calling for the removal of President Pérez from office.[1]

While Pérez was touting Venezuela's political stability to foreign investors at Davos, a group of army officers led by Lieutenant Colonel Hugo Chávez Frías plotted to capture him when his official plane landed at the Francisco de Miranda Air Force Base in downtown Caracas. The plan went awry because the president's plane arrived after dark. The downtown airstrip did not have landing lights, so the plane diverted to the Simón Bolívar International Airport in Maiquetía, about 13 miles away.[2]

The rebels then attacked La Casona, the presidential residence. Alerted minutes before the attack, Pérez managed to escape across town with the rebels at his heels to Miraflores Palace, which houses the presidential offices. As a rebel personnel carrier rammed through the front door, Pérez fled through a secret tunnel to the garage. His military chief of staff shoved him into an armored car and flung a raincoat over him for camouflage. Blasting through red lights, the vehicle raced to the nearby studios of the country's leading television channel, one he knew supported democracy: Channel 4, aka Venevisión.[3]

The coup had begun at about 9 at night. José Antonio Ríos remembers seeing airplanes flying — "and nothing in Venezuela flew at night" — so he knew something was happening. At the time, he was the COO of Cisneros. As reports of the coup began coming in, he called the station's general manager, Manuel Fraiz-Grijalba, and the chief engineer, and they immediately hustled to the Venevisión studios. Fraiz-Grijalba even brought his wife, which turned out to be a smart move.

I had already called my brother Ricardo to warn him that something was happening, to urge him to be careful and get to the Venevisión studios as quickly as possible. I had also been in touch with Fraiz-Grijalba; we had a plan to put the signal out from Miami, if necessary, and different places in South America. That was our business; it was something we knew how to do.

The car carrying Pérez reached Venevisión shortly before midnight.[4] *Pérez was given an office from which he could make and receive phone calls. José Antonio Ríos was already on the line to the U.S. embassy. Within 15 minutes, Pérez received a call from President George Bush affirming his support. An hour later — just as the day was dawning in Madrid — Prime Minister Felipe González also expressed his solidarity, as did other international leaders in Europe and Latin America.*[5]

191

Meanwhile, Ríos and his small team frantically worked to make possible a live transmission to the entire country in the middle of the night, despite the chaos and interference created by the coup attempt. My brother Ricardo handled one camera, Fraiz-Grijalba's wife was on a second and the deputy general manager handled the third. The duty technician punched out the signal and opened the microphone, while the chief engineer ensured the transmission would be broadcast not only on Channel 4 but also on Channel 2 and Channel 8, reaching practically everyone in Venezuela.

Not incidentally, this confused the insurgents about Pérez's real location, thereby ensuring that Venevisión wouldn't be shelled — at least, not immediately. (It later turned out that the insurgents approached Channel 8, the state channel, to air their own proclamation, but weren't able to broadcast it because the tape had been recorded in the wrong format.[6])

Pérez appeared on air, sitting at a desk in a studio and proving that, despite statements from the insurgents, he was undoubtedly alive. But he was just shy of 70 years old, and had just come off a 10-hour flight from Europe and survived multiple assassination attempts. He was sweaty and disheveled and looked, Ríos recalled, "totally broken."

At 4:30 a.m., Pérez appeared on TV a second time. A clean shirt had been found for him and he had showered and shaved. The Venevisión team readied a larger studio with a more substantial desk. He looked presidential and in charge.

Only one key element was missing from the scene: a Venezuelan flag to be placed next to him. Someone ran to the special storage unit where flags for newscast backdrops were folded and shelved, grabbed a yellow, blue and red banner, sprinted back to the studio and hoisted it on the flagstaff ... only to discover that it was the Colombian flag. (Both flags display the same colors but the width of the stripes is different and the Venezuelan flag also has an arc of eight white stars and a coat of arms.) After another sprint to the storage unit, the right flag was produced and hoisted just before Pérez went on air.

The second broadcast made the difference. National political leaders, labor leaders and community leaders saw the message and started arriving at the Venevisión studios or calling Pérez to affirm their support of democracy. A few hours later, he walked back into the Palacio de Miraflores and at 11:30 that morning, Hugo Chávez surrendered and was arrested.

Throughout the night, Patty manned the phones, providing a bridge between me and the family, our executives and international contacts, and the station, relaying information as it came in in a calm, controlled manner. That was extremely significant. Patty was a well-regarded public figure in Venezuela because of her work with ACUDE and Mozarteum; the family knew I trusted her 100%. Leveraging that platform of trust, she was the best conduit to transfer information from me to key people in the country until I could get to Caracas myself. (As soon as I heard the news when we landed in Madrid, I had the plane refueled and flew immediately to Miami. I went to my mother's house in Coral Gables, assessed the situation and quickly determined that my place was with Venevisión and my family in Venezuela. We landed at Maiquetía early the next morning.) There was a lot of improvisation but we got the signal out very quickly. That was critical in putting down the coup.

Venevisión had, from its inception, been an unequivocal supporter of democracy. When the coup attempt happened, there were no other alternatives for our company and me to defend the government. I may not have supported Pérez's policies, but the alternative was the overnight demise of democracy in Venezuela. There was no choice. Now, though, we paid a heavy price — and would pay an even heavier one later.

The populist rejection of Pérez — a response to a deadly combination of widespread government corruption and an economic policy so harsh that barely half (57%) of Venezuelans could afford more than one meal a day[7] — was so intense that a poll taken soon after the coup was put down found that 81% of respondents had "little or no trust" in Pérez' government.[8] One way in which they manifested their disgust with Pérez was by rejecting the television network that had served as his platform. Viewer numbers plummeted. It would take two years for Venevisión to recover its top spot.[9]

But there were more pernicious and enduring ways in which the attempted coup resonated. As José Antonio Ríos recalled, "The day after the day after, a rumor started: 'Cisneros put Pérez back into the presidency.' How many enemies does that make you?"

In the following months, a presidential commission was appointed to analyze and confront the social problems that led to the golpe de estado.[10] *But the commission's proposals were neither listened to nor implemented with any urgency or efficiency, leading the public to become further disillusioned in, frustrated with and distrustful of the government.*

A second coup d'état was attempted later that year, on November 27, 1992, this time by senior officers from the Marines and the Air Force. Once again, there was little popular support and the insurrection was put down. But the uprising seemed to confirm the belief that the longer Pérez remained in office, the more volatile the political situation would become and the more painful the economic and social crises would be.

In March 1993, impeachment proceedings were begun against Pérez on the charge of embezzling 250 million bolívares (about $2.7 million) from a presidential discretionary fund. Pérez would be permanently removed from office on August 31, 1993.

Powerful partnerships

Some 18 months before the first coup attempt, we had begun what would become a massive reinvention of our organization, one that would define us for the next three decades and continues to be a hallmark of our identity today.

We took our first steps into the field of telecommunications in November 1991 by founding Telcel, the first cellular telephone company in Venezuela. Telcel was a partnership between Ricardo, our cousin Oswaldo (who was appointed president) and me in a joint venture with the U.S. telecom giant BellSouth — I was on the board of directors — and some smaller telecommunications firms.[11]

Telcel was a practice test for us in many ways. It fit with our dream of expanding our presence in technology and telecommunications, in alliance with a large multinational that could provide operational expertise and give us hands-on experience. It was a business that we could grow fast and eventually sell for U.S. dollars.

The deal was also practice for a new form of financing for us. We were used to managing businesses with intensive cash flow that could, essentially, fund themselves. This was different: It required a lot of capital upfront.

We needed to understand how to set up the financial structure of the company so that we could borrow larger amounts of money than we had been accustomed to. That meant we needed a new investment source: not a bank or an LBO but a major corporation that would want to partner with us and put their skin in the game. This would be a recipe for more ambitious transactions in the coming years.

Telcel became the leading cell phone company in Venezuela. But the Telcel success was also bittersweet. The venture marked one of the final deals by "the three *amigos*" — Oswaldo, Ricardo and me. We had complemented each other immensely well but we had reached a point in our lives — we were all approaching our 50s — when we were beginning to go in different directions.

Oswaldo was like another brother. He was very good at day-to-day operations and finance, and was a key reason that our Pepsi and Hit bottling business remained so profitable. But after we sold the bottling business to Coca-Cola in 1996 (which I'll describe below), Oswaldo wanted to make a big bet in Venezuela's oil sector. I'd always wanted to be in the oil business, but I didn't think the politics of the country were reliable enough to take the risk at the time. Oswaldo wanted to gamble. I tried to convince him not to do it but he was stubborn — a quality that had made him such a good counterpart to me. We parted ways amicably and always remained very close.

Ricardo, too, was looking to take a different path. He had dedicated himself to the organization from the time he graduated from Babson College even though, unlike me, he was never comfortable working nonstop. Increasingly, he wanted to relax and enjoy life more while he was young enough to enjoy it. He would gradually step back and, after a complicated separation, eventually officially retired from the organization in 2008.

Some partnerships you wish would last for generations. But when there's no equal will to continue, it's best for both sides to break up.

* * *

"Good partners offer the opportunity for something bigger and different"

When I became the head of Venevisión in 1970, I had a clear vision of our mission: I wanted to turn the business into an enterprise of regional and even worldwide scope. And what would be the wind under our wings? Love — or, more precisely, the stories of hope and heartbreak embodied in the soap operas called telenovelas.

Thanks to *La Revancha, Las Amazonas, Cara Sucia, Esmeralda* and other *telenovelas*, by the beginning of the 1990s, we had a fantastic calling card: One out of every four soap operas transmitted to the Spanish-speaking world was produced by Venevisión, with additional markets in Turkey, Greece, Hungary and the Philippines.[12] Between 1991 and 1992, sales of Venevision International increased 150%.[13]

Once we were approaching 50% of the market in Venezuela, I had begun looking for growth opportunities outside the country but still in Latin America: in Peru, Argentina and Brazil, to name a few. But I encountered a situation similar to Venezuela: The market size was so limited that one company's growth came at the expense of its competition, which, in turn, upset the political equilibrium.

I thought, "Let's go for broke. Let's enter the biggest market with the greatest room for growth, a market where we could make a difference with the products and talent we had." There was really only one candidate. I thought, "What if we moved to the United States?" I wasn't the first person to come up with this idea.

Emilio Azcárraga Milmo was a Mexican entrepreneur and principal shareholder of Televisa, the Mexican counterpart of Venevisión. By 1991, Televisa controlled 97% of the Mexican market and exported some 38,000 hours of programming, mostly news and *telenovelas*.[14] Azcárraga, too, saw expansion across the border into the U.S. as a natural next step. However, he had already tried it some 20 years earlier — and been severely burned.

197

What happened was that in the 1970s, Azcárraga launched Spanish International Network (SIN), a channel to carry Televisa programming to the millions of Spanish-speakers who lived in the United States. However, U.S. law required that the channels — like NBC, ABC or SIN — be owned separately from the network of stations that distributed the signals in each city. Without control of the stations, there was no guarantee they would air SIN's programming.

Consequently, Azcárraga formed a partnership with a group of investors under the leadership of René Anselmo, a broadcasting entrepreneur, to found the Spanish International Communications Corporation (SICC), which began to buy stations that would broadcast SIN programming to a Hispanic population that was rapidly growing from 9.6 million in 1970 to 14.5 million in 1980 and would burgeon to 22.6 million in 1990.[15] By the mid-1980s, SICC/SIN comprised more than 400 broadcasts, satellite and cable outlets.[16] The future seemed bright.

Then, in 1986, SICC slammed into a wall. The Federal Communications Commission ruled that the corporation's close connection with the Azcárraga family violated rules against ownership of U.S. networks by foreigners.[17] The FCC refused to renew the licenses of the SICC stations and Anselmo was forced to sell SICC to a U.S. company. The buyer: Hallmark Cards, Inc.

A major manufacturer of greeting cards and stationery, Hallmark was also known for its award-winning — and often tear-jerking — movies produced for television. (The Hallmark Hall of Fame, first aired in 1951, was the longest-running prime-time series in the history of television.[18]) It had recently embarked on an ambitious program of diversification and television programs targeting the booming Hispanic audience fit right into its strategy. Hallmark began acquiring additional SICC stations not included in the original purchase, including purchasing SIN from

Televisa. In 1987, the company — including both the TV stations and network — was renamed Univision.[19]

Hallmark had little experience in creating programming for Hispanics. It launched Spanish-language versions of English-language hits such as "Saturday Night Live," "Entertainment Tonight," "The People's Court," and various talk shows and celebrity magazine-format programs. It hired more news correspondents and became noted for its coverage of current Latin American events.[20] However, the new programs were not as popular as the Televisa *telenovelas* or the Venevisión programs, and the expenses of developing original content weren't matched by advertising revenues. Boosting sales in an attempt to reach a wider audience demanded even greater expenditures. The cash flow wasn't enough to pay the debt Hallmark had taken on to finance the purchase of Univision.

Hallmark's problem was an opportunity for us. We had been closely watching both Univision and Telemundo, its competitors in the United States. Telemundo had only seven stations, however, while Univision had 13, plus a greater number of affiliated channels.[21] That meant that no matter how popular Telemundo's programming might be, it lacked Univision's broader coverage and, consequently, could never command the lion's share of advertising dollars.

Venevisión had sold programming to Univision but we didn't have enough content to fill an entire network. If we partnered with Televisa, however, between the two companies, we would. And with our combined strong management experience and the quality of our programming — especially the *telenovelas* — we could make that network #1.

I knew and admired Emilio Azcárraga. (Among our various connections, I later became a member of Televisa's board of directors.) I knew that just as I wanted to expand out of Venezuela, he, too, wanted to be independent of Mexico. We shared good chemistry and an appreciation of good tequila. I invited him to my house in the Dominican Republic, where we ate an immense lunch, drank many tequilas — somehow, I held my own — and shook hands on the idea.

Transforming the idea into reality was an exercise in soft power and hard practicality. I asked some good friends in Washington, D.C. for advice on how to structure the deal to win approval from the FCC. "Are you going to become a U.S. citizen?" they asked. (Back then, you needed a U.S. passport to buy or hold more than 20% of a U.S. network. That's what had sunk Azcárraga and SICC.) I said no. "Then find an American to hold the licenses — preferably a Republican." (They knew it would be easier to get the FCC's approval for a Republican under a Republican administration.)

Carlos Barba, whom we had recently hired to be the president of Venevision International, had previously run Channel 47 in New York, one of the flagship Spanish-language networks in the U.S. Under his leadership, Channel 47 had eclipsed the SIN channel in audience ratings in prime time. Barba suggested we approach the station's owner: A. Jerrold Perenchio.

Jerry Perenchio had previously worked at Music Corporation of America (MCA) under the legendary Lew Wasserman before becoming a top-name talent agent on his own, then branching out into television and motion pictures. He had never bothered to learn Spanish but he was convinced that Spanish-language television had a promising future in the U.S. He was a maverick, but I liked mavericks. And he was a dyed-in-the-wool Republican.

I went to see him and said, "Jerry, Emilio Azcárraga and I are thinking of buying Univision. We think you're the right person to be the chairman and CEO." He said, "I hate Azcárraga!

Never!" Then I went to see Emilio in Mexico. I said, "Emilio, this is the way to work in the U.S. I found a Republican, a former talent agent, who worked for Lew Wasserman. His name is Jerry Perenchio." Azcárraga said, "That son of a bitch? I hate that guy!"

Next, I called Bob O'Hara, my lawyer at Milbank and Tweed. I said, "Can you write a contract that protects the company against the *mala leche* (bad blood) between these two? I don't care if we have to spend all the money in the world but make sure that if they fight, nothing happens." Bob promised he could, and Azcárraga, Perenchio and I all got together. Sure enough, our first meeting was terrible. All they wanted to do was argue about the past and who did what to whom. I finally snapped, "Enough about the past! Let's talk about the future."

We finally did, and the result was that we agreed to buy Univision from Hallmark for $550 million.[22] Only $100 million was in cash; the rest would be covered by debt we would assume.[23] Perenchio received 75% of the ownership of the stations — the old SICC — and 50% of the SIN network; Azcárraga and Venevisión split the remainder, as well as receiving warrants enabling us to acquire 50% of the station group if U.S. laws changed to permit greater foreign ownership of broadcast outlets.[24] Perenchio would co-manage and there was a quid pro quo to protect the minority partners: Perenchio could not sell the operation without the approval of Azcárraga and Cisneros, and there were limits on the amount of debt the company could assume.[25]

We spent millions on the best lawyers because of the underlying animosity between Azcárraga and Perenchio. We had to write everything down so that it was impossible for Azcárraga to fire Perenchio and vice versa. For example, the partners had to agree on issues as minuscule as the choice of managers of even the smallest local station. And we had to plan meetings

201

between them to last no more than 25 minutes, because after half an hour in each other's company they would explode.

Sure enough, they began to fight before the ink was dry on the contract, but it didn't matter: We had a rule book as big as the old Manhattan telephone directory and we had Bob O'Hara to make them follow the rules. The FCC approved the sale on September 30, 1992.[26] We now owned the premier Spanish-language network in the largest Hispanic market outside of Mexico.

It's difficult to underestimate the significance of the Univision acquisition for Cisneros. From a purely financial standpoint, selling Venevisión programming to Univision would be a cash cow for Cisneros for many years. Participating in the largest Spanish-language network in the U.S. boosted Cisneros' prominence on a much bigger stage, and not just in the U.S. It provided a potential launch platform for expansion into Latin America, at the very least, and maybe even Spain.

Between 1990 and 2000, the U.S. Hispanic population exploded by over 50%, from 22.6 million to 35.7 million.[27] Within a year of our acquisition, Univision reversed its slumping cash flow; its EBITDA (earnings before interest, taxes, depreciation and amortization) nearly doubled from $34 million in 1992 to $60 million in 1993.[28] Within five years of our acquisition, Univision's share of Spanish-language television viewing in the U.S. grew from 57% to 83%. Each of its 13 stations, as well as its 10 affiliates, ranked first in Spanish-language television viewership.[29]

By 1996, of the 20 programs most watched by Hispanics, 15 were on Univision. A Merrill Lynch analyst noted, "Nobody approaches the control of 80% of the market that Univision enjoys — not even in the English-speaking market."[30]

That September, Univision went public, at a price of $23 per share. In a single day, the price per share shot up to $30.[31] Not a bad return for an initial investment of only $33 million — and the realization of a long-held dream.

What I was especially proud of was what we did for Hispanics in the United States. Many of the new immigrants, such as those from Guatemala, were marginalized in their home countries and new communities because they weren't fluent in Spanish; many of the Mexicans who came to the U.S. at the time were laborers with little income and less education. Lacking a common ground of language and culture, they were locked out of the existing Hispanic community. With satellite or internet technology still in its infancy, they were isolated from their home country; if something happened in Mexico or Guatemala, they didn't find out about it until days later.

"Concentrate on commonalities," my father used to preach. Our idea was that Spanish-speaking people in the U.S. should see themselves and be seen not as Mexicans, Guatemalans or Venezuelans but as one group of people: Latinos. We made sure that we provided the Puerto Ricans in New York, the Cubans living in Miami and the Mexicans in Chicago with common topics of conversation and shared music to party to.

We also had to convince advertisers that this was a huge untapped market and that we possessed the magic formula to access it. And we did. Today, that common culture and melting-pot market is huge. We were the first to reveal its power.

We took a marginalized group of people and helped them become part of the mainstream of U.S. life. We wanted to be an agent of change. The heart of this initiative was our decision to use neutral Spanish — rather like the BBC's standard English — rather than the rainbow of dialects. As a result, Univision gave everyone a common vocabulary and a common language. With over 1,400 repeating stations in places ranging from North Dakota to South Carolina, it provided a common meeting place:

Everyone could watch the same soccer game at the same time in the same language.

Furthermore, all the lessons we had learned from ACUDE, we put into our television programming in the U.S. Our programs encouraged viewers to learn to read and write, to get an education, to become good citizens and to vote. Thanks to Univision, awareness of the Latino audience — in fact, of the Latino *identity* in the United States — was created.

Good partners offer the opportunity for you to move into something bigger and different. But, of course, all good things eventually come to an end. Emilio Azcárraga died in 1997, and there was tension among all of the partners. My daughter Adriana, who was increasingly involved in the organization, was making noises that we were in the wrong business: Broadcasting was a thing of the past, she said, and we should turn our attention to the digital world.

By then, I was used to the idea that you buy, improve and sell. If Univision had only one owner, I would have taken the long-term view and kept it through good times and bad. But you owe responsibility to your shareholders and you cannot do what you want all the time. In the short term, the markets were saying, "Sell." I thought, "Let's get our money out and put it into something else."

In 2007, Univision was sold to a group of investors for $12.3 billion.[32] Our initial investment from 1992 returned 31%. (Cisneros did not own a majority stake.) We continued to supply content through Venevisión until 2014, including our wildly popular *telenovela Eva Luna*, which aired from November 2010 to April 2011, a programming agreement that boosted our return on investment to 49% overall.

Six months later, the stock market tanked and the business was worth half of what they had paid. We'd gotten out just in time.

* * *

"Partner with companies that can teach you something"
Soon after we bought Univision, both Televisa and Cisneros
began to explore the idea of creating a pan-regional television
network. Azcárraga bought channels in Chile and Peru; we
bought an interest in Channel 11 in Chile, which we renamed
Chilevisión. But very soon, a new technology became available:
direct-to-home (DTH) satellite television.

We'd been intrigued by satellite-transmitted television for
over a decade. In 1986, we'd even considered launching a satellite — the *Simón Bolívar* — to provide television and telecommunications services to the Andean region and the Caribbean.
It just wasn't feasible at the time: The cost of placing a satellite in
orbit was over $100 million and the satellite had a lifespan of
barely seven years, not to mention that the receivers on the
ground were the size of a backyard wading pool and cost
$3,000.[33] Skeptics joked that the acronym for Direct Broadcast
Satellite actually stood for "Don't Be Stupid." We had to wait for
the technology to catch up with the dream. But we knew that
when it did, it would revolutionize the industry and expand the
market on a global scale.

Fast-forward to the mid-1990s. The first internet browsers
appeared: Mosaic, Netscape and, in 1995, Microsoft Explorer.
America Online was taking the country by storm, with 3 million active users in the U.S. by 1995 and millions more floppy
disks — remember those? — landing in mailboxes every day.[34]
Doubts about DBS began to disappear.

Meanwhile, a few years earlier, Steven Bandel happened to
pay a visit to Hughes Electronics to negotiate an opportunity
to buy or lease one of their satellites. Why Hughes? Because at

the time, most satellites held only one transponder with a capacity of one television channel per transponder. Hughes had the technology to stuff a satellite with four transponders. That meant we could transmit Venevisión to Venezuela, Colombia, the Netherlands Antilles and perhaps one of the countries in Central America. In addition, Hughes had figured out how to concentrate the satellite signal to target very specific points on earth; instead of needing a huge receiver, you could pick up the signal with all the channels on a very small dish.

Bandel recalls,

On my way out [of the Hughes offices], I saw a sign for DirecTV. I asked a guy, "What's DirecTV?" He explained that it was a service based on a new technology focusing and multiplying the transmission from a satellite to specific geographies, and that once Hughes had acquired the appropriate orbiting position, they were planning to launch DirecTV in the U.S. and then maybe Latin America.

I called Gustavo and said, "You have to come here. This is the future of TV."

Gustavo did a presentation and tried to convince Hughes that Latin America was the next big opportunity. We felt it was even more promising than the U.S. because of the immense landmass and the lack of wiring for conventional television and cable TV.

They didn't want to do it.

But Gustavo knows everyone, so he got in front of the board of General Motors, which owned Hughes, to explain why Latin America made sense. GM went back to Hughes and said, "You need to do this with Cisneros in Latin America."

In March 1995, we announced the launch of DirecTV Latin America, the first all-digital, direct-to-home satellite television service in Latin America.[35] Hughes would control 80% of the business; the remaining 20% was divided among a local partner in each country, each partner contracting for a different share of the business: Grupo Clarin owned 50% of the Argentina service; Santo Domingo took 50% of Colombia; and Cisneros went all in with 100% in Venezuela.

Finalizing the contract with our local partners was delayed for days because we insisted on a clause stipulating that one transponder on the satellite be dedicated exclusively to educational programming and that it would be distributed for free. (Actually, it was the first clause in the contract.) We used it to build Cl@se, the first pan-regional Spanish-language educational channel. Cl@se allowed teachers and students to access free educational programming all across South America, including the South Pole.

In April 1995, I began a trip around the region to promote DirecTV in each of the countries where it would be available. My daughter Adriana, who was then 15, was on spring break from school and accompanied me. She sat in on many of my meetings with the local partner and listened carefully. Afterward, she asked a lot of questions. I could see that she really got it.

Adriana recalls the trip as a life-changing experience, both from a business standpoint and because it sowed the seeds of her own future network of relationships:

> We went to all these countries in Latin America that I had never seen before. I learned the power of structuring businesses from a pan-regional standpoint. As a result, when I became CEO of Cisneros, our focus from the beginning was pan-regional. And when I launched our digital business — we're now the largest digital advertising network in Latin America — even in countries where the group had never had any business dealings, I always knew one

207

person from the network of people I grew up with in Latin America. And that was all that was needed to initiate conversations.

In mid-1996, all the partners gathered at Cape Canaveral to watch the launch of the satellite. Adriana was there, too. She remembers, "I was never, ever, ever so nervous in my life. I could feel it in my stomach — the excitement and the nerves."

She wasn't the only one on edge. Launches were chancy things. Our main competitor, Rupert Murdoch's Sky, which had formed a partnership with Brazil's Grupo Globo media conglomerate and the Mexican counterpart owned by Emilio Azcárraga, had intended to put their satellite into orbit before us but it crashed during the launch, a loss of valuable time and millions of dollars.

Adriana said, "I remember being really shocked by the cost of the insurance — and that our Brazilian partners decided to take the risk of not paying it. Instead, they all wore string bracelets with little knots tied in for good luck. They even tied some to the satellite launcher. That was their insurance policy."

The good-luck charms must have worked because the launch went off flawlessly. DirecTV was a go, transmitting 300 channels (with the potential for 600), all available with digital high-quality through a small receiving dish on the roof of your house.

Of course, there were plenty of glitches and hiccups along the way, and we learned a lot of useful lessons. The most important was that we learned about the satellite business from a fantastic company — and Adriana saw it first-hand. That experience was invaluable, for us and for her. It's not exaggerating to say that experience would shape the future direction of our organization.

Another lesson was about the push-me/pull-you dynamics of partnership. Since DTH was a new industry and new technology for us, we initially let Hughes take the lead in selling the service to consumers. Their U.S.-based procedure dictated that the equipment be sold in specialized stores, such as RadioShack or Circuit City. This was convenient for Hughes because it allowed DirecTV to avoid hiring salespeople and shifted the cost of inventory to the store.

The strategy worked in Vermont but was bombed in Venezuela. Specialized stores simply didn't exist. The conventional sales channel was weakened by pirated content. And there was a more basic problem: Many Venezuelans did not understand the concept of pay television, let alone the benefits of "direct to the home," "digital" and "pay-per-view," because traditional cable television barely reached 3% of the viewing public.[36]

Hughes insisted on following the U.S. model. The result: While the business plan called for selling 3,000 subscriptions per month, only 300 were sold.[37] We needed a different sales model: Instead of expecting consumers to come to us, we had to go to them. Hughes initially balked but we pushed back.

Victor Ferreres had been designated by Cisneros to head DirecTV in Venezuela. As president of our Apple computer franchise in Venezuela, he knew how to sell a high-end product there. Ferreres set up kiosks in upscale shopping centers patronized by people who could afford the service. A phalanx of televisions demonstrated the advantages of DirecTV. He also deployed teams of salespeople to wealthy neighborhoods, where they would set up a stand on a busy corner and, with lots of fanfare, invite residents to see the wonders of DirecTV for themselves. If they subscribed on the spot, they received a special promotional price of $8 per month and an installer was sent to their house immediately. Sales skyrocketed[38] and this method became the model for selling DirecTV in other countries in Latin America.

We learned that even when smart people tell you, "Our way is the only way," their way may *not* be the best way. We gained the confidence to stand up for ourselves in the partnership. The results proved our point: In the countries where we managed the sales process, we did well; in countries where we relied on local partners, we did less well. It was a lesson we took to heart and would apply with AOL in Latin America.

DirecTV satellites revolutionized communications. By providing one signal for the entire continent, they delivered a unique opportunity to reach millions of people at once. As is often the case, it took longer than expected for the new technology to catch on, especially given the economic challenges of the Latin American market. I took the long view and wasn't too concerned. Hughes was owned by General Motors. I thought that meant unlimited support for eternity.

But then the unimaginable happened: Five years in, GM, the biggest company in the world, was running out of cash. When they began to make noises about selling the business, I knew we'd have trouble. There was no way we could fund $500 million a year on our own. As the saying goes, "Prepare for the worst, because it almost always comes."

DirecTV was fundamentally a desirable business and there's always a buyer for a good business, especially at a discounted price. In 2003, GM agreed to sell its stake to our competitor, Rupert Murdoch's News Corp. We sold our shares to News Corp. four years later, in 2007. We didn't make money but we came away with something much more valuable: knowledge and experience about the new field of international telecommunications. You always want to partner with companies that can teach you something.

Changing the fundamentals

Back on the ground in Venezuela, new presidential elections had been held in December 1993. With 18 candidates running for the office, Rafael Caldera won with a plurality of less than one-third (30.5%) of the votes. Caldera was both the founder and long-standing public face of COPEI, *one of Venezuela's two main political parties. In order to get elected, however, Caldera solicited support from proponents of the anti-political party sentiment that had been fermenting since the 1992 golpes, further eroding the stability of Venezuela's two-party system.*

Caldera was inaugurated on February 2, 1994. Like his predecessor, Carlos Andrés Pérez, Caldera had previously served a five-year term as president (1969-1974). Like Pérez, whom he preceded in his first term, Caldera had presided over enormous investments in infrastructure and education fueled by petrodollars. His second administration, however, inherited the economic crisis that had knee-capped Pérez: a sharp decrease in oil prices coupled with soaring inflation, rising interest rates and economic contraction.

Making matters worse, in January 1994, less than a month before Caldera's inauguration, Banco Latino, the second-largest bank in Venezuela, collapsed and was taken over by the government. Five years of financial deregulation and minimal government supervision allowed Banco Latino and many other banks to offer unsustainably high interest rates. Rates as high as 70% attracted deposits from the pension funds of government institutions like PDVSA[39] *and Fogade, Venezuela's federal deposit insurance fund, which had put 33.6% of its resources in Banco Latino and 13% more in another bank largely owned by Banco Latino, as well as more than a million ordinary people who entrusted Banco Latino with their life savings.*[40]

In most countries, when a bank gets into trouble, the government and/or an industry regulatory agency intervenes and the

211

institution works out its problems under supervision. (Think of Barclays's $2 billion fine for selling toxic mortgage-backed securities in the U.S.[41] or Bankia in Spain.) Closing one bank is a disaster. The Venezuelan model amplified the problem, putting the entire sector at risk.

Banco Latino's collapse was the beginning of a financial catastrophe for the country. Within six months, nine more banks failed, accounting for more than one-half of the banking assets in Venezuela, costing taxpayers a $6.1 billion bailout bill — 75% of the Government's 1994 national budget.[42] Additional bank failures ensued and by the following January, more than half of the country's 47 commercial banks needed bailing out.[43]

The Cisneros organization owned 3.5% of Banco Latino. My brother Ricardo was on the board of directors of Banco Latino, a non-executive position he had been persuaded to accept by Pedro Tinoco, who had been president of the Central Bank until 1993.[44]

The bank's failure was a public relations nightmare for our family, our company, and our country. Some people said our close relationship with Tinoco, who had died the previous March, had been a back-door play to gain more power; others blamed us for the bank's collapse.[45]

We felt there was only one thing to do: pay back all of our loans, in cash and at their full value, to all 25 Venezuelan financial institutions, including the Banco Latino, with which we did business. Some of our senior people were against it: They thought it was crazy to bring hard currency to an unstable country. For example, in the U.S. it's typical to say, "I'll buy your debt for 60 cents on the dollar." We probably had an opportunity in Venezuela to get some discounts.

But we committed to paying 100 cents on the dollar. It was the right thing to do, and the only thing to do to clear our family name and the name of the organization. Cisneros was able to raise cash *by calling on lines of credit from the US and slowly selling certain businesses in Venezuela. Our loans with Banco Latino alone were some $23 million, the rough equivalent of 13% of our total liabilities in Venezuela.[46] Ricardo and I were willing to supplement the available cash with our own money but it still wouldn't be enough.*

We were already moving ahead with our plan to sell many of our companies in Venezuela as part of our strategy to internationalize. Now, we sold off some of our Venezuelan consumer companies. These were the legacy companies that had helped build our organization: Yukery, Tío Rico and others. CADA and Maxy's went on the block, too, and were sold to the Colombian Cadenalco group for $70 million in December 1994.[47]

Selling them made sense: The Venezuelan government was freezing prices and restricting imports; we couldn't provide the service or supplies that had been our hallmark. Still, as Ricardo said when we sold CADA, it was like saying farewell to a beloved child.[48]

It took a while but we repaid every cent of every loan.

* * *

"A partnership has to be a gas pedal, not a brake"

The Cisneros organization that emerged from Venezuela's financial crisis was very different from what it had looked like going in. Instead of focusing on consumer products, we were now clearly reinventing ourselves as a media and entertainment company. There was, however, one fundamental business that had remained stalwart throughout the decades: our soft drinks conglomerate, anchored by the Pepsi-Cola bottling operation.

Even that was about to change. The partnership had been mutually beneficial for close to 50 years. But productive partnership has to continue nurturing both sides, otherwise it becomes a brake rather than a gas pedal. You always have to be prepared for that possibility.

Despite the warm personal ties between Don Kendall, the CEO of PepsiCo until 1986, and our family — Don and my father were close friends, and he and I regularly fished together — there had been strains in our partnership with Pepsi for years. Every time we wanted to expand our geography outside of Venezuela, we met with tepid interest, indifference or outright rejection.

For example, when my father and my brother Carlos set up our bottling business in Brazil and Colombia in the 1960s, we were starting from zero against the all-powerful Coca-Cola. We established a sizable foothold but could have really benefited from Pepsi's support. Instead, they pretty much left us to fight it out on our own. The same thing happened again in 1972 when we bought a bottling factory in Málaga, Spain, that made La Casera, a very popular drink.

When our dream of becoming the largest bottler in Latin America was thwarted by Pepsi's intransigence, we switched our ambitions to the United States. We made our wishes clearly known to Pepsi with our acquisition of All-American Bottling (AAB) in 1982: As the eighth-largest bottler in the U.S., we would have the capacity to bottle Pepsi-Cola. We certainly had the desire. Pepsi asked us to wait… and wait. Ultimately, it offered us a bottling plant in New York and another in Tennessee. It was a slap in the face: The New York plant was infested with the corrupt Teamsters union and both operations were in such bad financial shape that they were known as "junk" plants.

Roberto Goizueta became the CEO of Coca-Cola in 1981. Cerebral and reserved, he was also laser-focused on flipping countries from Pepsi blue to Coke red. Venezuela was one of the few countries in the world where Pepsi outsold Coke. It was a "pebble in his shoe" — *una piedra en el zapato* — and Goizueta was eager to remove it.

We popped up on Goizueta's radar screen closer to home with our acquisition of AAB. One of the brands included in the sale was Royal Crown Cola, also created in Georgia. A favorite among African-American customers, RC Cola wasn't selling particularly well. We switched the advertising agency to an African-American-owned firm that better understood the market. Sales skyrocketed and Goizueta took notice.

I first proposed the idea of selling Pepsi-Cola-Hit Bottlers of Venezuela to Coca-Cola to my cousin Oswaldo in the mid-1980s. The son of my uncle Antonio, Oswaldo had grown up in and ran the bottling operation; we couldn't consider any major changes without his consent.

Oswaldo was a personal friend of Roger Enrico, who headed Pepsi-Cola's global beverages division. He, too, was frustrated by Pepsi's intransigence but hoped that things would improve. I told Oswaldo, "When you have no more hope, we'll go to Coca-Cola, because PepsiCo is *never* going to solve our problems."

By the early 1990s, Oswaldo ran out of hope. He had turned 50 in 1990 and was in bad health. He'd seen the toll that stress had taken on my father. If he needed further warning, in 1990, his good friend Roger Enrico had suffered a heart attack while dancing at an Istanbul nightclub when the Enricos and Cisneroses were vacationing together.

Enrico recovered but stepped back from worldwide operations. Meanwhile, his successors paid little attention to Venezuela. When Oswaldo raised his concerns about the future and proposed that Pepsi or Enrico buy his shares in the bottling operation, Enrico was noncommittal. Oswaldo was ready to pull the trigger.

My initial agreement with Goizueta was a handshake deal. Goizueta made the mistake of asking his lawyers to analyze it and they came up with so many legal hurdles that the whole thing collapsed. But it gave us both a taste of what we could do.

In 1994, we were ready to try again. Oswaldo, Ricardo and I met with Goizueta and his right-hand man, Douglas Ivester, in Goizueta's private dining room on the 12th floor of Coke headquarters in Atlanta. This time we agreed to push forward.

Secrecy was absolutely paramount. Over the next two years, we met some 50 times — but never again at Coke headquarters. Instead, our teams got together in anonymous hotel conference rooms or airplane hangars. The team working on the deal was forbidden to fly in planes belonging to the Cisneros Group or use the company travel agency to make reservations.[49] The negotiations were referred to as "Project Swan" — *cisne* is the Spanish word for "swan" — and Pepsi and Coca-Cola were called by their code names of Blue and Red, for their respective corporate colors. Even Weldon Johnson, Coca-Cola's group president for Latin America, was kept in the dark.[50]

The deal was signed at 10 a.m. on Wednesday, August 14, 1996. Coca-Cola agreed to buy Pepsi-Cola-Hit Bottlers of Venezuela for about $500 million. Pepsi was informed two days later through papers filed with its lawyers.[51]

Even as the successful conclusion of Project Swan was being toasted in Atlanta, Project Switch was launched. Every vestige of PepsiCo in Venezuela had to be erased and replaced by Coca-Cola. All the red paint in the country was used up painting over Pepsi blue, with more specially imported from Colombia.[52] That Saturday morning, a 727 jet carried thousands of Coke bottles to Caracas, to be distributed to the bottling plants.[53] Employees who came to work on Saturday were surprised to be told to turn in their Pepsi-Cola uniforms and don ones from Coca-Cola.[54]

My daughter Adriana recalls:

I was in boarding school in Massachusetts. These were the days before cell phones and we didn't have email. I just got a message: "Come to Atlanta for the weekend." I was told a lot of the cousins would be there but I had no idea why we'd been summoned. When we all arrived, we were told that Cisneros had sold our Pepsi business to Coca-Cola.

A whole floor in a hotel had been set up with fax machines. The job of the cousins — my uncle Ricardo's kids and Cousin Oswaldo's daughters, as well as my brother Guillermo and sister Carolina — was to send out 200 faxes each, announcing that Coca-Cola would be replacing Pepsi in Venezuela. The news was so hot that 'the adults' couldn't even trust their assistants or secretaries. The only people they could trust were their kids.

Pepsi-Cola was more than a business; it was a part of my family. Pepsi ran through our veins. It shaped the environment I grew up in. Of all the businesses we had had, the one business no one ever thought we would sell was Pepsi. I remember my father telling us at the time, "All businesses are for sale. It's just a matter of the right time and the right price." That was a big lesson.

The ramifications of the deal were earthshaking. Pepsi owned 40% of the market in Venezuela, compared to Coke's paltry 10% share. Hit and other brands comprised another 45% share, giving Cisneros 85% of the soda market. Overnight, Coca-Cola took control of 55% of the market, plus the bottling capacity to power Coke 40% higher.[55] Pepsi's share plummeted to zero, with no bottling capacity — although Coke placed six bottling plants that it didn't need in a special trust and agreed to offer Pepsi the chance to buy them[56] — and no distribution. "I can't remember a more dramatic switch since Leo Durocher of the Brooklyn Dodgers went overnight to manage the Giants," said Jesse Meyers, founding director of industry newsletter Beverage Digest.[57]

Oswaldo and I had agreed that I would handle any calls from Pepsi. Sure enough, on Monday morning, I got calls from Don Kendall and Peter Warren, who had run Pepsi's international business for two decades before retiring in 1985.[58] They had been close to my father and, not surprisingly, they were furious. But I pointed out that it was a matter of strategy as much as choice: If we had allowed the status quo to continue, we would have eventually been eaten up by Coca-Cola. We wanted to modernize our plants and expand geographically but Pepsi wouldn't provide the resources. I said, "Between my family and Pepsi, I'm choosing my family. I need to think of my family and I need to grow outside of Venezuela, and Pepsi refused to understand that." They couldn't argue.

The deal would resonate in other ways throughout the extended Cisneros family. Oswaldo became the chief executive of Embotelladoras Coca-Cola y Hit de Venezuela, the new name of the group of 18 bottling plants.[59] (It was a temporary holding position, due to his concerns about his health. The following year, the bottling operations were sold to Panamerican Beverages, aka Panamco, Coke's anchor bottler in Latin America, for $1.1 billion.[60])

Over half a century earlier, Oswaldo's father, my uncle Antonio, had first tasted Pepsi at the New York World's Fair; he and my father founded Pepsi-Cola of Venezuela on May 8, 1940.[61] Pepsi cemented our families together. That would no longer be the case.

Oswaldo, Ricardo and I also signed a private transaction. Oswaldo gave us his shares of Cervecería Regional — a brewery we had bought together in 1992 — and, in exchange, we gave him our shares in Telcel.

The deep and productive partnership between the two branches of the Cisneros family was coming to an end. Although our relations remained warm and affectionate, from then on, we would go our separate ways.

* * *

"Beware the cult of the converted"

As the 1990s unfolded, it was clear that the internet was the invention of the century: It offered a new mode of communicating, a new boost to creativity and a new opportunity to make money. For most Americans, the road to this magical future was built by one company: America Online.

By 1995, more than 3 million Americans were dialing up (yes, that was the way to connect back then) to send emails, argue in online forums, flirt in chat rooms, play games, learn through news and education sites, and explore the exciting new universe of the worldwide web.[62] Thousands more were signing up every day, thanks to AOL blanketing the country with CD-ROMs and 3.5-inch diskettes. According to *PC World*, "You couldn't open a magazine (*PC World* included) or your mailbox without an AOL disk falling out of it."[63] By the late 1990s, AOL was adding almost half a million new subscribers every month and had become the de facto operating system for the internet in the United States.[64]

We had been discussing the idea of forming an alliance with AOL to offer internet service in Latin America since 1996. At the end of 1995, AOL announced a joint venture with German media conglomerate Bertelsmann AG to launch its service in Europe. AOL would provide the technology and Bertelsmann would contribute the money and their knowledge of the European market.[65] We were the Bertelsmann of Latin America. We felt it made sense for AOL and Cisneros to work together.

219

By the mid-1990s, our strategy for the future was clear: to invest in media and telecommunications. Thanks to selling off many of our legacy businesses, we were sitting on a massive treasure chest of over $2 billion in cash.[66] (We'd sold Spalding and Evenflo in August 1996.) We were primed and ready to enter this exciting new world.

It took two years to hammer out a deal but America Online Latin America (AOLA) was finally announced on December 15, 1998. AOL and Cisneros would each contribute up to $200 million in a joint venture to bring a Spanish- and Portuguese-language version of AOL to Brazil, Mexico and Argentina, the three largest and fastest-growing markets in the region.[67]

It seemed like we were doing the right thing at the right time. AOL was a dream come true. It had the power to transform Latin America. This was the best business proposition in the world at the time, with the best partners and the best management.

But I made a terrible decision with AOLA. We had the wrong formula for the region. Like Hughes, AOL thought they could apply the formula that worked so well for them in the U.S. to Latin America: mail free CDs to everyone. In Latin America, though, the mail is not reliable. We tried to convince AOL that sending CDs wouldn't work. They said, "It works in the U.S."

Furthermore, their playbook was to charge customers for their service. In Latin America, though, customers aren't used to paying. The company makes money from advertisers who pay to reach customers. You build up the network and sell it to advertisers.

We knew that, yet there was not a single person in my group who said no. That should have been a signal to me. To be fair, at the beginning, there *were* many Cassandras. But the internet was so seductive and we were seduced. It was a fresh new way of doing business and we were persuaded that we had to abandon our parochial methods. We had joined the cult of the converted.

It's hard to stay converted when your investment is going down the drain. When our losses hit $25 million, we went back to AOL and tried to convince them to change their system, to sell advertising and to make money that way. It was something we knew how to do. They said no.

We had many people on the ground inside the company, who warned us that things weren't working as predicted. Fortunately, our contract allowed us to revisit our commitment if losses hit $100 million. I said, "If the company loses $100 million, we're out. We'll give AOL all our shares." And that's what we did.

The best decision I made in that deal was to pull the plug at $100 million. We could have lost a billion dollars. We learned a valuable lesson: If you don't agree with the business plan, don't do it.

It was the wrong business plan and we should have known better. Thankfully, we put in a floor. When you gamble, you always have to ask yourself how much you're willing to lose. You have to know to what extent do you cover and when do you get out. With AOLA, we needed a lot of capital but I had mentally decided that $100 million was enough; I wasn't going to waste $200 million.

I wrote earlier about the need to have an exit strategy. In addition, you need a sense of timing: to know when to hold and when to fold. That comes down to judgment. I wish I could tell you that judgment can be taught. I helped my father in all the decisions that were important to him and I certainly learned a lot as a result. But judgment ultimately is a function of experience. You have to have maturity.

I certainly didn't have the judgment 25 years ago that I have now. I've seen thousands of presentations. To spot the gold in the dirt, you need information, experience and street smarts to be able to tell when people are trying to pull the wool over your eyes. Ego, too, can be a blinder; as my father often admonished me, you have to put your ego in the closet, so you see all the facts, not just the ones you want to see.

The whole experience with AOLA left a bad taste in my mouth. I knew instinctively it wouldn't work but I went along with it because everyone told me to. I should have thrown a tantrum. It's not the $100 million that I was angry about; it was the decision-making process where I found fault with myself.

I question myself a lot more now. I ate a big helping of humble pie. Now, instead of double-checking and triple-checking on big decisions, I check ten times — with more people and with outsiders. If there's a general positive consensus on the inside, I get suspicious. I bring in a designated Cassandra, an outside consultant, lawyer or technical expert, whose purpose is to question our thinking.

And we always have a clearly articulated mission. That's extremely important. Everyone knows how much risk we'll tolerate — or not.

"Reorganize, relocate and reinvent"

On December 6, 1998, Hugo Chávez Frias was elected president of Venezuela with 56.2% of the valid popular vote.[68] Back in 1994, one of President Caldera's first actions as president had been to pardon Chávez and other army and air force officers who had planned and participated in both coup attempts.[69] Chávez subsequently became a symbol of the opposition to the long-standing two-party political system that upheld Venezuela's democracy. Tapping into popular discontent about declining standards of living and widespread political corruption, he promised to dissolve the Congress and reorganize the country and its laws to restore national pride and prosperity.

Venevisión was continuously polling throughout the country. We knew that 15% to 20% of the population in the shanty towns were poor people from Bolivia, Peru, Colombia and other Latin American countries who had come to Venezuela as laborers. We gave them work and we gave them citizenship, but the political parties didn't bother to educate them, provide decent healthcare or teach them about democracy. These were people who had been downtrodden for centuries and had inherited hatred for eons. The chavista *message of class warfare and social resentment gave them a voice — and their vote was enough to swing the election.*

* * *

"Manage uncertainty as a way of life"

I wasn't going to give up the fight for democracy in Venezuela. I used all the connections I had —the Catholic Church, open-minded *chavistas*, even former U.S. Presidents Jimmy Carter and George Bush — to try to persuade Chávez that waging war against businesspeople and the media wasn't good for anyone: not the people being attacked, not Chávez and certainly not most Venezuelans. We did everything we could to convince Chávez that capitalism was not his enemy. We failed miserably. If anything, the attacks became more frequent, more personal and more virulent. Everything we represented came under attack.

Leonard Lauder had come to visit before Chávez won the election and warned me, "You're a target." All capitalists and so-called imperialists came under attack but Venevisión had been instrumental in helping to put down the 1992 coup, so I was Public Enemy #1. A systematic campaign was launched against me, my assets and the companies in our organization. There was constant institutional harassment from the tax authorities, the

Ministry of the Interior and other government entities. I was attacked by name in speeches on television and in daily broadcasts on all the radio stations; pamphlets and placards were distributed on the streets in downtown Caracas showing my face and labeling me as an enemy of the state. Some of our Venevisión reporters were physically assaulted.

The attacks were ferocious and they just kept escalating. We were in crisis management mode all the time. It was enough to make you question the future. Instead of going crazy, we reorganized completely so I could live and work outside of Venezuela. We already had a home and office in the Dominican Republic with a guesthouse, where Patty and I hosted friends and family, as well as heads of state and many distinguished people. I thought about making it our corporate headquarters. But Adriana said, "Close the office in the DR. Move everything to Miami."

I didn't agree with her decision initially. We were so established in Venezuela and the Dominican Republic. And we had a satisfactory foothold in Miami and Coral Gables, where the Venevisión Studios were located. But Adriana pointed out that Miami was just more of a happening place than Coral Gables and would be more attractive to young talent. She was 100% right and I was eventually convinced 100%.

As we began to prepare to leave Venezuela, I thought, "We have to give the impression that *nothing* has changed for us except our address and phone number." We had been gradually shifting our management to Miami in the wake of "el Caracazo" in 1989. By March 2000, the transition was complete and we announced that henceforth Miami would be the site of our operational headquarters. It was an immense operation and very expensive, but it was worth every penny. Setting up our headquarters there gave our executives and me peace of mind. We needed their brains more than ever. (We would shut down

224

our New York office and make Miami our official corporate headquarters when Adriana became CEO in 2013.)

We were in a holding pattern. Then, suddenly, everything accelerated. There had been an abortive coup against Chávez in April 2002, forcefully suppressed, followed by a series of nation-wide strikes paralyzing the petroleum sector and other main-stays of the now-shaky economy. Demonstrations called for Chávez to step down. In August 2003, a petition with 3.2 million signatures demanded that the National Electoral Council (Consejo National Electoral, or CNE) oust Chávez. After the CNE rejected it, a second petition with 3.6 million names was pre-sented three months later, in November 2003. When the coun-cil rejected that, too, claiming that half of the signatures were invalid, riots erupted across the country. Public sentiment was further inflamed when the list of signatures was published and many government workers who had signed lost their jobs in retaliation. The CNE eventually agreed to set aside five days in May 2004 for people to verify their signatures; if the require-ment of 2.4 million signatures was met, a recall vote would be scheduled for August 15, 2004.[70] The country was on the brink of an explosion.

We had a beautiful fishing camp in Manaka, in the Venezu-elan Amazon region. We had hosted George H.W. Bush and Jimmy Carter, both avid fishermen, to fish for *pavón* (peacock bass), as well as the Walton brothers, Barbara Walters and World Bank president James Wolfensohn. Just after Easter, armed Black Hawk helicopters from Miraflores, the presidential house-hold, swooped down without any warning. Forty-eight Special Forces troops jumped out. They shot our two dogs and our par-rots, terrified our staff and ransacked the camp.

I knew immediately that we had to leave the country. I was taking care of the final preparations when, on May 11, I received word that 500 armed troops had raided our organic coffee farm at Carabobo, on the pretext that I was arming Colombian guerrillas to attack the presidential palace, the military barracks and other strategic enclaves.[71] This, of course, was completely false. Fortunately, I was able to send people there to prevent the troops from planting any weapons on the property.

There was no longer time to delay. Our plane was standing by at Maiquetía. Patty, Adriana and I boarded. (Carolina and Guillermo were out of the country at the time.) Our luggage was loaded and … nothing happened. We sat on the runway and waited. And waited. The pilot told us that he hadn't received clearance for takeoff. With armed soldiers all around the airport, we didn't dare try to take off without permission. There was nothing to do but wait. No one said anything.

Eventually, an Army vehicle drove up to the plane. A man in uniform climbed out and came on board. I recognized him as one of the officers who had participated in the 1992 coup attempt, a die-hard *chavista* who was in charge of the area around Caracas. He walked up to where I was sitting, stared down at me and paused. "*Un mensaje de mi comandante,*" he said. (A message from my commander.) "*No regrese.*" (Do not return.) Then he turned around and got off the plane.

The door was immediately shut and secured. We taxied to the end of the runway, the pilot gunned the engine and the plane leaped into the air. Within minutes, we were flying over the Caribbean, into the protection of international waters.

We were safe but at what a cost. We were thankful beyond words to be alive but the loss was almost too big to encompass. Patty and I and our family would now be exiled from the country we loved and had worked so hard to help. We were leaving behind a heritage that went back generations, the people and places at the heart of our family's most cherished memories:

friends we had known since childhood; the church where our children were baptized and married; the farm where Patty and I had planned to spend our later years; Venevisión, the business I fell in love with and grew up with.

We had left Venezuela before for months at a time, but we always knew we could return. Not now. It was clear we wouldn't be coming back for years. Patty and Adriana thought it might be six or eight years. I knew deep down it wouldn't be for at least a generation.

I mourned not just for me but for my family and my beloved country. Patty, too, suffered immensely. We were both scarred by the trauma of the previous few years, more deeply than we initially realized.

Eventually, we both sought professional help. My father was open to psychotherapy and I had already established a long-term relationship with a psychologist to help me deal with the many losses my family had suffered over the years. Patty and I also have very good friends who are priests and ministers. They made a difference; our faith makes a difference. When you're experiencing pain or grief, it's very helpful to have a conversation with God.

Meanwhile, hard work, physical exercise and meaningful projects were our medicine. We left Venezuela but we didn't leave the world. Patty had already established the Colección Patricia Phelps de Cisneros and was deepening relationships with the Museum of Modern Art in New York, the Fogg Art Museum at Harvard University and the Blanton Museum at the University of Texas in Austin. If anything, I traveled more, following up on old connections and making new ones. Opportunities help concentrate the mind on the future.

I began to think, "We can renew."

Notes

1. *The History of Venezuela*, p. 152.

2. Brooke, James, "Venezuela Recounts How Coup Failed," in *The New York Times*, February 6, 1992. https://www.nytimes.com/1992/02/06/world/venezuela-recounts-how-coup-failed.html?searchResultPosition=2

3. *Ibid.*

4. *Gustavo Cisneros: Pioneer*, p .120.

5. *Ibidem*, p. 121.

6. *Ibidem*, p. 122.

7. "Venezuela Crushes Army Coup Attempt," in *The New York Times*, February 5, 1992. https://www.nytimes.com/1992/02/05/world/venezuela-crushes-army-coup-attempt.html?searchResultPosition=3

8. "Venezuela Recounts How Coup Failed."

9. *Gustavo Cisneros: Pioneer*, p .123.

10. *The History of Venezuela*, p. 154.

11. "US$20 million line of credit for Telcel Celular of Venezuela," CAF Development Bank of Latin America. January 31, 1992. https://www.caf.com/en/currently/news/1992/01/us-20-million-line-of-credit-for-telcel-celular-of-venezuela/

12. *Gustavo Cisneros: Pioneer*, p .126.

13. *Ibid.*

14. *Ibidem*, p. 129.

15. "U.S. Hispanic population surpassed 60 million in 2019," in *Pew Research Center*, July 7, 2020. https://www.pewresearch.org/fact-tank/2020/07/07/u-s-hispanic-population-surpassed-60-million-in-2019-but-growth-has-slowed/

16. Johnston, David Cay, "Rene Anselmo, 69, the Founder of A Satellite Network, Is Dead," in *The New York Times*, September 21, 1995. https://www.nytimes.com/1995/09/21/obituaries/rene-anselmo-69-thefounder-of-a-satellite-network-is-dead.html

17. *Ibid.*

18. "Hallmark Hall of Fame," Wikipedia. https://en.wikipedia.org/wiki/Hallmark_Hall_of_Fame#History

19. "The History of Serving Hispanic America," Univision Communications. https://corporate.univision.com/timeline/#close

20. https://www.company-histories.com/Univision-Communications-Inc-Company-History.html

21. *Gustavo Cisneros: Pioneer,* p .131.

22. https://www.company-histories.com/Univision-Communications-Inc-Company-History.html

23. *Gustavo Cisneros: Pioneer,* p .133.

24. https://www.company-histories.com/Univision-Communications-Inc-Company-History.html

25. *Gustavo Cisneros: Pioneer,* p .133.

26. "FCC Approves Sales of Univision Stations," UPI Archives. https://www.upi.com/Archives/1992/09/30/FCC-approves-sale-of-Univision-stations/8887717825600/

27. https://www.pewresearch.org/fact-tank/2020/07/07/u-s-hispanic-population-surpassed-60-million-in-2019-but-growth-has-slowed/

28. *Gustavo Cisneros: Pioneer,* p .135.

29. https://www.company-histories.com/Univision-Communications-Inc-Company-History.html

30. *Gustavo Cisneros: Pioneer,* p .136.

31. *Ibid.*

32. Villafañe, Veronica, "Univision is Exploring Selling the Company," in *Forbes,* July 3, 2019. https://www.forbes.com/sites/veronicavillafane/2019/07/03/univision-is-exploring- selling-the-company/?sh=37c05751edcc

33. *Gustavo Cisneros: Pioneer,* p .151.

34. Nollinger, Mark, "America, Online!," in *Wired,* September 1, 1995. https://www.wired.com/1995/09/aol-2/

35. *Gustavo Cisneros: Pioneer,* p .161.

36. *Ibidem,* p. 164.

37. *Ibid.*

38. *Ibid.*

39. Tejera, María, "Venezuela's Oil Industry Hit Hard by Failure of Nation's Banco Latino," in *The Journal of Commerce,* January 18, 1994. https://www.joc.com/venezuelas-oil-industry-hit-hard-failure-nations-bancolatino_19940118.html

40. Freed, Kenneth, "Venezuelan Bank Collapse Threatens Nation's Future," in *Los Angeles Times,* February 14, 1994. https://www.latimes.com/archives/la-xpm-1994-02-14-mn-22878-story.html

41. White, Lawrence, "Barclays $2 Billion Fraud Fines Resolves Major U.S. Legal Issue," in *Reuters,* March 29, 2018. https://www.reuters.com/

article/us-barclays-mortgages-fine/
barclays-2-billion-fraud-fine-resolves-majoru-s-legal-issue-
idUSKBN1H51WY

42. Brooke, James, "Failure of High-Flying Banks Shakes Venezuelan Economy," in *The New York Times*, May 16, 1994. https://www.nytimes.com/1994/05/16/us/failure-of-high-flying-banks-shakes-venezuelaneconomy.html

43. "Chaos in Caracas," in *The Economist*, April 10, 1997. https://www.economist.com/special-report/1997/04/10/chaos-in-caracas

44. *Gustavo Cisneros: Pioneer*, p .141.

45. *Ibidem*, p. 146.

46. *Ibidem*, p. 15.

47. "Venezuela: Grupos colombianos compran supermercados y tiendas," Inter Press Service, December 22, 1994. https://ipsnoticias.net/1994/12/venezuela-grupos-colombianos-ompran-supermercados-y-tiendas/

48. *Gustavo Cisneros: Pioneer*, p .148..

49. *Ibidem*, p. 178..

50. Sellers, Patricia, "How Coke Is Kicking Pepsi's Can," in *Fortune*, October 28, 1996. https://money.cnn.com/magazines/fortune/fortune_archive/1996/10/28/203906/index.htm

51. Frank, Robert, "Coca-Cola Steals Bottler in Venezuela from Pepsi," in *The Wall Street Journal*, August 19, 1996. https://www.wsj.com/articles/SB84040964045778500

52. *Gustavo Cisneros: Pioneer*, p .180.

53. "How Coke Is Kicking Pepsi's Can."

54. *Gustavo Cisneros: Pioneer*, p .180.

55. Collins, Glenn, "How Venezuela is Becoming Coca-Cola Country," in *The New York Times*, August 21, 1996. https://www.nytimes.com/1996/08/21/business/how-venezuela-is-becoming-coca-cola-country.html

56. "Coca-Cola Steals Bottler in Venezuela from Pepsi."

57. Collins, Glenn, "A Coke Coup in Venezuela Leaves Pepsi High and Dry," in *The New York Times*, August 17, 1996. https://www.nytimes.com/1996/08/17/business/a-coke-coup-in-venezuela-leaves-pepsi-highand-dry.html

58. D'Souza, Charles, "Peter K. Warren, 94, of Wilton, Former Pepsi International CEO," in *Wilton Daily Voice*, July 15, 2014. https://dailyvoice.com/connecticut/wilton/obituaries/peter-k-warren-94-of-wilton-former-pepsi-international-ceo/474045/

59. "A Coke Coup in Venezuela Leaves Pepsi High and Dry."

60. "Panamerican Beverages," in *Reference for Business*. https://www. referenceforbusiness.com/history2/93/Panamerican-Beverages-Inc.html

61. *Diego Cisneros: A Life for Venezuela.*

62. Nollinger, Mark, "America, Online!," in *Wired*, September 1, 1995. https://www.wired.com/1995/09/aol-2/

63. Tynan, Dan, "The 25 Worst Tech Products of All Time," in *PC World*, May 26, 2006. https://www.pcworld.com/article/535838/worst_ products_ever.html

64. *Gustavo Cisneros: Pioneer,* p .198.

65. *Gustavo Cisneros: Pioneer,* p .191.

66. Vogel, Thomas T., Jr., "Cisneros Group Scours Globe for Media Deals," in *The Wall Street Journal,* September 18, 1996. https://www.wsj.com/ articles/SB842997056506259000

67. "AOL, Cisneros Form Online Joint Venture," in *Los Angeles Times,* December 16, 1998. https://www.latimes.com/archives/la-xpm-1998-dec-16-fi-54457-story.html

68. *The History of Venezuela,* p. 161.

69. "President Caldera Pardons Officers Who Led 1992 Coup Attempt in Venezuela," in *Latin America Data Base,* April 29, 1994. https:// digitalrepository.unm.edu/cgi/viewcontent. cgi?article=12459&context=notisur

70. The History of Venezuela, p. 173.

71. Hernandez, Clodovaldo, "Chávez Denuncia una Conspiración Internacional contra Venezuela," in *El País,* May 11, 2004. https://elpais. com/diario/2004/05/13/internacional/1084399224_850215.html

Part V

PLANNING THE TRANSITION

Patty and I never wanted our kids to feel obligated to join the family business. Nonetheless, I'd often thought about the topic of succession and how to plan an orderly transition. That's natural when you lead a family company.

My father had never really asked me to take over from him. Because of the suddenness and severity of his stroke, it just happened. There was no warning and no chance to prepare either myself, the family or his business partners. After he began to recover, he made it clear that I should continue to run the company. I was extremely fortunate that my mother, brothers, sisters and cousins all supported his decision — 100%.

It could have been so different. The history of family companies is rife with stories of internecine feuds. Survey after survey shows that about a third of family business leaders are apprehensive about the transfer of control to the next generation.[1] The period when one generation anticipates the transition to the next is especially perilous: That's when old conflicts arise and buried resentments can emerge, leaving a lasting dividend of rancor and bitterness. I was well aware of that danger. It was the last thing I wanted to have happen in my family.

I was also aware — how could I not be? — of the adage about the rise and fall of family businesses: "Shirtsleeves to shirtsleeves in three generations." Fewer than half of U.S. family-owned businesses transition into a second-generation business; barely one-tenth smoothly pass to a third generation.[2] I was always interested in why one family succeeded in surviving this rocky passage when another family failed, what steps they took to designate and train their successors, and whom they turned to for advice.

Patty and I have three children, each of whom is distinctly talented in his or her own way. As they grew up, I would have liked a third generation of our family to lead the organization my father founded. But not at the cost of their — or our — happiness.

* * *

"Put your kids in places that engage their interest and they'll do the rest"

We rarely talked about business when the kids were little, and almost never discussed work over the dinner table. That was a principle Patty and I agreed on in the first years of our marriage, when my father was so ill and I was trying to save him and the company at the same time. I'd said to Patty, "When I come home, I don't want to repeat everything that happened today. Home is a haven and I just don't want to deal with business concerns until tomorrow."

That didn't mean we didn't have lots of interesting guests around the dinner table: politicians, artists, financiers, businesspeople, diplomats, orchestra conductors — you name it. Guillermo, Carolina and Adriana met Presidents and Prime Ministers of countries large and small, the Dalai Lama, Nelson Mandela, Zubin Mehta, Carlos Fuentes, Barbara Walters, diva Celia Cruz

236

and the pop duo Los del Rio, who came up with their mega-hit song "La Macarena" at a party we hosted with them.

Nor did Patty and I build a moat around our work. The kids could see how much enjoyment and satisfaction we got: I from the business and Patty from our social responsibility projects.

I always offered the kids the opportunity to get to know the business. I might have them meet me after school at the Venevisión offices; if I were running late, they were welcome to roam around, watching how the news was produced or how *telenovelas* were created. Adriana, our youngest, particularly loved learning how things were made. Cisneros owned factories producing everything from Tío Rico ice cream and Yukery juices to the giant bakery that supplied bread for CADA supermarkets. It was easy to arrange for her to take a tour.

Those visits offered a breadth and depth of exposure to business and the arts unavailable to most kids. But there was never any formal indoctrination, rarely a grand tour with the *jefe* and certainly no Faustian promise that "this, too, can be yours." Instead, the kids were given carte blanche to explore whatever piqued their interest. I followed my father's approach in this: "If you're curious, the door is open."

As the kids got older, I invited them to accompany me on business trips, when appropriate. I never said, "I want my children to join me so they can see how I do this deal." It was more like, "I'm going here. Would you like to come along?" As I described earlier, Adriana joined me on our "12 countries in 12 days" tour of South America when we launched DirecTV. That would have a huge impact on how she would view the potential for our work in that region. At the time, though, it was just pure fun to have her there. I was sowing seeds and, to my delight, many of them started sprouting. That's really the trick: Put your kids in places that engage their interest, and they'll do the rest.

When Guillermo, who is our eldest, began attending college at Yale University in the late 1980s, he organized his schedule to spend half of his time in New York City, where Patty and I were living. Guillermo has a very engaging personality and invited many of his friends. Between them, they asked a lot of questions — not only about business but also about art and the creation of the Colección Patricia Phelps de Cisneros, which was then just getting off the ground. It was as if we were running an open seminar. Carolina often came to art openings. And Adriana, who is eight years younger than her brother and four years younger than her sister, would be hanging out with the crowd of older kids — always listening, always asking questions, always interested in what was going on.

New York was the center of the world in the 1990s. When you're in the center of the world, the world comes to you: My European friends visited, my South American friends visited, and many friends in the art world came, too. The kids were always part of the picture.

After Guillermo graduated from Yale, he went to Columbia University's business school. In 1998, he launched Vale TV in Venezuela, an educational and cultural entertainment channel we created in partnership with the Catholic Church that was like a combination of PBS and A&E. That gave him hands-on experience of setting up a business. He then shifted to Florida, where he was the founder and chairman of Venevisión Studios, which gave him insights into what production was like in the United States. He learned what he liked about business — and what he didn't. That's invaluable.

He worked in the business for about 15 years, then one day, he came to me and said, "Dad, I love you very much but I'm not interested in doing this. I'll help you long-term but right now I'd like to take a break." He was married by then, with kids. He's a very involved parent and wanted to devote a lot of time to his children. I could see he wouldn't come back. He's a very active member of the Family Council, which I'll describe in more detail, and works closely with Adriana.

Meanwhile, Carolina, our second child, had graduated from Georgetown University. After a stint at Venevisión in Caracas and working in our new media business in Florida, she, too, made it clear that she didn't want to be a businesswoman: Creating a family was where her interest and talents lay. She had five kids very quickly — three of them triplets — and motherhood was a full-time job for her. She also became a loyal member of the Family Council.

I had time to think — and to change speed.

Adriana had decided on her own that she wanted to be in New York. She was always fascinated with media. After she graduated from Columbia University in 2002, she went to New York University's Journalism Institute, from which she would graduate with a Master's degree in journalism in 2005. I think she wanted to be a producer and have her own production company.

By this time — it was soon after we left Venezuela — Ricardo and I had gone our separate ways. (It wasn't official but for all practical purposes, we were no longer partners.) We had always run the different businesses within the organization as if they were public companies; that way, if someone wanted to buy one, we didn't have to waste time sorting out the finances. I think if Adriana had said, "I want to go out on my own," I would have taken advantage of the soaring stock market in the U.S. to take the organization public; certainly, I would have sold off parts of it to secure the family's financial future. My philosophy has always been: If the price is right, you have to sell. You may not like it but you have to do it.

239

But then Adriana and I had a conversation. And everything changed.

"You have to own your ideas"
Adriana recalls:

> I always knew I would work for Cisneros but my plan was to work on my own for about 10 years before joining the family business. I had aspirations of setting up a television news agency for Latin America, including Brazil. (I moved to Brazil to learn Portuguese.) In 2004, during my final year at journalism school, when I was 25 years old, I applied for a fantastic two-year training program at NBC. Some 1,500 students applied and I made it to the final round: one other candidate and me, being grilled by all the top executives of the news organization.
>
> At the end of the process, I was called by one of the program administrators. She said, "We just realized who you are and we can't offer you a job." (At the time, Cisneros owned Univision and NBC owned Telemundo, its arch-rival.)
>
> I was heartbroken. I felt stupid — and angry. I thought the U.S. was a meritocracy: If you earned the right to a position, you could have it.
>
> I wasn't shy about saying so to two close family friends: Bill Luers, the former American ambassador to Venezuela, and Albert Ibargüen, the publisher of The Miami Herald. They both told me the same thing: Even if I decided to move to a small town and bury myself in a college radio station, the trend towards media consolidation meant my name would always be an issue. If I wanted to work in media, they both said, I should go into the family business — and do it sooner rather than later.

Bill Luers further pushed Adriana to think about what she wanted to accomplish with her journalism degree. "I didn't think [journalism alone] fit with her abilities," he said. "She was already ambitious and had a vision of what she wanted to achieve. She wanted to be big in whatever she did."

Luers had known our kids since they were small. They regarded him as a beloved uncle. He could see that Adriana was hesitant to make any move that might challenge her brother. Luers was the only person who could say what needed to be said and do what needed to be done, and he stepped up to the plate. "Guillermo doesn't want to be Gustavo's successor," he told her. "You're not only the logical choice but a good choice." Luers recalls, "I think that opened her mind to the possibility [of succeeding her father] and gave her the courage to demonstrate her interest."

That started a series of quiet conversations between Adriana, Steven Bandel, our CEO, and me.

* * *

"An opportunity and a laboratory"

In fact, Adriana wasn't starting from scratch. She had long been active in the Cisneros Foundation, and the Cisneros family business activities were closely linked to the Cisneros Foundation's goals of improving education throughout Latin America and fostering global awareness of the region's heritage and many contributions to world culture.

Patty and I had never differentiated between the Foundation and the business. The leadership of both requires the same abilities: the same financial strengths, the same talent to oversee operational details, and the same people skills — maybe even more so, as is often the case in the non-profit workspace.

241

At the time Adriana expressed her interest in joining the business, the Foundation was managing three programs: the Colección Patricia Phelps de Cisneros (CPPC); Cl@se, our original teacher training program (although the program was being phased out); and Actualización de Maestros en Educación, or AME, a program similar to Cl@se but online. (We focused on training teachers rather than teaching kids directly because it had more impact: One teacher could reach many children.)

Adriana literally had front seat at the creation and launch of our Cl@se and AME education initiatives. She recalls:

My parents didn't discuss work in front of us kids but they often spoke about how to use their social capital to make the world a better place. When the DirecTV deal was coming together, my parents realized they had an opportunity to reform education through connectivity. That led them to launch Cl@se, the first pan-regional educational television channel. This was a topic of many dinnertime conversations: how to ensure that one node out of 800 on the satellite was dedicated to an educational signal and that each local partner would commit to distributing educational programming without advertising revenue.

You can imagine how exciting it was. And I was right there: at the dinner table as they brainstormed the topic and with my father as we toured Latin America and signed the contracts with the partners in each country. That was my first exposure to Fundación Cisneros.

When we launched AOLA (AmericaOnline Latin America), we had a similar epiphany: Online, everyone can talk to each other and be in the same space without passports. We had a similar conversation about educational opportunities online. That led to AME, the first online teacher-training program in the region. We worked with different universities to develop curricula for everything from how to be a better math teacher to conflict resolution in schools. Teachers from the highlands of Peru who might never have left their region now were classmates with their counterparts in Chile and Colombia. Having seen the differences between those countries when I visited them during our DirecTV launch, I could now see the potential to build bridges through technology.

In 2007, Adriana assumed the role of the President of the Cisneros Foundation. Both Cl@se and AME were dormant at the time, so being President essentially meant taking charge of the CPPC, which was growing fast. It was a transitional moment.

* * *

"As an agent of change, nothing is more important than culture"

Patty and I purchased our first work of art together — Spanish artist Manuel Rivera's Tiritaña — soon after we were married and continued collecting contemporary Venezuelan artists, as many well-off Caracas families did. But there was no plan for a collection at the time.

That began to change as Patty accompanied me on business trips to other countries in Latin America. While I was in meetings, Patty would visit galleries and artists' studios. Patty recalls that I encouraged her to think beyond the boundaries of Venezuela, to consider the commonalities of Latin American culture. "That wouldn't have happened without Gustavo urging me not to stay local and to become more aware of international trends," Patty says.

"It was not an expensive collection," Patty recalls. "For the first 25 years, I never spent more than $5,000 on a work of art.

Fortunately, geometric abstraction was the type of art that appealed to me." That was the nucleus of what became known as the Colección Patricia Phelps de Cisneros, or CPPC.

Many people create private collections as a status symbol, a way to diversify their investments. Very few have a mission-led collection. Patty's idea was to build a collection that at the time didn't exist: one that would describe the history of Latin America through its art, from its indigenous peoples through the present day, and demonstrate that 20th-century Latin American artists didn't so much mirror artistic developments in Europe and the United States as create their own identity in dialogue with the rest of the world, an identity that deserved to be seen as an integral part of global art history.

Led by Patty, we launched an active and determined philanthropic commitment to educating people everywhere about the value and excitement of Latin American culture: endowing teaching chairs at universities; providing fellowships for students to study in Latin America; starting a series of publications, both analog and digital; and financing a fund for museum curators to travel to Latin America to meet artists and see their work *in situ*.

The CPPC also offers grants to support artists in Latin America. Because most artist-run spaces are run on a shoestring, especially in Latin America, a few thousand dollars goes so far. In return, we got a front-row seat to the most innovative arts ideas in the region. Our investment was modest but the impact was huge.

One thing we did *not* do was build a museum. If you build a museum, people visit once or twice, but it's a challenge to make them come back. If your mission is to rewrite and expand the canon of art history, however, you need to go where the great art already is: New York's Museum of Modern Art in New York, the

Getty Museum in Los Angeles, the Royal Academy in London, the Museo Reina Sofia in Madrid, and the Moderna Museet in Stockholm. We always tried to partner with the force multipliers: We gave them the know-how and access to Latin American art, which they needed, and they gave us a bigger platform, which *we* needed.

We also sowed our seeds in smaller places through a wide-ranging program of exhibitions that traveled around the world. At one point, we had Fundación Cisneros activities "from pole to pole," as we liked to say — the Orinoco collection at a beautiful cultural center in northern Finland and a teacher training program at the Argentine navy base in Antarctica.

Half of what we were doing was collecting objects and being good custodians, and the other half was activism, outreach and education. And the great thing was that it was *much* less expensive than building a museum and *far* more effective.

Adriana came in with a digital mindset and applied it to art. That was unique. Under her direction, and with a new director, Gabriel Pérez-Barreiro, the cppc underwent a major restructuring and implemented a new strategic plan.

At Adriana's urging, we tried out new technologies, as well as developing our own. We hired new, younger staff. We engaged with the public in new ways: a comprehensive website, ebooks, online exhibitions, interactive seminars, public dialogues about issues in modern art, free lectures available to everyone, and a visual arts education program. We repositioned Piensa en Arte/ Think Art, our arts education program, for a global audience and made the material available in English. For the "Invención Concreta" exhibit at the Reina Sofia in 2013, which explored the development of geometric abstraction in Latin America, we developed a technology platform that was integrated into the curatorial aspect of the show: Visitors could access geolocated audio tours on their mobile phones; iPads were distributed in the museum gallery with video interviews with the artists and views of Caracas in the 1950s. We weren't just hanging art on the walls. We were trying to show and share the rich history of the country that produced the art. We became a museum without walls.

The Foundation was both an opportunity for Adriana to test the waters and a laboratory in which she could experiment with developments she wanted to implement in the business, while gaining the experience and confidence to take on the leadership of the business.

Adriana was named President of the Cisneros Foundation in 2009. By that time, she was well on her path to succeeding me in the business. But she had one stipulation, she recalled:

> One of the few conditions I gave my father before I was named his successor was: You have to let me run both the business and the foundation. He didn't want to do it; he thought it was too much. But our Foundation was and still is very important to me. I said, "My heart beats both ways. I won't feel complete unless I can do both."

* * *

"Structure is your friend"

When Adriana had that conversation with Bill Luers about joining the family business, she recalls, "He planted the seed. But it was my father and Steven Bandel who proposed the idea of me taking over as CEO."

Her response: "I said no. On the one hand, I was surprised and wondered if I was up for the job. On the other, I was just beginning to understand how being head of the company would affect our family dynamics and how complicated that could be."

What was so daunting to Adriana was that in taking over the family business, she would also be taking over as the leader of the family. "I was the youngest, and at the time I was very young," she recalls. "So there was the question of how to get my older siblings to support me as the leader of the family and CEO. I told my dad, we have to make sure we do all the work in the family so that I will never have to fight with my siblings over money or family power. No job is ever worth me being in that position."

Then, in October 2007, Adriana attended a seminar about succession in family businesses, led by Professor John Davis, the founding chair of Harvard Business School's Families in Business program. "I had an 'aha!' moment. I realized we have a typical problem that is often solvable. And our family is not as dysfunctional as many families trying to deal with succession."

John Davis recalls, "Adriana told me that she was tasked to think about whether she wanted to be the successor and whether she could do it. She said, 'Could you help us figure it out? First of all, I need to know whether I really want to do this. I know some things about the company but I've got to get my arms around this new experience I may be signing up for before I decide.'"

The following month, Adriana and I had a conference call with John to discuss getting to know one another through a family workshop. In January 2008, everyone gathered at our home in the Dominican Republic and the work began.

John pointed out that when a successor takes over, family relationships start to change — sometimes subtly, sometimes with more of a bang — because one person now has a role the others don't have. Whoever gets the baton will be in a special role and have special decision-making responsibilities and powers. The others will have different roles. So you want to make sure every family member has a voice and is able to participate in meaningful conversations about what we were moving to.

John introduced the concept of a formal Family Council. In many families, business is discussed informally over the dinner table or over a beer on the weekend. If you do it around a conference table with formal presentations from family members or a company executive, he explained, everyone will learn more, they'll be updated more thoroughly and, most important, they will feel more respected. They're not bystanders who will learn "what we've done" after the fact.

"A key ingredient was to try to build support in Adriana's generation, among her brother and sister," John says. "I think Gustavo's early go-to choice was Guillermo. He is a really smart, interesting person, but he made it clear this wasn't for him."

Adriana adds, "John explained that it was great that Guillermo had the courage to say, 'I don't want this.' My father just hadn't been listening. John said, 'I've seen too many cases where the successor didn't have the courage to say that, and then they do the job for 30 years and don't do it well and are miserable.' The work we started doing with John gave my father the framework to understand that there would be another, also valuable place for Guillermo, as well as for Carolina. It freed my father from his expectations."

The conversation helped me realize that Adriana's brother and sister weren't the only members of the family who had to readjust their roles in the family dynamic. Patty and I had to alter our assumptions and start thinking of the next generation as adults, not children, as stewards and advisors, not just shareholders. (The traditional Latin American model, Adriana explains, treated the family members as children who obeyed the patriarch's dictates without much actual knowledge of the business.) That was a huge mind shift, for me even more than Patty. Fortunately, Patty was already working through her own transition at the Fundación Cisneros, so she understood how I would feel. She played an important role as a well-informed supporter of both Adriana and me.

John describes the formal process we instituted to bring all five family members together and have frank and open discussions. "I tell families, 'Structure is your friend.' Left to their own devices, families skirt issues, and leapfrog processes they should go through because they can be uncomfortable or because they just don't know how to do this. You rely on the structure because it helps keep you disciplined and more honest. You don't need too many rules and meetings but a certain amount of formality enables you to say, 'I looked at the real data. We had the conversations we needed to have.'"

At John's prompting, we established a Family Council where we get together to exchange views, analyze issues and discuss new projects. It is not a formal decision-making body but rather a sounding board and a structured communication channel. In the Family Council, we think as a family about our goals and consider what we want to accomplish. The Family Council made possible the sweeping changes Adriana would make to the business.

John played a key role as a facilitator. It helps to have a facilitator when dealing with sensitive, high-stakes topics. You need to make sure issues are addressed systematically and emotions are expressed in a constructive way. A facilitator ensures that you have the tough conversations and no one can say, "No one asked me."

We have Family Council meetings four times a year. Adriana makes a presentation about the business; we often invite outside trustees to make presentations on particular topics. Initially, John attended all of the meetings. These days, he comes less frequently, although he is informed about what goes on. He compares his role to that of a spotter in a weight room: He's there to make sure your form is correct. If a problem is bubbling up and the family could use some help, he can step in.

The formal structure of the Family Council did more than provide Patty, Guillermo and Carolina with a better perspective of the company's evolution: It also kept them informed about Adriana's own development on the path to becoming CEO. It gave them the opportunity to ask questions, make suggestions and provide support. They came to recognize that her taking over could work — maybe even before she did herself.

* * *

"You're going to need to not sleep"

My father often said, "Give me the right people and we'll give them the skills." I had no doubt that Adriana was the right person to succeed me. But she needed to acquire the skills to become CEO.

Thanks to John Davis, we created a program that addressed one of the two fundamental challenges: organize the family office so that the family could accept her as the next leader, even though she was the youngest child. Now, we needed to create a program that addressed the other fundamental challenge: organize a course of study that would prepare Adriana to become CEO. These were two different areas she needed to feel confident she could manage: the intellectual and the emotional.

Adriana had initially dismissed Steven Bandel's and my proposal that she succeed me. We insisted that she at least consider it. As Adriana later said, "I've learned that when smart people say you can do something *you* don't think you're capable of, it's usually because *they* think that you *are* capable." Eventually, we all agreed that she would learn what was involved in being the CEO so that she could make an informed decision.

One key question Adriana asked before we could move forward: Why do it now? After all, she pointed out, she had intended to work for Cisneros eventually, perhaps 15 years from now, when she was in her 40s. What was the rush? She said to me, "You're in good health, your brain is sharper than ever. Why don't you demote yourself from chairman to CEO and take over from Steven?"

I reminded her that I had taken over the business from my father when I was 25, just about the age she was now. I needed every ounce of my energy and passion to fix things and grow the business in the way I thought was best. "You're going to need to not sleep," I warned her. "You'll be running a marathon but you'll be running it at sprint speed. The only way you can do that is to start now, when you're young, not when you're in your 40s."

Adriana had already applied to the MBA program at Columbia University. It was a two-year course of study. Adriana recalls, "My dad said, 'You cannot take two years off and go to school. Absolutely not!' That's when we began to think about a customized program. I would not get a diploma from Columbia but I would be prepared to run the family business for 30 years."

John Davis, Steven Bandel and I put together a plan to determine Adriana's existing skills and knowledge, and complement them with the specific skills and knowledge she would need to take on the CEO position. The plan was a combination of coursework and real-life involvement at Cisneros.

She learned the fundamentals of business through MBA courses at both Columbia and Harvard, as well as being tutored privately in finance by a graduate student at the Harvard Business School. In order to develop the perspective of a general manager, she also took courses in marketing, finance, sales and the like. Every single course and case study was scrupulously analyzed through the lens of a family business.

I had warned her that the pace would be grueling and it was. She crammed the finance classes of a two-year MBA program into six months. At the same time, she was mother to a one-year-old and had a second baby.

"I gave birth to my daughter in December 2008 and went back to Boston at the end of January 2009," Adriana recalls. "I found myself Fedexing frozen milk to New York. I said to my husband and my dad, 'Why did you think I should go back to school? Am I crazy?' They both said, 'You think we could stop you? *That* would be crazy!'"

John Davis identified a handful of people he knew who had gone through similar processes and introduced them to Adriana. "I started having incredible conversations," she remembers. One in particular stood out. "John Elkaan [the grandson of Giovanni Agnelli, who became the head of the Agnelli Family group of businesses in 2004] asked me, 'What do *you* want to do?' He told me that he wanted to create EXOR, a holding company for the Agnelli businesses that would last 30 years. That conversation was critical. I thought, If I'm going to take over, I'll need a lot of space to reorganize the company, not just its managerial structure but the businesses I want to be involved with for the next 30 years."

In addition, Steven Bandel and Miguel Dvorak, our COO, directed her hands-on learning in business. "The challenge was that she was young and the daughter of the boss," Bandel explained. "How could people respect her as a leader while Gustavo and I were still there?"

Adriana was officially designated my successor in 2009, with the titles of Vice Chairman and Director of Strategy. (I would remain the Chairman and Steven Bandel would remain the CEO until she was ready to take his place.) The position of Director of Strategy was invented specifically for Adriana with no specific brief. "No one knew what I was doing, which was great," she recalls. In practice, the title was a passport to explore every aspect of the organization.

Beginning in 2010, Miguel Dvorak became her personal tour guide:

> My role was to take Adriana by the hand and introduce her to everybody and every detail of the business. I tried to have Adriana attend every single meeting with every single team of every single company, from the smallest to the biggest: monthly reports, yearly budgets, strategy meetings, brainstorming meetings to solve problems, create new products or consider acquisitions. That way, she could interact with everyone and become familiar with every detail of every operation.
>
> I'd prepare Adriana before each meeting, describing whom she would meet and the highlights that we needed to discuss and resolve. As a form of discipline, I made sure to ask everyone in the meeting to share their opinion of each point on the agenda before moving on to the next topic. That made meetings a little long, but I figured the first six or so times we did that were worthwhile, because Adriana would start to understand how each of us thought about things.

Adriana recalls:

> Those first meetings were me asking questions about why we were organized a certain way and who did what. For example, when the organization left Venezuela, we set up mirror companies here to do the functions of those in Venezuela. But because we thought

253

we'd eventually return to Venezuela, we never collapsed the Venezuelan structures. Consequently, we had double functions in most of our media operations. I started questioning the "why" behind that: the structure, people's roles, and the objectives of certain units. They were happy to have me be the one who was doing it. It would have been difficult for them to do it on their own and, honestly, they were so used to the format that they might not have been able to see what needed to change.

Meanwhile, behind the scenes, Bandel groomed her to take over his job. "From Steven, I learned that patience is a powerful virtue, that passion paired with discipline is a winning combination, and that human capital is the most valuable asset in our company. Above all, he showed me that as an organization, we thrive on challenge."[3]

There was a lot of information to digest and digesting it took a couple of years. Adriana says, "I was trying to go from zero to 100 miles per hour, while asking a million annoying questions." As people saw her interacting, reacting, giving her opinions and getting to know the organization, they slowly started to respect her because her opinions were right on target. And, Bandel adds, "They saw that Gustavo trusted her. That was very important."

It was mostly up to Adriana to step into and occupy the space we were giving her, and to demonstrate that she had the capability and interest. As Bandel and I saw her participating more and wanting more engagement, we were happy to let her get more involved. As for Adriana, she says, "The more I learned about family businesses and *our* business, the more convinced I was that I had something strategic to offer and the more this crazy idea of my father and Steven started making sense to me."

It also helped that Adriana was not obligated to become CEO. Every step forward was *her* choice and her choice alone.

She essentially had an escape clause. That's not always the case with family companies. Succession can be complicated in some family businesses by the pressure of having to have a family member on the leadership team. We don't have that mandate. Adriana says, "Had I not wanted it, we would have been okay with having a CEO who was not a family member. After all, Steve Bandel wasn't a family member. Nothing bad would have happened if I had said no."

Ultimately, the transition functioned relatively smoothly — although there were naturally a lot of ups and downs — because all of the players were aligned: There was an alignment of expectations and a common understanding of what needed to happen next. Adriana drove the process; my role was to facilitate it.

I was happy to do it. Adriana is a lot like me — and a lot like her grandfather. If she hadn't seen this opportunity as a real responsibility and hadn't been so committed to it, I might have been less comfortable with the prospect of her succeeding me. Of course, I knew she needed experience but John Davis often reminded me — and her! — that it's impossible to make the successor as accomplished as the outgoing leader on day one. Instead, you want to make sure she is as prepared as possible. And everyone gets better after they take the job.

I could see her confidence growing day by day, which, in turn, increased my own confidence in her. My challenge now was to give her the space she needed to spread her wings. But the headwinds were much rougher than either of us had anticipated.

* * *

As Director of Strategy, Adriana had an insider's knowledge of the challenges the organization encountered as we began to regain our equilibrium in the wake of our abrupt departure from Venezuela. As a relative newcomer, she brought a fresh set of eyes to how we were addressing them.

The years since Chávez had assumed power in 1999 were traumatic, both for me personally and for the organization. We were under constant attack, a ferocious blitz of calumny and criticism targeting everything we had accomplished. It was relentless, escalating in concert with the catastrophe overwhelming our country. We felt as though we were trapped in a chaotic surf zone, trying to catch a breath before the next wave crashed down on us, unable to break free.

Adriana pointed out that when you're in a crisis, day after day after day, crisis management becomes the modus operandi. What made it worse was that we had initially thought, "It's a lousy situation but it's only for six months, maybe a year." But the months turned into a year, and the year turned into two, then three, then four. The vicious attacks only intensified, coming from all quarters. We never knew what to expect next. I was the primary target, with Venevisión a close second.

The day-to-day challenge to survive the political firestorm was all-consuming. We didn't have the time or the strength or the mental capacity to think beyond fighting the conflagration happening outside our door, let alone protect ourselves from the psychological and emotional damage. We were all scarred in ways we didn't realize.

Planning for the future was set aside for "later." When you're scared that the government will shut down or take over your main asset in Venezuela, there's not a penny to spare for other investments. Identifying areas for potential growth got shoved down the priority list. Innovative thinking? No one had the energy or imagination for it. We were so focused on surviving that we couldn't escape survival mode.

As if the outside political circumstances weren't bad enough, soon after we left Venezuela, another series of events slammed us onto the ropes. They were a complete surprise; I really don't think anyone could have foreseen what happened or how things played out. By the time it was over, Cisneros was in a fight for its life.

It's a very complicated story but, basically, the issue boiled down to beer and my brother. Even before we left Venezuela, Ricardo had made it clear that he had no interest in the firm — with one exception: our brewery business, Cervecería Regional. He viewed the beer business as a personal launch pad for expanding into other enterprises in Venezuela and Latin America.

Beer can be a great source of cash flow but you need very good professionals in charge. Ricardo had put in new managers and when the business didn't produce the results Ricardo wanted, he became upset and defensive. His decision-making became skewed. He started playing one business against another. He would complain about the cost of the media business and nitpick the expenses of producing the telenovelas, which were our cash cow. If we wanted to invest any money in the business, he insisted that it had to be in beer.

Operationally, things became very problematic. Managers were getting opposing — and even antagonistic — messages from one of the co-chairmen. Loyalties were called into question with every decision. The ugly situation went on for several years. I suppose I kept hoping that some sort of solution would emerge, but the company became more divided and Ricardo became increasingly resentful.

Things came to a head when a large conglomerate offered us $800 million to buy Regional. It was an enormous amount of money for a business in a country that was in financial trouble. We really could have used an infusion of $800 million for new investments in the United States. The economic situation in Venezuela

257

was getting worse and advertising revenues for Venevisión were plummeting. At the same time, Univision was insisting on changes in the way we produced our content, threatening our greatest stream of income. Ricardo blocked the transaction, demanding $900 million. As a result, the conglomerate withdrew its offer.

I could no longer ignore the handwriting on the wall. Ever since I took over from my father, my responsibility had been to protect our company, our family and our people. But now our family company's future was threatened by a family member. I had to choose. I chose our company.

Ricardo didn't have shares that I could buy out. The only option was to break up the company and save what we could. The Gustavo/Ricardo partnership was a hallmark of our company, a permanent part of our corporate landscape, and as much a source of pride as Venezuela's great Guri dam. Now the dam was cracking. It was one more loss to take on, one more source of pain and grief.

Implementing the separation was a massively complex undertaking. In Venezuela alone, Cisneros owned 220 different companies: There were in different industries and different geographies, with different corporate structures, different fiscal and regulatory limitations, and different people attached to different enterprises. Venevisión alone was at the center of an enormous web of related businesses.

We had to inventory all 220 companies and define whether it was an independent company or a subsidiary, which other companies it owned shares in, and what was the status of its accounting. We didn't have much of a database — this was when Excel was state of the art. The inventory ran to pages and pages and pages. Then we had to map out all the connections and interconnections and correlations. Every wall of the dedicated conference room was papered with print-outs, festooned with snippets that had been taped on top, and further complicated by circles and arrows scrawled in colored markers to indicate intertwined businesses. It looked like a police diagram of a murder investigation.

The negotiations took about six or seven months, and the separation another three or four. For close to a year, we were trying to run a business while simultaneously slicing it up and spinning off its component parts. Nobody won. We knew we would lose fundamental synergies and economies of scale: Regional would lose a major advertising outlet a hard blow for a business dependent on advertising; Venevisión would lose one of its best advertising customers. We always kept a very good cash reserve — a lesson George Moore had hammered into me — but with our business literally cut in half while legal fees and other costs went through the roof, we were hemorrhaging an eye-popping amount of money in Venezuela.

Managing our people was the most difficult part. Everyone knew that if the economies of scale disappeared, some of the businesses they had justified could no longer exist. People were anxious: Would they still have a job? Or if they retained their job, would they have a different boss? With everyone defending their turf, behavior ran the spectrum from nitpicking to knife-fighting. Loyalties were compromised and opportunism reared its ugly head. For example, there was a question about who owned the office furniture: When a lawyer was spotted removing the television set in his office, people accused him of stealing it. (In fact, it was his own television.) It was a melee.

In the end, I don't think we lost any of the managers we wanted to keep. Maybe five people out of 150 employees in corporate decided they wanted to do something else. But that meant Cisneros carried more people than we needed for our new size. We would need to create new businesses to employ them.

The separation contract was signed in 2008. But the repercussions would reverberate for years.

Our brains were battered and bruised; our emotions were shredded raw. Few family businesses can survive this process because there is such a substantial elimination of value. In our case, the business diversity, and the great number of jurisdictions and geographies involved only increased the complexity of the undertaking and the severity of the hit we took. I give enormous credit to Steven Bandel and Ariel Prat, who ensured that the separation was executed cleanly and with no regulatory consequences. The private consequences of the rupture of the GURI partnership — well, that was my own affair.

This was the situation when Adriana came in. It was a critical moment. We were already experiencing a severe cash crunch as a result of the split, then came the global financial crisis and a critical downturn in the business. Our entire strategy had to be rethought, our organization restructured and our business reinvented.

Sometime in 2012, Adriana wrote a strategy paper outlining her observations and proposing changes. It took someone with an outside perspective to recognize that most of the members of our leadership team were in their 50s and that during the turmoil of the previous years, succession planning had been completely ignored. There was no one being trained to take over from Steven Bandel, our CEO.

Furthermore, Adriana noted that the crucible we had endured had annealed the leadership team into a close-knit circle of crisis managers, a true "band of brothers." It would have been difficult for any outsider to become CEO, because whoever it was would inherit a very complicated tangle of problems related to Venezuela. "I could see how exhausted many of the executives were," Adriana recalls.

Her strategy paper was the wake-up call we needed to envision and prepare not just for survival but for whatever transformations we would need to enact to thrive in the future. But honestly, we were too exhausted to rise to the challenge. Someone else would have to lead the way.

Adriana now likes to joke that the good news was that her strategy paper was well-received. The bad news? "They said, 'You have to own your ideas. Can you implement what you recommended?'"

* * *

"Make the bed you want to get into"

Let's go back a few years to when Adriana was still deciding whether to become CEO. When Adriana said, "Okay. I think I'll do this," we — Adriana, Steven Bandel and I — had another frank conversation. The topic was: What were the conditions under which she would be willing to be named my successor?

Adriana proposed some radical changes. I have to confess, I was initially startled. But then I realized that she is very much my daughter — and very much my father Diego's granddaughter. Bold thinking and new ideas are in her DNA.

I'll let her describe the changes in her own words:

I realized I couldn't lead the company the way Steven Bandel had structured it. He spent 30 years at the company; he could manage it perfectly because he grew up in it.

If I had taken over the company as he structured it, I would have 28 direct reports. They were mostly men, mostly over 50, most of whom had worked in the company for 20 to 30 years. I knew that would make my job really difficult. I'd have to convince 28 people, many of whom had known me from when I was a little girl, that this young, female CEO was the boss. That would take a lot of effort. Plus, everything I'd read said that the optimal number of direct reports is 8. I certainly didn't want 28.

With Steven's help, we got rid of that entire structure: all those silos and fiefdoms that had developed. We unified the units that should have been working more in unison.

It's never a good idea to restructure for the sake of restructuring. It's much better to restructure for the sake of a new business opportunity. So, we mixed the two things. That also made it easier to bring in new people.

We decided that we would get rid of all but one of the legacy businesses. All of them. The only legacy business that would stay in was our media business, i.e., Venevisión. And we would launch two brand-new divisions, which I would create from scratch: the digital division (an off-shoot of our media business) and real estate.

One of the smartest things my father and Steven did was to allow me to make major changes before I took over as CEO: to sell companies and dismiss people who hadn't done anything wrong but were redundant for the new direction I wanted to go in. I didn't have to arrive as CEO and dive into the uncomfortable work; I had done 80% of the hard work before I took over. I was able to make the bed I wanted to get into.

* * *

"Give everyone the same tools for the toolbox"

Adriana likes to say that the tough thinking and heavy lifting were accomplished in the years leading up to when she took over as CEO. "From the first day I became CEO, I could concentrate on building new business," she says.

The digital shift had started long before she became CEO. Facebook was created in 2004. "Google" officially became a verb in 2006.[4] Apple released the first iPhone in 2007. By the time Adriana wrote her strategy paper, digital mania was in full swing.

"There wasn't a clear road map in the Cisneros media division, but I knew I wanted to push our digital strategy and push it hard," Adriana recalls. "I wanted to make some pretty radical changes in terms of content and how we were thinking about media." She quickly identified a hurdle: "We didn't have the common ground or common language to talk about all the concepts I wanted to implement."

She discovered a company called Hyper Island, a digital creative business school that helps effect digital transformation for non-digital companies. The Cisneros Foundation was the ideal vehicle to experiment on. "I invited Miguel Dvorak to come with me for a four-day course in New York. Afterward, we could speak in the same language. When I started talking about what I wanted to do, he could now talk to me and see the potential in what I proposed." What she was proposing was a complete mind shift. "We used to think about TV in terms of broadcast," Adriana explains. "I was pushing a 360-degree approach to all our content."

The next step was to convince other key people in the business of the opportunities and buy into the new direction. It actually wasn't difficult, she recalls. "Everyone was eager to learn about the digital shift. "We brought Hyper Island here, to Miami," she says. "We included everyone in the same class: our lawyers, our engineers, everyone in middle management and up. Everyone was given the same tools for the toolbox. And that's when things started to change."

With everyone speaking the same language, Adriana could put together the kind of multidisciplinary ad-hoc teams that I used to create to brainstorm ideas and solve problems. These hackathons have become her modus operandi. "All our new lines of business came from those, especially in media," she says. "When you have younger guys from the legal team talking with digital producers talking with script writers, the power of collaboration is amazing. We came up with so many new ideas and interesting solutions that we now do this across all units whenever we feel stuck."

* * *

"Learn to step back"

John Davis says that good succession planning is always a matter of generosity. You're surrendering something that you created and nurtured and love, and you're bestowing it on someone that you created and nurtured and love. It's one of the most profound gifts you can give.

I didn't want to be possessive. Once again, I looked to my father for a role model: I had taken over an organization he had built out of nothing and, with his support and approval, changed it pretty radically. I was aware that Adriana would want to change things in her way. The best gift I could give was to help her succeed.

John Davis pointed out that I hadn't built a monument for Adriana to protect and preserve. I was giving her an opportunity to establish her own mark: to step beyond the shadows of those who stood before her, and to find new ventures for expansion while building on the legacy that supports her. It was up to her to figure out the right way to do that. (He had to remind me of that frequently.)

Looking back, Adriana says that I carved out the space so that she could take over. Patty had a different perspective: She says I had to sit on my hands and let Adriana learn for herself. I had to learn to step back so Adriana could step forward.

There were plenty of awkward moments between us, especially at the beginning, as we figured out our new roles and responsibilities and responses to fundamental questions like, "What are the priorities? How much leeway is there to reshape them? Where will the resources to accomplish them come from?" To ease the friction, we both turned to Ariel Prat, the Cisneros Chief Financial Officer, who became a wise counselor, a sounding board for both of us and a valuable go-between.

"Being a family member and the one who is taking over, you are touching not only business elements but family sensibilities," Prat recalls. "That's a key element they both worked to solve, but it wasn't easy.

"When there were issues, the message I got was not so much to mediate as to go back and forth between Gustavo and Adriana to lay the groundwork for negotiation. At those times, what I heard was, 'You have to convince my father' or 'You have to convince Adriana.' If you put them in the same room when they were hanging on to those poles, the situation could escalate quickly.

"Instead, I would talk to Adriana to get her point of view and talk to Gustavo to get *his* point of view. Playing the middle man allowed both to envision and engage in a better way; it was a way to stimulate discussion and calm things down. Then, having got that out of their systems and heard the other person's perspective from me, they came into the same ballpark; they could communicate and decide."

I had to learn to allow her to do things her own way and not blink an eye — at least, not where people could see me. Even when I didn't always agree with her, I would try to tell her why not. But if she wanted to do it, I would let her. And I never said, "I told you so." My contribution was my whole-hearted and open support.

I gave her a lot of space to make mistakes. Adriana says I wanted her to fail hard very early, when the ramifications have quite as much impact and she could learn important lessons to apply later. That was the most difficult challenge for me.

Early on, she dismissed two very senior people. They had been with us for years — decades. Both were smart guys but they both made the mistake of not taking Adriana seriously as a boss. I could have stepped in. But if I had, it would have been terrible for her and for the business. As a young person, she needed to be confident in her skills and decisions. You can make people insecure very quickly, if you want to, by overshadowing them. I needed her to be very secure in everything.

I always take a long-term view and I knew if I interfered, it would trigger something that would cause problems for years to come. I didn't want to create any doubts in the minds of other executives, bankers or stakeholders. I wanted everyone to know: There's one boss and it's Adriana.

When Adriana took those actions, everyone wondered, "What's Gustavo going to do?" What I did was take a couple of aspirin. That was unusual: Normally, I don't take aspirin — I usually dispense it. In this case, though, I followed my own advice: I took a couple of aspirin and went to bed. Adriana made her point, and everyone understood it.

A meticulously planned, well-coordinated succession process is like adding drops of color into a pail of paint. At first, nothing seems to change. Then, you observe a gradual shift in the spectrum until, one day, you realize that the original color is now a different color entirely.

I could see the metamorphosis proceed with each meeting where the managers reminded me, "You have to include Adriana. We can't make this decision without her being included." With each successful deal Adriana accomplished inside and outside the company, my confidence in her grew.

There was no particular act of transition, no *Godfather* moment when the *capo* kisses Michael Corleone's hand and calls him "Godfather." Instead, at a certain point, I realized that people were calling me and instead of asking me to make a decision, they wanted to discuss a decision Adriana had already made. There were no lateral or rear-guard battles to fight: no drama, no trauma. Adriana was in a secure spot. That's when I understood that our succession plan had, indeed, succeeded.

Seven years after she initially said no to the idea of becoming CEO, Adriana said yes — with one provision. In December 2012, she wrote me a letter. After describing the arrangements, she and her family had made to move from New York to Miami, she laid out her requests and her reasoning:

> I want to ask for your support. Not as a father or a mentor, but as the Chairman of our company. I am moving to Miami because our company is there and we need to reinforce our presence in Florida. We have worked hard to fix what was broken and have been growing our businesses incrementally. The time has now come to make our next big move. We need to be disruptive, to make our new mark and make money.
>
> [There] are four opportunities that we are now ready to act on. They are good, solid, money-making opportunities. I need to know that I will be fully endorsed before I move my family to Miami.

I was happy to agree. In August 2013, she officially assumed the role of CEO.

* * *

"A thinking partner and early warning system"
When we embarked on this journey, John Davis warned us that most family relationships would change. I'm really happy to see

my relationship with Adriana has been enriched. I derive the same pleasure from talking with her about business that I did with my father. I think she enjoys it, too. I became a very active chairman and I'm very happy with the role.

Adriana calls me her "thinking partner." She says, "We connect in a way that's very special. It goes beyond love; we 'get' each other intellectually. I often feel alone in the room when I have ideas that no one else has come up with. The only one who 'gets' me is my father. When we make the biggest bets, the boldest moves, and the most audacious changes, it takes a few months for everyone else to get on the bandwagon. With my father, though, I don't have to do a lot of explaining. It's more like, 'How will you execute this?' That's really fun."

She also regards me as an early warning system: "The knowledge he brings in terms of the right ingredients to make a deal float is very valuable." I'm a very active counselor. We try to talk at least three or four times a week, usually very early in the morning. We have only one rule: Adriana is not allowed to *not* answer my calls. Ever. But that's the only rule.

As things started to fall into place, Adriana noticed an evolution in the pattern and frequency of my calls:

There would be times we wouldn't talk about work for days, then times when he would call 14 times in one day. I realized that his interest wasn't linked to the magnitude of the problem I was trying to solve. He wasn't asking, 'How do you feel about taking on the biggest loan of your life?' Instead, he was calling to talk about things he thought were intellectually stimulating.

When I was setting up our digital business, I wanted to buy a small company in Argentina. The company was comprised of just two guys with Ph. D.s who were building interesting algorithms, what we now call artificial intelligence. My father kept calling me:

"Can I come to Argentina with you to meet them?" I said yes, then asked, "But where are you?" He said, "I'm in Spain." He wasn't just being supportive in suggesting he fly across two oceans. His enthusiasm went way beyond cheerleading. He understood that we were on to something that would redefine the group forever and he wanted to be part of that ride.

Adriana and I apply the same rule that Patty and I do: Never go to bed mad at the other person. If there's a difference of opinion, we try to resolve it that day.

There will always be give and take, because that's how ideas develop. I still bite my tongue a lot. I'm sure Adriana does, too. But ultimately the chairman and CEO have to be happy with each other. And I believe we are.

Building bridges

Even before Adriana and I started paving a path to our organization's future, I was building other bridges across geographies and generations through two organizations I helped create: the Foro Iberoamericano and Padres & Hijos. Both organizations still exist and, to my immense satisfaction, Adriana is an active participant in Padres & Hijos.

* * *

"We should be talking, not fighting"

I've always seen myself as an Iberoamerican. I've always believed in combining Spanish, Portuguese and South American culture: as my friend, the esteemed Mexican novelist Carlos Fuentes said, a transatlantic businessman as well as an inter-American one.[5]

Fuentes was a bridge-builder. He always said, "We should be talking, not fighting." For example, he always made a point of speaking well of other authors. He was always a positive guy. Fuentes said, "We need more integration between Portugal, Spain and Latin America. We need to strengthen our similarities." That was the seed of the Foro Iberoamericano, a think tank like no other. Fuentes left no heirs, but the Foro Iberoamericano became his enduring legacy.

The Foro was created in 2000. It was — and still is — extremely significant. It was the first and is the only forum I know of where leaders from the political world, the intellectual world and the business world who never spoke to anyone outside of their own circle could meet and have a rational discussion about major issues affecting our world — in Spanish.

It's hard to over-emphasize how mind-blowing this was then and how relevant it will continue to be. Intellectuals, especially in the Spanish-speaking sphere, normally challenge the status quo. The Foro was one of the few places they could meet representatives of the status quo. Similarly, politicians and business leaders don't always see eye to eye. The Foro provided common ground, a place to speak on or off the record as you chose. It was like the Davos conference for the Spanish-speaking world.

It was new and fresh and, quite frankly, we didn't know whether it would work. Fuentes was the soul and because of him, everyone took the time to come: King Juan Carlos, who was a sponsor; presidents Fernando Cardozo from Brazil and Ricardo Lagos from Chile; prime ministers Felipe Gonzales from Spain and Mario Soares from Portugal; the heads of Brazil's Globo, Argentina's Grupo Clarín, Spain's Grupo PRISA, Carlos Slim from Mexico and me.

Fuentes was a great director. He never let his ego control him, so he was a great role model for everyone to check their egos at the door. You could really let your hair down. The Nobel Prize-winning novelist Gabriel García Márquez was famous for his partying. We would be in Cartagena for one of these meetings and he would invite everyone to join him for *una parranda* — an open-ended party that spun from bar to bar, picking up more people at each stop, with singing, dancing and *el maestro* inventing poetry on the spot. (A secretary followed along and wrote it down.) We'd end with breakfast and more music, then go to bed at 8 a.m.

The Foro met once a year for three days. But the connections we forged were so meaningful that we'd get together with our *Foro Compañeros* after we went home. I was always looking to expand my horizons — both my intellectual perspectives, as well as my network of political and business acquaintances.

I have to confess that I was initially hesitant to get to know people on the far Left but I always admire a good IQ and when I got to know these artists and writers through the Foro, I admired them even more. By the end of a meeting, I had moderated my point of view and I think they had changed their own point of view, too. Most other people had a similar experience. That's really an accomplishment.

* * *

"Change how families talk to each other"

At one of the early meetings of the Foro Iberoamericano, Carlos Slim, Julio Mario Santo Domingo, a Colombian industrialist, and I were tossing around ideas about the Foro when Slim said, "Why don't we do something similar for our children?"

We thought how good it could be if we could bring together the families of the top business families in Latin America to talk

271

off-the-record about common issues. It would nurture relationships between countries that didn't really exist: While there were plenty of official organizations that fostered connections among businesspeople, there were none that focused on families.

I believe in inclusivity: the more people, the merrier in this kind of conversation. We invited Joseph Safra of the Brazilian investment firm Banco Safra to join us — Brazil accounts for half of the economy in Latin America, so we wanted to include a Brazilian — as well as colleagues in Argentina and Chile. We all agreed to meet a few weeks later in New York City to talk further and things quickly began to mushroom in a good way.

The result was Encuentros de Empresarios de América Latina: Padres & Hijos (Encounters of Latin American Families in Business: Parents and Children). It's an alliance with the goal of sharing experiences across industries, countries, markets and generations, with a focus on affecting change across the region.

We discuss subjects specific to Latin American family businesses and business families: from succession planning and how business can promote social mobility and strengthen education to protecting yourself from kidnapping and other security issues. Sometimes we bring in experts; sometimes *we* are the experts. As with the Foro Iberoamericano, the meetings are held in Spanish. We meet once a year in person; in between meetings, we have a very active WhatsApp group.

When Padres & Hijos launched in 2004, Carlos, Julio Mario, me and our peers ran the organization. Now it's run by our kids. The generation that followed us are adults, running their own companies, so it's *their* forum.

Adriana describes how it has evolved:

Padres & Hijos was started by my father and others with the idea that the younger generation needed to get to know one another. It was very useful; if not for those meetings, that wouldn't have happened. Now that we've all grown older, the kids have taken over the family businesses and the padres are like patriarchs. There's still a council of the founding members, but you can see the younger generation pushing the boundaries of the topics that we think are important to us.

These are responsible people who are committed to enhancing the health of the countries where we're raising our own kids and the health of Latin America as a whole: whether through education or strengthening democracy or leveraging corporate social responsibility to move from charity to strategic philanthropy.

Recently, we've become more focused on new economies and the new players. We invite new leading entrepreneurs to join us. And the padres are attending the meetings. You can see Carlos Slim and others saying, "Wow, these guys are amazing! How can we get to know them?"

The DNA of the conference is shifting as the age group shifts. But just as we hoped, it has changed how Latin America's business families talk to each other.

Notes

1. Cited in "Family Business Facts," SC Johnson School of Business, Cornell University. https://www.johnson.cornell.edu/smith-family-businessinitiative-at-cornell/resources/family-business-facts/

2. *Ibid.*

3. Quoted in "Adriana Cisneros: The New Face of Cisneros Group," in *The Miami Herald,* October 27, 2013. https://www.miamiherald.com/news/business/biz-monday/article1956732.html

4. Lombardi, Candace, "Google Joins Xerox as a Verb," in *CNET,* July 6, 2006. https://www.cnet.com/culture/google-joins-xerox-as-a-verb/

5. Quoted in *Cisneros: A Family History.*

"Be open to the possibility of wonder"

None of our businesses should be museums of our personal memories. They should be dynamic entities that can evolve without changing the organization's essential genetic makeup. My father, Diego Cisneros, understood the importance of generational change. I also embrace it.

I'm a firm believer in the right of the next generation to do things according to their own vision. I also believe it is necessary to have a healthy respect for the achievements of our predecessors and for seeing relevance in the past as we plan for the future.

The fact that the company bears our family name is really important. Our organization is, literally, a name brand. The businesses we're in may change but our values remain the same as when my father bought his first dump truck. These are:

- Resilience in the face of adversity.
- The will and ability to reinvent ourselves as circumstances change.
- Responsibility — to our family, our employees, our partners, the communities in which we operate and, most of all, our customers.

- A sense of curiosity that inspires us to dream bigger and constantly seek out new opportunities.

That last trait is invaluable. A business is nothing without a constant inflow of new ideas. Otherwise, it will wither and die, and the family will suffer. We must continue to open our minds, to adapt and evolve, if both the business and the family are to survive and thrive.

That's true of any organization with long-term ambitions. But a family business has a built-in advantage: It has a sense of purpose that directs our decisions and shapes how we put them into practice. We look to the lessons of the past to guide us into the future. And what those lessons boil down to is this: If you intend to stay in business for 100 years, there's only one way to do business, and that's the right way.

I am so pleased that our younger daughter, Adriana, is enthusiastically perpetuating the family's business tradition. She shares her grandfather's curiosity about new developments in the world as well as the flexibility to take advantage of the opportunities they present. I am equally pleased that her brother and sister are so involved in our Family Council, where they help ensure that the business stays true to our family's values.

* * *

"The only way to truly fail is by not trying"

My father lacked fear. He took chances that other people wouldn't dare to take. He had some failures, of course, but he taught me that the key thing is to have a good batting average. The only way you will truly fail is by not trying. You'll fail in some instances, of course, but as long as you win more than you lose, you'll do well.

I was — and am — a risk-taker, too. But I never leave anything to pure chance. As has been said, hope is not a strategy. I've learned to double-check and triple-check, to consider the changes that may confront us and to calculate the response. Following that precept is what has enabled us to adapt to a changing world and reinvent the organization to thrive in new circumstances.

Adriana inherited those traits, combined with Patty's attention to detail. As a result, while Cisneros is at heart the organization her grandfather founded, it looks very different from the one I helped build. Cisneros today is comprised of three divisions: — media, interactive and real estate — as well as an investment in AST SpaceMobile.

Cisneros Media traces its roots back to my father's launch of Venevisión in 1961. It continues to develop stories and produce and distribute premium content in a range of genres and languages, from *telenovelas* to live-action to animation, for both adults and kids. Its platforms reach over 50 million subscribers around the world.[1]

I'll let Adriana explain:

Previously, with Venevisión, we owned the physical studio and produced content on those premises. As part of the digital transformation of the division, we created a new studio model that is 100% digital. We don't have to own physical assets and we can work with talent all over the world. We're now a key player across all platforms.

We continue to own and maintain Venevisión. My father started the network because he was a stalwart champion of democracy and believed that there is no better tool to support democracy than responsible media. We are the only independent news outlet in Venezuela. We take a completely clinical approach: all facts, zero opinions, no editorializing. In dark times, the best thing we can do is provide an outlet for reliable news.

Venevisión was once the center of a money-making dynamo. Today, we're lucky if it ekes out enough to cover its costs. All the revenues go to paying our employees' salaries and providing food for them and their families at our company cafeteria. That's not minor: Food insecurity is one of the major issues in Venezuela today. So we'll keep my father's legacy alive and continue to sustain minds, bodies and souls in the country we love.

Cisneros Interactive began because Adriana knew she wanted to do something big in the digital world. "I didn't know what that meant but I was willing to explore," she recalls. She began by investing in accelerators focused on that space. At the same time, she decided to hire someone to lead our digital effort. "Candidates would ask me what the mandate was," she says. "I would say, 'The mandate is to figure out what the mandate will be.' The world was so new that we could say that."

Adriana and Victor Kong, the new head of Cisneros Interactive who ultimately would be responsible for building this division, noticed that a huge amount of the content Cisneros was creating for Univision on television was being uploaded by viewers online. "We were generating so much traffic that had it been an organized platform, it would have been the largest platform for digital content in Spanish at the time. And no one was monetizing Spanish-language traffic while English-language content was being monetized for a lot of money."

Adriana questioned why that was the case. She explains:

In the U.S., Hispanics have always over-indexed in terms of digital consumption. That's been true from the early days. So, it seemed strange that there was no advertising agency specializing in the

278

digital Hispanic audience; in the big agencies, this enormous field was left to maybe one person in a corner. We thought, "Wow, there's a lot of money being left on the table."

We decided to do something about it. I remember the story of my grandfather bringing great American brands like Pepsi to Latin America and my father doing the same with Apple computers and Burger King and Pizza Hut. Those were a big part of our family stories as I was growing up.

I thought, "Why don't we do the same thing with Facebook?" When we pitched Facebook (now called Meta), we were so new to the space that we weren't even invited to be part of the RFP. We were the last people to be interviewed. The only way I could explain why I thought we could do a better job than the other, better-known groups was by describing our history of representing great American brands in the region. It was a very honest pitch. And we won.

At that point, I realized that the world had changed. Even the youngest companies understand that having a partner that's been around for nearly 100 years is not a bad thing. It's actually pretty cool.

Today, Cisneros Interactive is the leading digital advertising company serving the Latin American and U.S. Hispanic markets in 17 countries. We are the reseller partner for digital power-houses like Facebook, Instagram, Spotify and LinkedIn, as well as creating proprietary brands like Audio.Ad and JustMob to focus on specific digital niches, such as audio, video and gaming.

The hallmark of Cisneros Real Estate is Tropicalia, a sustainable luxury resort development on the northeast coast of the Dominican Republic, the country that we first came to know as one of our family's favorite vacation places and that we have come to call home. Tropicalia is both a way to give something back to the Dominican Republic and the realization of my long-held dream of investing in real estate. The first venture is a partnership with Four Seasons Hotels. The 24 residences were originally designed for personalization and privacy; since Covid-19, those attributes have become even more valuable.

We began to conceive Tropicalia in the early 2000s. This was a time when people were beginning to raise concerns about "enclave tourism" — the tendency of vacation complexes to become segregated spaces that rarely involve local communities in the functioning and benefits of their activities and limit visitors' interaction with the local economy.

I may have had the seed of the idea for Tropicalia, but its development is all Adriana. It was the first project I assigned her in her role as Vice President of Business Strategy in 2005 and it has been *her* project ever since. She managed the acquisition of over 200 parcels of land — 90% of which, she recalls, had discrepancies with their titles and issues with their ownership. You can imagine the sensitivities and headwinds involved in these transactions but she handled them with grace and perseverance. And, she now says, "I probably have the only clean land title in the Dominican Republic."

Tropicalia is located in one of the most beautiful and remote provinces of the Dominican Republic. Adriana wanted to leverage both our business and social endeavors to be mutually beneficial to the municipality of Miches. She recalls, "The same week we decided to create Tropicalia, we decided to create the Fundación Tropicalia. It wasn't an afterthought; it was a simultaneous thought."

The Fundación Tropicalia was founded as a registered NGO in 2008, long before we broke ground on the resort. Under Adriana's guidance, the Foundation began by focusing on education: fostering a favorable climate for learning by improving the physical infrastructure of schools and enhancing the quality of teaching through the Cisneros Foundation's own AME teacher training program and the "Piensa en Arte/Think Art" program run by the Colección Patricia Phelps de Cisneros. Over the past 14 years, the Foundation has developed and implemented over 30 programs, partnering with USAID, Fundación REDDOM, the Multilateral Investment Fund of the Inter-American Development Bank and other organizations that work in a range of areas: promoting sustainable agriculture, preserving the environment, boosting adult literacy and funding micro- and small businesses, to name just a few initiatives. Adriana personally serves as a role model for participants in the "Soy niña, soy importante" ("I'm a girl, I'm important") female empowerment program for local girls between nine and 12 years old.

Along the way, she not only elevated the notion of corporate social responsibility to a new level, but integrated it into the company. She explains:

> We don't think of CSR as a separate division. It's part of who we are as a family, as individuals and as a company. Every time we embark on a business venture, we try to figure out how to be the best possible stakeholders and responsible members of the communities in which we work. We take that mandate very seriously and are strategic about it.
>
> If we're not successful with Tropicalia, it will take us five years to finish. If we're successful, it will take us 40 years. Here's why: When you have a 40-year timeline and you work in a family business, you think about the local communities in a very different way. With a five-year timeline, you might think, "We'll work with one school and we'll try to figure out how to give it clean water." With a 40-year timeline, you're thinking about the next three generations of people living in these communities and how they'll relate to the project in a very different and meaningful way.

We do that kind of work not only because it's a good thing to do but because we think a big part of our success will depend on how we include the community in this project. That's why CSR is good business.

Tropicalia created about 2,000 jobs during its construction and will offer steady employment for 400 people when operational in one of the most economically depressed regions of the country. As Adriana says, "I want the Miches community to benefit from the project: to make sure the kids who are graduating from high school can be hired by the resort, that the farmers can sell their produce to the resort. When I drive into town, I want the locals to be really happy that I'm there.'"

Adriana's ideas and leadership in turning our dream of the resort and the foundation into reality showed me why she was the right person to become CEO of Cisneros. What started as a family project grew into an entire business division now known as Cisneros Real Estate.

Real estate is an important way to protect and preserve family wealth: It's a land bank. But my own dream is that Tropicalia will be a cherished legacy for all families, not just ours. We want to attract people who will want to stay long-term and build a community. We're also building a compound for my own family. I hope it will have an influence in keeping our family together for the next two or three generations.

Our investment in AST SpaceMobile is especially exciting. Adriana first became interested in satellites when she accompanied me to the launch of the DirecTV satellite when she was a teenager. Over the years, her fascination grew as she saw how a field that formerly was highly regulated by NASA and accessible to very few enterprises suddenly became democratized.

I'll let her describe what happened next:

My bankers at LionTree knew I liked satellites. One day, they called and said, "We have a new client, for whom we're raising $800 million." I didn't have that kind of money set aside for new projects, but I thought, "This client is Venezuelan, he's in Miami and he's into satellites. I'm extremely intrigued." So, I asked the banker if he'd be willing to talk for 10 minutes.

We didn't need 10 minutes. In five minutes, literally, we decided to become partners. We came in as Series A investors with $10 million for what was valued at $100 million. Then I took over as the head of strategy and organized the Series B round of investing.

That partnership only happened because we had context. I knew how my grandfather had done things in the past, I knew how my father had launched DirecTV. My partner could see there was so much value in the knowledge we could bring to the table that he was willing to rethink his entire strategy and bring us on.

The AST investment was a bold move but it was so obvious that we needed to be a part of it. I was willing to bet on the idea and the founder. And the bet paid off: The company is now valued at more than $2 billion.

Today, AST & Science and our global partners — we eventually made a significant equity investment — are building the first space-based cellular broadband network accessible by standard smartphones with 4G/5G connectivity anywhere on the planet — on land, sea or in flight. No one will ever have to build a cellphone tower again. Connectivity will no longer be a socio-economic or political issue. And we will be the ones to connect the world.

* * *

Back when Adriana agreed to be my official successor, she insisted that she wouldn't feel complete unless she was allowed to run both the business and the Cisneros Foundation. Under her leadership, our role as a platform and a springboard for Latin American art has also continued to evolve and reinvent itself.

Patty and I always viewed ourselves not as collectors but as custodians. To that end, the ultimate goal of the Colección Patricia Phelps de Cisneros (CPPC) was to share the art with as large an audience as possible to educate them about the rich heritage and exciting imagination of Latin American art.

Thanks to Adriana, we consolidated and sharpened our focus on education through the Fundación Cisneros. Our website became an editorial platform with eBooks incorporating video and audio components; our social media program spun off apps for exhibits and mobile websites. We became truly transnational.

Meanwhile, Patty had become a trustee of the Museum of Modern Art, where she founded the Latin American-Caribbean Fund (LACF) to purchase artworks for MOMA. At the same time, she sponsored a position for a curator of Latin American art, as a way to introduce this body of knowledge into MOMA, and created a travel fund for MOMA curators to visit Latin America. When the museum re-opened in 2004 after a massive renovation, 20 works from the CPPC were integrated into the display. Today, there are multiple works from the CPPC gift always on view in the permanent collection galleries.

MOMA became the vehicle for Patty to realize her dream about Latin American art and cement her legacy: not just by showcasing a valuable collection but by creating a research institute. Founded by the Rockefeller family, MOMA has been an advocate for Latin American modern art almost since its inception, so it was the perfect home for the Patricia Phelps de Cisneros Research Institute for the Study of Art from Latin America. The Cisneros Institute, as it's now called, was formally established in 2016 with a gift of more than 100 artworks from the CPPC. It hosts visiting scholars and artists, convenes an annual international conference and produces research publications on art from Latin America. With further gifts from Patty serving as an incentive, today MOMA's collection comprises more than 5,000 works from artists from Latin America — and Patty's dedication ensures those works will be shared and studied for generations to come.

(The Orinoco Collection remains part of the CPPC, which preserves more than 1,200 works as well as an archive of ethnographic research. Because it's part of Venezuela's heritage, it will be returned to Venezuela someday.)

* * *

As for me, I'm as busy as I've ever been. My father often warned me about the dangers of stagnation; I'm definitely not stagnating. I look forward to continuing the partnership with Adriana: It's been very rewarding for me and for her. But to keep out of her hair, I'm also involved with projects of my own outside of Cisneros, many of them pro bono.

One of the most exciting is my involvement with Barrick's Pueblo Viejo mining operation in the Dominican Republic. Barrick is one of the largest gold and copper mining companies in the world, with operations in 13 countries. Mining is a basic necessity: As long as our world needs copper, gold and other precious metals, people will dig into the earth to extract them.

But there are ways to do it that minimize damage to the environment while providing maximum benefits to neighboring communities. That's what we're doing with Pueblo Viejo.

Pueblo Viejo is one of the ten largest gold mines in the world by production[2] and with over 2,500 employees — 97% of whom are Dominican — Pueblo Viejo is one of the country's largest employers and biggest tax-payers. Thanks to our social development programs, though, we reach over 180,000 residents of nearby communities. These programs include literacy, vocational and leadership training, for men and women as well as boys and girls, with the aim of preparing them for jobs in the facility; a business incubator that helps local start-ups; sustainable agro-forestry projects; preventive health programs; and rural electrification. We've made Pueblo Viejo an example of "green" mining and we're seeing fantastic results.

I felt — and still feel — that it's important to do this right because I live in the Dominican Republic. It's my duty to a country that has been a place of relaxation, refuge and revival for so many years.

I sit on Barrick's international advisory board, where I serve as the recruitment officer for the board. That's a key way of ensuring that the men and women who lead the company share similar views about its responsibilities to stakeholders in the community as well as shareholders in the firm. These people come from every country where Barrick's operates so, not incidentally, my role provides me with another opportunity to strengthen my connections to people in power all over the world. I think of the board as a business version of the Council on Foreign Relations.

Speaking of the Council on Foreign Relations: In 2022, I rejoined the Global Board of Advisors of the Council on Foreign Relations. (I had the privilege of being a founding member, having joined at the behest of David Rockefeller and Pete Peterson in 1995, and served for 15 years, until the board was dismantled in 2010.) A distinguished group of business leaders and former government officials from all around the globe, the board is a think tank of the best kind: Its members are always up to date on whatever is happening in the world and share the most insightful opinions. Being on the board connects me with the whole world as well as the United States. If you are as curious as I am, there is no better place to expand your knowledge.

You may wonder what I *do* with this knowledge and these connections. Just as Adriana's responsibility is to lead the family business, my responsibility is to manage the family's money. Most families like ours pool their money in a fund which is then invested in a variety of ways. Our family investment office, run by Ana Teresa Arismendi, is independent of the company: It's modeled like a European private bank and I'm essentially the chief investment officer. It keeps me busy doing stuff I love for the people I love.

Life doesn't get much better than that.

* * *

Patty and I now live much of the year in the Dominican Republic. My office in our home there has a wide verandah, looking south over the ever-changing colors of the Caribbean. Just over the horizon is Venezuela, out of sight but always in the corner of my heart. That's not to say, though, that I spend my days dwelling on what might have been. Instead, most of my time and energy is focused on the future.

One hundred years ago, no one would have thought that a young man with a dump truck could build the most successful

Pepsi-Cola business outside of the United States. Or that his son would create a multi-billion-dollar global enterprise. Or that his granddaughter would literally be reaching for the stars.

As Adriana likes to say, "It's all about being open to the possibility of wonder. All of our great ideas in business have come from that."

Family companies often stall out in the second or third generation because that generation is just caretaking: They're not on a new quest. That has yet to happen in the Cisneros family. Our momentum has, for the most part, been unbroken. Our sense of curiosity remains undiminished. We continue to dream bigger.

Patty and I have 10 grandchildren. I'm hoping some of them will commit their curiosity, confidence and courage to our family company. When I dream about the future, I see myself sitting on the verandah with my grandchildren, exploring ideas for the next 100 years.

Notes

1. https://www.cisneros.com/divisions/cisneros-media

2. Conte, Niccolo, "Mapped: The Ten Largest Gold Mines in the World, by Production," in *Visual Capitalist,* May 19, 2022. https://www.visualcapitalist.com/mapped-the-10-largest-gold-mines-in-the-world-by-production/

ACKNOWLEDGMENTS

One of the most important lessons my father taught me was to park my ego in the closet. There's no way I could have written this book by myself. This book was a team effort and is immeasurably better for everyone's contributions.

Another enduring lesson was to hire the best people I could find. I was extremely fortunate to have worked on this book with Steve Bandel, Miguel Dvorak, José Antonio Rios, Johnny Fanjul, Ariel Prat and Beatrice Rangel. They helped make Cisneros into the business it is today, then generously shared their stories and wisdom to make this book the best it could be.

My father also taught me to recognize what you don't know, and then find experts who do. Ambassador William Luers provided invaluable perspectives on the politics and economy of Venezuela, in the process becoming a close family friend and honorary uncle to my children. Professor John Davis, a global authority on family businesses, has been a wise counselor, thoughtful consultant and tactful therapist to everyone in my family as well as the family as a whole. Thomas Shannon has been a helpful sounding board over the years.

A big hug to Leonard "Leonardo" Lauder. He combines hard-nosed business advice with a warm heart. I have benefited from both many times over many years and I am honored to call him a dear friend. His encouragement at the start of this project made all the difference.

I can't thank enough the two close collaborators who transformed a vague idea into the book you are now reading. Catherine Fredman, my writing partner, came into this project without any special knowledge of Cisneros or Venezuela, but by the end she was able to teach me things I didn't know. Her sensitivity and persistence extracted many nuggets of information, but perhaps more importantly, connections between them that I hadn't seen before. Gabriel Pérez-Barreiro is a perfect example of a general who didn't hesitate to step into a sergeant's shoes — in this case, as our project editor. He generously made space within his work with the Colección Patricia Phelps de Cisneros to shepherd this project through to completion. His deep knowledge of our company's and country's history is matched only by his gift for explaining complicated concepts in a clear and compelling fashion.

I also want to acknowledge the prior work done by Pablo Bachelet in writing *Gustavo Cisneros: Pioneer*, which was a valuable source of background material.

I am especially grateful to José (Pepe) Crehueras for his enthusiastic embrace of this project at Planeta, and to Cristóbal Pera, Mariana Marczuk and all their colleagues for their sensitive care of the book from manuscript to production.

Once we had a finished manuscript, Jonathan Blum, Luis Emilio Gómez, Eduardo Hernández and Luis Queremel filled in gaps and corrected the details of various business transactions. Especial thanks to Nicolas Griffin for sharing his writer's sensibility and sharp eye.

I also want to thank the staff at Casa Bonita, New York, and Madrid. They may work behind the scenes but their tireless care and cheerful efficiency created the atmosphere in which this book could come to life.

Last but never least, I would like to thank my wife Patty and my children — Guillermo, Carolina and Adriana — for their love and support. They are the source of all good things in my life. Just by being there, they constantly encourage me to always be open to the possibility of wonder.

GUSTAVO CISNEROS (1945-2023)

Until his death on December 29, 2023, Gustavo Cisneros was the President of the Board of CISNEROS — a private enterprise with over 100 years of experience operating businesses worldwide — of which he was the CEO for 50 years. In his role as CEO, he prioritized CISNEROS' strategic development to heighten Latin America's profile on the global stage, promoting education, the principles of democracy, and individual freedom.

He was also a member of the Board of Barrick Gold Corporation and a member of the Advisory Board of the Council of Foreign Relations, among other functions. For decades, Cisneros occupied a variety of executive and leadership positions in several key organizations in Latin America, the United States, and Europe, both in the private and non-profit sectors, and in academic centers and cultural institutions.

With his wife, Patricia Phelps de Cisneros, he established the Fundación Cisneros, a private, non-profit institution devoted to improving education in Latin America and increasing awareness of the contributions of Latin America to world culture.

EXHIBIT

The humble origins of D. Cisneros & Co. (Caracas, 1940). He was dedicated to importing automobile parts and other products, such as Norge refrigerators and Hamilton household appliances. Thanks to his energy and vision, an international conglomerate grew from this seed.

My father insisted on visiting all the company's facilities unannounced to ensure everything was in order. In this picture, at a Pepsi-Cola bottling plant in 1968.

On the left, I am with my brother Carlos Enrique, in front of the new 1952 Studebaker model. It was a very glamorous and attractive world for a young boy.

In the early 1950s, D. Cisneros & Co. represented Studebaker automobiles, among other brands, in buildings characteristic of Venezuelan modernism.

At Babson College, I learned to think and understand
the business culture of the United States, an understanding that has helped me for my entire life.

My father and me in 1969, a year before his illness.

CADA supermarkets symbolized modernity in a country accustomed to small neighborhood stores. The design, the quality of the supplies and the hygiene, all added to a new experience in harmony with a fast-growing country.

Galerías Preciados was an emblematic chain in Spain, which was on the verge of bankruptcy during the scandalous and ruinous management of RUMASA. After expropriation by the Spanish government and subsequent acquisition by my father, we managed to modernize the company in a few years and make it profitable again. This photo dates from 1984.

The sale of Pepsi-Cola to Coca-Cola in Venezuela was a delicate and silent operation. Here, Ricardo, Oswaldo, and me are signing the historic agreement with Roberto Goizueta, then global president of Coca-Cola.

The purchase of Spalding and Evenflo led us to explore production in China, anticipating what would become a global trend in the following years. Here I am with Deng Xiaoping in Beijing in 1988.

In 2022, my *alma mater*, Babson College, honored my family with the Babson-Camus Global Family Entrepreneurship Award. It was a very proud moment for all of us.

The Tropicalia project in the Dominican Republic is a dream shared by Adriana and me. What started as an idea of a rest house has become a holistic project of housing and luxury hotel, with a strong social and ecological concept.

Within Tropicalia, the Querencia farm is fundamental. Not only does it generate high-quality organic products, but it is also a social project for the inclusion of women at risk and education on sustainable agriculture.

Art continues to be a fundamental aspect of our lives, and Adriana has assumed the direction of Cisneros, and the Cisneros Foundation. In this photo, we are at the exhibition Chosen Memories (2022), with which the Museum of Modern Art in New York honored our donation of more than 100 works of Latin American art and the creation of a permanent research institute.

Satellites have been part of our business and family dreams since DirecTV. Adriana has continued this passion with her investment in AST SpaceMobile, a visionary satellite and telecommunications company. Here, we are at the first launch at Cape Canaveral with her husband, Nicholas Griffin.

Of the many philanthropic and social initiatives that Adriana has led, one of the most important is the summer camp "Soy niña, soy importante" (I am a girl, I matter), held in Miches, Dominican Republic. The camp instills values of self-esteem for pre-teen girls, a population at risk of early pregnancy and prejudice against women.